Special Edition

This copy of this special edition of

Supernatural Power

is presented to

J & K Naslund

with love and appreciation from the author

for the prayer and financial support of Omega Ministries.

I pray that this book will be a blessing to you and that you will receive new insights into the supernatural power that is available to Spirit-filled Christians. I pray that you will begin to let this power flow through you to the glory of Christ and Father God. Always love Him with all your heart, soul, mind and strength.

James McKeever

Special Edition distributed by:

Omega Ministries
P. O. Box 1788
Medford, Oregon 97501

"Another brilliant work by Dr. McKeever, who has got to be one of the most prolific writers around. An outstanding, solid teaching. I believe it will benefit everyone who reads it and I highly recommend it."

—Jack Hoskins,
Attorney

"Certainly this message is needed today in the lives of Spirit-filled believers to walk in the demonstration of His power. Perhaps the greatest contribution of this book will be the exhortation to the body of Christ of the need for a return of spiritual power in the life of the church. It certainly has a different tenor in style that denotes a prophetic call to preparation for spiritual battle."

—Jim Burck,
Counseling Director

"McKeever has combined the office of prophet and the gift of teaching to produce a seminal and yet practical work. It will greatly edify the body of Christ and help it fulfill its end times mission with the power of God."

—Daniel Biskind,
Executive and entrepreneur

"Your chapter on our 'spiritual diet' is conceptually brilliant."

—Jim Spillman,
Evangelist, Author and Greek Scholar

"I was extremely impressed with the beginning two sections. I think it is a dramatic book and one that is needed."

—Roger Minor,
Attorney

SUPERNATURAL POWER

How to let God's power flow through YOU!

DR. JAMES McKEEVER

SUPERNATURAL POWER

Printed in the United States of America
First printing June, 1990

Omega Publications
P. O. Box 4130
Medford, Oregon 97501 (U.S.A.)

ISBN #0-86694-121-5 (Hardback)

TABLE OF CONTENTS

DEDICATION

This book is dedicated first and foremost to the glory of God and His only begotten Son, Jesus Christ, with thanksgiving for the supernatural power that they give to us as Spirit-filled Christians.

This book is also dedicated to:

The Omega staff
The Omega Family
The Omega Team

Their faithful prayers and financial support made this book possible.

I would also like to dedicate this book to some men of God who move in the supernatural power of God and who were most helpful in interacting with me on this subject:

Terry Calkin
Stuart Gramenz
James Wesley Smith
Jim Spillman
Bill Subritzky

FOREWORD

By Terry Calkin

The one dynamic which is missing from the church today is the demonstration of the power of God. An examination of the early church's activities bears testimony to the promise of Jesus: "And you shall receive power after the Holy Spirit has come upon you." The book of Acts is a record of a church demonstrating the power of God.

I believe that the end-time church is going to evince the power of God in an even greater way than the early church, as God empowers it to stand in the last days. That is why I count it a privilege to write a preface for such a book as this. Dr. McKeever has rightly discerned that the demonstration of the power of God is the last missing ingredient that has yet to be restored to the church today. We know that God has given the church power; the question then to be answered is: *how is the church going to release this power?*

The power of God is released by Spirit-filled Christians stepping out in faith and obeying God's word. This is the great gulf which we must cross if we are to use and demonstrate God's power to an unbelieving world. We take a chance on failure, but there is no faith without taking a risk. We need to understand that our righteousness comes from faith, just as the use of the power of God also comes from faith. His power is so great and it is available to us:

> **19 And [so that you can know and understand] what is the immeasurable *and* unlimited *and* surpassing greatness of His power in *and* for us who believe, as demonstrated in the working of His mighty strength,**
> **20 Which He exerted in Christ when He raised Him from the dead . . .**
>
> **—Ephesians 1, *AMP***

I believe this book opens up the last great piece of God's jigsaw that needs to be in place as we approach the end of the age. I pray that as you read this book, you will be gripped and challenged by both the urgency of the hour and the necessity for every believer to be a channel through which God's power can flow.

Dr. McKeever has written many outstanding books, but this one, I believe, is the most important, with God's vital message for this age.

—Terry Calkin, Pastor
Greenlane Christian Church
Auckland, New Zealand

ACKNOWLEDGMENTS

Of course, the first and foremost acknowledgment must be to our Father God, who placed the concept of this book on my heart; to the Holy Spirit who gave me inspiration; and to Jesus Christ, my Lord and Savior. With my whole heart, I want only to glorify God in this book, and in everything that I do in life.

On the human level, I am greatly indebted to my assistant, Jackie Cunningham, who faithfully typed the book and labored shoulder-to-shoulder with me during its writing and preparation. I am equally indebted to my precious brother in Christ, Jim Andrews, who helped with the editing, did the technical work with the computers and the typesetting, and made valuable suggestions. Many thanks also to Jeannine Carvalho, who aided in typing corrections to the manuscript, to Judy McClure for the typing she did, and to Ellen Thorsen, who helped in the proofreading.

However, top billing must go to my precious wife, Jeani, who has spent more time on this book than I have. The quality of this book is the result of her careful and conscientious editing. However, she was not just the editor—she really would qualify to be the co-author. There are major passages that she wrote entirely. Her constructive criticism and suggestions of Scriptures to include helped round out the book, making it as full and complete as possible. Not only did we work together in this way, but she also gave constant, cheerful encouragement and the tender love that only a wonderful, caring wife can give. Without her, this book most likely would not exist.

I am also indebted to the men of God who read through the rough manuscript and gave me both encouraging comments and very valuable criticisms. Acknowledging them here does not mean that they agree with everything that is in this book. I love them deeply and appreciate them taking the time to read the manuscript and to give me their helpful comments.

Jim Andrews	Ed Gruman
Dan Biskind	Jack Hoskins
Carlton Booth	Roger Minor
Jim Burck	Carl Nine
Terry Calkin	Jim Spillman
Giff Claiborne	Harry Stiritz

I also want to express my love and appreciation to the Omega Family, the Omega Team and others who receive our monthly publication, *End-Times News Digest,* who have prayed faithfully with us as this book was being developed. Great things are wrought by prayers, and their prayers have been a protection for this book from the attacks of the evil one. They have also "held up my hands" when I was weary in writing. I want to personally thank each and every one of them, and pray God's richest blessings upon them.

I would also like to express my appreciation to some beautiful men of God who gave me some valuable insights for this book. Terry Calkin not only read the manuscript, but he spent a great deal of time with me while I was in New Zealand, discussing issues involved in the supernatural power of God. I appreciate the time Bill Subritzky spent with me discussing the way that God is mightily using him in a healing and evangelistic ministry. I appreciate Dave and Mary Clark, who have devoted their lives to missionary work in Africa and have been mightily used of God in works of supernatural power. I also appreciate the time that I had with Stuart Gramenz from Australia, who has a ministry of teaching people how to move in the supernatural power of God and then taking them out for hands-on experience. I am also thankful to Jim Spillman, who has an international ministry and whom God has used greatly in healing and other manifestations of the power of God. I appreciated the time that he spent with me interacting over the manuscript.

My last acknowledgment and word of appreciation goes to you, the reader; for a book would be valueless, if no one read or benefitted from it. I am really praying that the Holy Spirit will cause you to recognize the things in this book that are truth from God. I am also praying that, if I have missed the mark in any area and there is anything in this book that is not the absolute truth of God, the Holy Spirit will simply eradicate it from your mind and cause you not even to remember it.

However, the things in this book that are the truth of God, I pray that the Holy Spirit will burn deep into your heart and soul, and that these truths will transform your life into one characterized by supernatural power flowing out to do the mighty works of God.

James McKeever
P. O. Box 1788
Medford, Oregon 97501

"This book contains a wealth of material, and is certainly no minor undertaking. Difficult subjects are what you appear to thrive on. There should be 'double honor' for those who tackle such hard stuff head on. It caused me to examine some of my most deeply held beliefs much more carefully than I am unusually willing to do. This of itself speaks eloquently of the book's utility and value. I've enjoyed the book enormously."

—Ed Gruman,
World Vision Management

"A great book! I believe God will use it immensely in these times of travail in the body of Christ. The message of this book is straightforward and clear. God's supernatural character and power are the same today as yesterday. This book has the potential to help Christians understand and demonstrate God's supernatural power."

—Gifford Claiborne, Pastor
Advertising and Marketing Executive

"Stimulating reading. As members of the body of Christ open their hearts to the Holy Spirit as they read, I believe the Lord is going to speak through it in this day."

—Carlton Booth,
Retired Fuller Seminary professor

PREFACE

By Jeani McKeever

The message of this book is truly exciting! If Christians were to put in practice the truths contained herein, they truly could turn the world upside-down.

The early Christians of the first century indelibly affected history. Through lives sold out for Jesus, the good news of how man could be reconciled to God was spread through the known world. How did they do it? They were witnesses of what they had seen and heard and of what Christ had done for them ***and*** the gospel was confirmed by signs and wonders accomplished by their hands. In other words, the gospel went out not in words only, but truly in demonstration of the supernatural power of God.

Working on this book has affected my life profoundly, and I know that I will never be the same. I strongly suspect it will do the same for you. I pray that you will be challenged to walk in the fullness of what God has prepared for you and that this book will be but the start of an exciting new adventure with God.

Part I

POWER IS AVAILABLE NOW

Chapter 1

POWER AND VICTORY—NOW!

Most Christians would like to have more power in their lives and to see more victory. At the Olympics, we all enjoy seeing the power of the weight lifters, the pole vaulters, the gymnasts and the runners.

IT TAKES POWER TO HAVE VICTORY!

It is exhilarating when we see someone come through a challenge as a real victor. Our hearts thrill with such an individual as he throws up his arms in triumph.

Unfortunately, most of us do not appreciate the price that Olympic champions have to pay for their victories. The victory is sweet, but there is indeed a cost. There are many long, hard, daily hours of practice, which means sacrificing in studies and social life. There is actual physical pain at times, as weight lifters and long-distance runners push their bodies beyond previous limitations. And yet, they each are willing to pay that price in order to have that sweet taste of victory.

Most Christians seem to be waiting for "something" to happen to give them instantaneous power and victory. We are so accustomed to "instant" cereals, "instant" dinners and a pushbutton life, that somehow we have almost deluded ourselves into a sense that our power and victory should come simply by "adding water and stirring."

A friend of mine who is a pastor, Carl Nine, passed on to me one of his sayings on this subject that reflects many people's attitude:

"Instant coffee,
Instant tea,
Instant God
For you and me."

Unfortunately, in order to have real power and victory, we must first exercise an act of the ***will*** and then there is a subsequent price to pay. It is the same for an Olympic athlete who must decide that he is willing to pay the price of daily workouts and other sacrifices in order to become a champion. But I have good news for you. You need not wait. Jesus Christ Himself said that if you believe in Him, you will do the works that He did:

> **12 "Truly, truly, I say to you, he who believes in Me, the works that I do shall he do also; and greater *works* than these shall he do; because I go to the Father. . . ."**
>
> **—John 14**

He did not say that if you were a pastor, an evangelist, a prophet or an apostle you would do the same works that He did. He said that if you believed in Him, you would do the ***same*** works that He did. Jesus has already decided that you can have that power, and He is offering it to every true believer. He wants every Christian to have it. That power and the victory that follows is available to you, and it is available to you now! You do not have to wait for anything. Go for it! You can have a gold medal!

You need this power now and you will really need it during the end times of this age! Real power brings victory. Supernatural power accomplishes much.

IT TAKES POWER TO HAVE VICTORY

POWER IS AVAILABLE TO YOU NOW!

I would like to begin discussing the concept of power by asking you a question. While He was here on earth, do you think that Jesus Christ utilized power not available to you and me? Your answer to that question could actually change your life. I have asked that question of thousands of Christian audiences around the world, and almost uniformly I get the same answer: "HE RESTRICTED HIMSELF TO USING ONLY THE POWER THAT IS AVAILABLE TO YOU AND ME."

Christ had divine creative power, but Philippians 2 tells us that He laid that aside when He came down to the earth and He humbled Himself as a man. Most of us have an easy time accepting Christ's divinity, but we have a hard time accepting His humanity. Stop and think about it for a moment. Every miracle that Jesus did was also performed by someone else somewhere in the Bible.

Jesus raised the dead, but so did Peter and Paul and prophets in the Old Testament (Acts 9:36-41; 20:8-10). Jesus multiplied food, but so did Elijah with the meal and the oil in the situation with the widow (1 Kings 17:11-16). Jesus walked on water, but in the Old Testament a prophet caused an iron axe head to float to the surface of a river (2 Kings 6:5-7) and Moses caused the water to part. Jesus Christ had words of knowledge, but so did many others throughout the Scriptures. He healed the sick and cast out demons, but so did Peter, Paul and the other disciples.

In addition, the book of Hebrews tells us that Jesus was tempted in all points as we are (Hebrews 2:18). If

He had power to meet those temptations that is not available to us, that would have given Him an unfair advantage. Obviously, this is not true, because Hebrews also tells us that He experienced those temptations so that He could understand us (Hebrews 4:14,15).

While He lived here on earth, Jesus limited Himself to using just the supernatural power that is available to every born-again believer. Do you think that we need that power to lead a victorious Christian life? I do.

WE NEED POWER

When I say that we need power, I am not talking about physical power, such as the power or strength needed to lift weights, to hammer nails or to push a heavy vacuum cleaner. (Although, it may be that some of us are physically out of shape and God would like us to get back into shape, so that we can do physical things with more ease, to His glory.)

Here we are not talking about physical power, financial power, electrical power or any other "powers" in the natural realm. We are addressing *supernatural power*. Things done with supernatural power cannot be explained by natural laws. They are *"super"*-natural or "above and beyond" the natural. These are things that occur totally outside of the laws of nature. There is nothing natural about them—that is why they are called *supernatural.*

I have been having encounters with supernatural power since I was a child. When I was two years old, I turned a tub of boiling water over on myself and was scalded from my waist down. My legs were extremely badly burned. The doctor said that I would not live and, if by any miracle I were to live, there was absolutely no possibility that I would ever walk again, because of the depth of the burns in the muscles in my legs. Mother, who was a devout Christian, prayed the prayer of

Hannah and said, "Lord, if You spare him, he's Yours." By miraculous, supernatural power, God not only saved my life, but healed my legs so that I could not only walk, but run track, play football and participate in all of the other major sports.

About thirteen years ago, I was at a meeting in Oklahoma. At the end of the meeting, the man who was speaking had several words of knowledge for healings. One of them was that someone had impacted wisdom teeth. I knew that I had four impacted wisdom teeth, because my dentist in the Los Angeles area had been wanting me to have oral surgery on them for several years. Many others went up in response to every other word of knowledge that was given and they got healed. At the end of the meeting, he said, "Everyone came up except whomever it was who had the impacted wisdom teeth."

I went up to him after the meeting and shared with him: "I was the one with the impacted wisdom teeth, but I was a little embarrassed to come up." In a booming voice, he announced, "Hold it everyone—here are the impacted wisdom teeth!" He then prayed for me. Within the next few days, I noticed some sensitivity at the extremities of my lower teeth and found a little bit of blood when I would put my finger back there to check it out. It was about that time that we moved to Oregon and the dentist here examined my teeth. He asked me, "Did you ever have lower wisdom teeth?" I said, "Of course, and I still do. In fact, they're impacted." He told me that I had no lower wisdom teeth, and there was no evidence that I had ever had any!

Praise God! Evidently, He had simply dissolved them. The earlier X-rays from Los Angeles show impacted wisdom teeth, and now there are none. Later, I had my upper wisdom teeth extracted, but Jesus Christ was the Great Dentist (in addition to being the Great Physician) who extracted my lower wisdom teeth! This cannot be explained by any natural methods; it was "supernatural" power that accomplished it.

Another incredible thing happened to me for which there is physical, scientific evidence. I had a major heart attack in the early 1980's. I first had inferior damage on the right side of my heart and later massive anterior damage on the left side. It showed up on the EKG every day while I was in the hospital. My wife, Jeani, contacted a great number of the faithful supporters of Omega Ministries and asked them to pray that God would not only heal me but give me a brand new heart.

About six weeks later, I went in for a treadmill test, and they gave me an EKG prior to it. The doctor said, "All the EKG's we took at the hospital must have been wrong, because this EKG shows no anterior damage." Some of you may not be aware that once you have damage to your heart (part of the heart muscle dies in a heart attack), it will normally show up on your EKG for the rest of your life. Our doctor knows where I stand with the Lord, and I told him that we should give credit where credit is due—God was giving me a new heart! I then was able to stay on the treadmill far longer than the norm for a man my age who had never had a heart attack.

Then a couple of years later, I went to a heart specialist in southern California, Dr. Julian Whitaker, who has authored a number of books, including *Reversing Heart Disease.* I told him the story and he smiled. He then gave me an EKG. About halfway through the treadmill test, he said, "I have news for you: the inferior damage on your EKG is gone as well. The way you're handling this stress test, unless I'd seen your old EKG's, you would never have convinced me that you had had a heart attack." The EKG's from the hospital and these subsequent visits actually physically prove the fact that God miraculously gave me a new heart.

Medical doctors cannot explain such an occurrence that is not a "natural" or normal event. As you and I know, God did something *through nature*—He intervened into nature, and this is why we call it "*supernatural*."

Another example of supernatural power occurred when a dear friend of mine, James Wesley Smith, was praying for people to be healed in a service in Ireland. At a particular meeting, a girl came up whose arms had not fully developed. Her hands were about where our elbows are. When she came up for prayer, he thought, "O Lord! Let it be a cold or a backache!" When he asked her what she wanted prayer for, her reply was, "Isn't it obvious?" So he commanded her to be healed in the name of Jesus Christ. The power of God came upon her such that she was knocked to the floor. He went on to pray for the next person in line, when all of a sudden behind him, he heard gasps and exclamations from the Methodist ministers, who were there with him. This girl's arms were growing out at such a rate that in about five minutes they were of normal length. There was no fakery here; the people in the community knew her. That cannot be explained by our logical minds.

In our minds, we may try to figure out where the extra skin came from, and how the nerves, muscles and blood vessels grew so quickly. Sadly, many Christians try to analyze such an event logically and scientifically, rather than rejoicing and praising God for a supernatural happening—one that cannot be explained by our logical minds.

James Wesley Smith has an international ministry emphasizing praise and worship, and the Lord uses him extensively in healing, especially through words of knowledge. He may be contacted at this address:

P. O. Box 2114
Melbourne, Florida 32902-2114

We are not talking here about "powerful preaching" and things of that nature. If you listen to some of the senators and congressmen who do not know Jesus Christ as their Savior, it is evident that they are very powerful, persuasive speakers. There are also Christian speakers and teachers who speak very powerfully and persuasively, but that is not the supernatural power of God. Powerful preaching can be explained by human minds.

Christians today seem almost afraid of supernatural power. I believe the reason is "fear of failure." In many Charismatic meetings, there are the regular two or three who pray for healings. If you asked the average member to come up and pray for a blind person to gain his sight, he would likely panic. Why? He is afraid that he will pray and nothing will happen. This means he has no faith. Faith involves risk.

IF THERE IS NO RISK,
THERE IS NO FAITH.

The church today must quit trying to avoid the supernatural; we must accept it and learn to operate in it. Most churches are afraid they will be classified as "kooky" or "drunk with wine." Let's face it, Christianity is based on a supernatural event—after having been dead and buried for three days, Jesus Christ spontaneously came back to life (by the power of God). This cannot be explained or understood scientifically. It is said that the brain begins to deteriorate after eight minutes without oxygen. After three days, it would be so badly deteriorated that, if someone came back to life, he would be a total imbecile. Yet Jesus Christ miraculously rose from the dead and was even more of a glorious, powerful being than He was before His death. When we preach Jesus Christ and Him crucified and raised from the dead, we are preaching a supernatural event. The four Gospels are full of supernatural events that Jesus Christ accomplished, such as healing lepers, blind men and deaf people, or having "words of knowledge," such as the one about the fish with a coin in its mouth which he foretold that Peter would catch (Matthew 17:24-27). All of those are supernatural happenings that cannot be analyzed or explained scientifically.

The early disciples walked in supernatural power. An angel came and opened the prison doors, took Peter out and closed the doors again (Acts 12:5-19). God sent an earthquake to release Paul and Silas from prison (Acts 16:23-34). Not only was it a normal earthquake that shook the foundations of the prison, but He also caused the chains to fall off the prisoners and all the prison doors to be opened. Peter healed the lame man at the gate of the temple when he said, "Silver and gold have I none; but such as I have give I unto thee: In the name of Jesus Christ of Nazareth rise up and walk" (Acts 3:6, *KJV*). Paul raised a dead man and brought him back to life (Acts 20:8-12).

Christianity is a supernatural religion. Did it ever stop being a supernatural religion? If so, when? The answer is obviously *no.* Even those who think that the gifts of the Spirit stopped during the first century will agree that, through the centuries, there have been miraculous things happening by the supernatural power of God. Let's accept it, flow with it and enjoy the power that God wants to give to us. Of course, He wants us to use it only for His glory and His kingdom, and not for selfish purposes. He wants to give us that supernatural power so that we can help others and help expand His kingdom.

I have recently met a precious brother, Stuart Gramenz, who has an outstanding ministry based in Australia. In one of his books, *How to Heal the Sick*, (available through Omega Ministries, P. O. Box 1788, Medford, Oregon 97501) he tells of how he started moving in the power of God :

As a young Christian I excitedly read of the wonderful healings and miracles which Jesus did. I expected that God wanted to, and would heal people the same today.

After all, Jesus Christ is the same yesterday, today and forever (Hebrews 13:8). My mistake however, was to think that He would only use a priest, pastor or the evangelist for this task, while I was to take on the role of an excited spectator.

One day back in 1979, a Scripture that I had read many times suddenly leapt out at me. A Scripture that was ultimately to change my direction and give me the extra joy and excitement that had been missing from my Christian experience.

Jesus had this to say in John 14:12:

"Most assuredly, I say to you, he who believes in Me, the works that I do he will do also; and greater works than these he will do, because I go to the Father."

What Are 'The Works'?

Acts 10:38 tells us: *"How God anointed Jesus of Nazareth with the Holy Spirit and with power, who went about doing good and healing all who were oppressed by the devil, for God was with Him."*

Two areas of works are given here:

1. Doing good;
2. Healing all.

Firstly, we are expected to exhibit a Godly character doing good works. This is an area which has received the majority of instruction in the Church at large. Most of us are very much aware of our role in this area of helping mankind. We feed the hungry, provide for the poor, look after widows and orphans, and the like.

However, the second part is just as important, if we wish to be obedient to all of the Scriptures. By "healing all that are oppressed by the devil" we certainly would be helping mankind in another form.

Notice the emphasis that Jesus uses in John 14:12: *"The works that I do will you do also."*

Just as we are to exhibit Godly character and to do good works, we are to heal. This was not an optional extra, it was a command. That knowledge really released me. Not only was I supposed to heal the sick, but I was EXPECTED to do it.

His Disciples Only

For years, I was under the impression that Jesus was only talking to Peter, John and the other disciples. I thought it must have been so great and exciting to live back in those days.

But the revelation of John 14:12 impacted on me: *"HE THAT BELIEVES ON ME"* will do my works!

Jesus was not only talking to His immediate disciples, but to me and every other believer!

I noted most importantly, that it did not say a group of Christians together with collective works, would do the works. It meant the individual, he or she who believed on Him could do these works.

Other translations of the Scripture only confirmed my excitement:

"I assure you that the man who believes in Me will do the same things I have done . . ." (J.B. Phillips).

"In most solemn truth I tell you that he who trusts in Me . . . the things which I do he shall do also . . ." (Weymouth).

"I tell you the truth, anyone who has faith in Me will do what I have been doing." (N.I.V.)

Truthfully, most definitely, most assuredly anyone who has faith in Jesus has an opportunity to pray for and to see the sick healed!

The realisation of this promise was the beginning of a new life for me with the opportunity of praying for, and seeing, thousands and thousands healed.

Since that time, our organisation has taken over 1,500 everyday Christians on our crusades into India and other Third World countries. They have not been full time missionaries, just ones with a heart to reach the lost and see the power of God work through them.

The majority knew very little about power ministry when they came. On these training trips, we teach them how to preach, how to heal and cast out demons and then release them on the streets during the day and the crusade crowds at night. Everyone has seen results in the miraculous.

After this training and experience, they return to their hometown to continue the ministry.

—Sovereign World Ltd., pp. 18-20

POWER OVER NATURE

Most of the "supernatural" events that come to mind for Christians are in the realm of healing. Healing is one of the gifts of the Holy Spirit, but another one is miracles. There are many miracles which have nothing to do with the human body that the power of God working through a Christian can, and does, achieve.

I will give you just two examples out of my own life. I share this in no way to exalt myself or to try to pretend that I am something special. Rather I share this to show you the kind of power—miracle-working power—that can operate in any Christian's life. At the time this event occurred, I was a businessman and simply attended a church.

Jeani and I were going to have our wedding dedication ceremony at her parents' home in Penticton, B.C., Canada, in June, 1976. At that time of year, there is seldom any rain there. Therefore, it was planned to be held outdoors on the large lawn area of my wife's parents' home. There was absolutely no provision to have this wedding dedication and dinner inside.

Unexpectedly, the day before our wedding dedication, it began to rain torrents. Everyone began to pray that the rain would stop. The morning of our wedding dedication (which was scheduled for 3:00 in the afternoon), there was still a torrential downpour. Everyone was still praying, asking God to stop the rain.

I was out walking back and forth underneath the carport off her parents' home, praying. This was one of the few times the Lord spoke to me audibly, and He said, "Prayer is not enough; you must take dominion over the rain." This was an absolute jolt to me. I had never even considered anything of this nature. I had to do about 15 minutes of confessing and cleaning up things in my life before I felt I was in any position to take dominion over the rain. After getting myself squared up with God and cleansed from all unrighteousness, in the power of the name of Jesus Christ, I took dominion over the rain and commanded it to stop and not to start again until after the wedding dedication and the dinner were over. I did this with full authority, exercising supernatural power, and I had total assurance that it was going to occur.

Within an hour, the rain had stopped. When the time for the event came, the grass was even dry, and we had a glorious wedding dedication which was officiated by the Baptist pastor who had led Jeani to the Lord. Many of Jeani's relatives and hometown friends were there and commented to her that they had never seen anything that glorified the Lord so much. We had a wedding dinner afterward out-of-doors, on large folding tables with paper tablecloths. After the dinner was over, when they were beginning to take off the paper tablecloths, the rain began again. Praise God! His supernatural power, working through me—a vessel willing to listen and then ***act***—caused the rain to stop for that period of time, and God received the glory through it.

A similar instance occurred in the late 1970's after we were married. We were living in Oregon by then and we were having a Bible study in our home. It was one of the rare times in southern Oregon when we had several weeks of rain. One lady in our group, whose faith was a bit weak, said that she hated the rain and wished it would stop. Once again I felt the Lord telling me to take dominion over the rain. I told her that it would not rain for three weeks and then it would start raining again. After the people left, I went outside and in the name of Jesus Christ commanded the rain to stop and not to start again for three weeks.

You guessed it! The supernatural power of God was at work to His glory! The rain stopped for exactly three weeks. Then three weeks and one day later, the rain started again in real earnest.

Obviously I cannot go out any time that I want to and command the rain to stop. I can only do so when God tells me to, when He wants to let His supernatural power work and flow through me to achieve ***His*** deeds.

> **30 "I can do nothing on My own initiative. As I hear, I judge; and My judgment is just, because I do not seek My own will, but the will of Him who sent me. . . ."**
>
> **—John 5**

Perhaps you have wondered if supernatural power was for all Christians or just for the apostles of yesterday, the evangelists of today, or those with the gift and ministry of healing. God does indeed desire all Christians to have supernatural power and to have it now. It does not matter if you are a blue-collar worker, a housewife or a business or professional person—God wants you to operate in supernatural power. It does not matter if you are a Sunday school teacher, a pew-filler or a pastor—the power of God is there for you to use, and God wants you to learn how to use it and then to do so. This may be a little frightening to you. But don't let that stop you. His perfect love casts out fear.

As you move forward into this exciting area, we want to look together at how you can have that supernatural power of God and how it can be working through you. After that, we will take a look at some of the things that might hinder God's miracle power from flowing through you. God wants to use you mightily and to exhibit His power through you, both now and as the end of this age occurs. It can happen. It ***will*** happen, if you are willing. Do you desire this? Are you willing?

God's supernatural power is for every Christian.

Chapter 2

THE SHOELESS TOWN

The following story appeared in the book, *Why I Am a Christian,* in 1928, written by Frank Crane.

Some years ago there was printed an article, which I think was written by Hugh Price Hughes, entitled "Ubique." This is the Latin word for "everywhere" and the story was intended to be a satire upon professed Christians.

The gist of it was that a man had occasion to go for the first time to the town of Ubique on business. He arrived at the railroad station on a blustering December day. There was a cold wind and a flurry of snow. As he walked along the street he saw women dressed in costly furs and gentlemen in fur coats, but all having bare feet. The population seemed respectable and well-to-do, but no one wore shoes. They limped along, were afflicted with chilblains and bruises and suffered great pain.

When he went to the hotel he found the clerk at the desk, the bellboys and other attendants all barefoot. At the dinner table he sat next to a prosperous looking old gentleman and fell into conversation. As this new acquaintance seemed so kindly and open-minded, our traveler said to him:

"Pardon me if I seem intrusive, but I notice that nobody in this town seems to wear shoes, yet everyone appears to suffer from cold and bruised feet. Would you mind telling me why?"

"Ah!" said the old gentleman, raising his eyes piously, "why indeed!"

He talked further with his companion, but could never get past that point. The old gentleman was perfectly willing to admit that shoes were desirable above all things, and that everybody ought to wear them, but he could not tell why they did not do so.

The traveler took a walk through the town and found that here and there were beautiful buildings, more elaborate and larger than the ordinary. Seeing the janitor sweeping the steps of one of these structures, he stopped and talked to him.

"What is this building? I am a stranger in the town and notice there are many buildings like this."

"This is a shoe factory," said the janitor.

"Oh! Then they make shoes here."

"Oh, not at all," was the reply. "They just talk about making shoes, and sing about shoes and pray about them."

Pointing to a sign by the door he saw an announcement that the chief official of the factory was going to give a lecture every seventh day on shoes. The subjects listed included "The Origin of Shoes," "The History of Shoe Making," "Varieties of Leather," etc. He was informed by the janitor that once every seven days every other business in town was required by law to close, that nothing was allowed to be open but the shoe factories and the people all gathered in them to sing and pray and hear lectures about shoes. But no shoes were produced and nobody wore them.

Finally in a little side street he found a small shop inside of which was an old German cobbler making a pair of shoes. He bought a pair and took it back to his hotel to present to the old gentleman with whom he had become acquainted.

> To his surprise the old gentleman declined the gift, assuring him that none of the best people ever wore shoes, and in fact it was considered a sign of fanaticism and hypocrisy ever really to wear them.
>
> —Wm. H. Wise & Company

I trust the application is obvious. I hope I will not be insulting your intelligence when I point out how most Christians meet once or twice a week to talk about our supernatural God, the things that He did in Egypt, the things Jesus did when He was here on earth, and the supernatural things that He said He wanted us to do.

Without the supernatural, the Bible would be so thin that we would not need a concordance!

We keep meeting and talking about these supernatural things, but not doing them. I pray that this book will help you to begin to put this power to work in your life, so that you can begin to actually *"wear shoes,"* instead of just talking about them.

As we will see in the next chapter, you receive the power of God when you are filled with the Spirit. So very many Christians have this power, but they are not using it. God has given us the shoes. Now we must act. We must put on the shoes.

Chapter 3

POWER AND THE HOLY SPIRIT

There are many Christians today who confuse or equate the power of God with the Holy Spirit. We need to examine this so we can understand and use the power of God. One of the reasons for this confusion comes from Acts 1. To help eliminate this confusion, let us take a look at the time when the disciples became Christians. I believe the disciples became Christians in John 20, if not before. Jesus had been buried and resurrected, and then this happened:

> **20 And when He had said this, He showed them both His hands and His side. The disciples therefore rejoiced when they saw the Lord.**
>
> **21 Jesus therefore said to them again, "Peace *be* with you; as the Father has sent Me, I also send you."**
>
> **22 And when He had said this, He breathed on them, and said to them, "Receive the Holy Spirit.**
>
> **23 "If you forgive the sins of any, *their sins* have been forgiven them; if you retain the *sins* of any, they have been retained."**
>
> **—John 20**

Here we see that Jesus breathed on them and said, "Receive the Holy Spirit," and He gave them spiritual authority. Everything that was necessary for the disciples to become Christians was in place at this time, and when Jesus breathes on you and says, "Receive the Holy Spirit," *you receive Him.* All Christians have the Holy Spirit indwelling them.

> **9 However, you are not in the flesh but in the Spirit, if indeed the Spirit of God dwells in you. But if anyone does not have the Spirit of Christ, he does not belong to Him.**
>
> **—Romans 8**

> **16 Do you not know that you are a temple of God, and *that* the Spirit of God dwells in you?**
>
> **—1 Corinthians 3**

> **14 Guard, through the Holy Spirit who dwells in us, the treasure which has been entrusted to *you.***
>
> **—2 Timothy 1**

However, Jesus knew that the indwelling of the Holy Spirit was not enough; the disciples also needed to be baptized or filled with the Holy Spirit in order to have supernatural power. He knew that to do the work of God, they had to have this miracle-working power. We read this in Acts:

> **4 And gathering them together, He commanded them not to leave Jerusalem, but to wait for what the Father had promised, "Which," *He said,* "you heard of from Me;**
>
> **5 for John baptized with water, but you shall be baptized with the Holy Spirit not many days from now." . . .**
>
> **8 but you shall receive power when the Holy Spirit has come upon you; and you shall be My witnesses both in Jerusalem, and in all Judea and Samaria, and even to the remotest part of the earth."**
>
> **—Acts 1**

Here Jesus told the disciples not to leave Jerusalem, not to go out witnessing in Samaria, Judea and other parts of the earth, but to stay right in Jerusalem until they had received power, and they would receive the power when and only when the Holy Spirit had come upon them. In verse 5, Jesus is talking about being baptized in the Spirit. He details what will happen when you are baptized in the Spirit, in verse 8. In no way does this equate the Holy Spirit and power. Verse 8 says "you shall receive power when the Holy Spirit has come upon you."

This is like saying that you will receive an ice cream cone when the bell rings. We cannot equate the ice cream cone and the ringing of the bell; it is simply that the ringing of the bell tells us when we are going to get the ice cream cone. Acts 1 tells us that when we are baptized with the Holy Spirit, that is when we get the power, but the two are not the same.

To help us understand that these are two different things, in writing to the Corinthians, Paul said this:

> **4 And my message and my preaching were not in persuasive words of wisdom, but in demonstration of the Spirit and of power,**
>
> **5 that your faith should not rest on the wisdom of men, but on the power of God.**
>
> **—1 Corinthians 2**

We see in verse 4 here that Paul's message was given in demonstration of the Spirit and also of the power. These are two separate things: the Spirit and the power.

When Paul wrote to the Christians in Thessalonica, he told them that the gospel came to them in both the Holy Spirit and in power:

> **5 for our gospel did not come to you in word only, but also in power and in the Holy Spirit and with full conviction; just as you know what kind of men we proved to be among you for your sake.**
>
> **—1 Thessalonians 1**

We need to take a lesson from this. When we present the gospel, we should present it both in the Holy Spirit and also in the power of God.

It is exciting to know that Jesus Himself was anointed from God the Father with the Holy Spirit, and He was also anointed with *POWER*:

> **38 *You know of* Jesus of Nazareth, how God anointed Him with the Holy Spirit and with power, and *how* He went about doing good, and healing all who were oppressed by the devil; for God was with Him.**
>
> **—Acts 10**

We are to be filled with the Holy Spirit, but we are also to be anointed with the power of God; these are two separate things. The Holy Spirit is a person; power is a force.

Most people reading this book already will have been filled with the Holy Spirit. The emphasis of this book is not on being filled with the Spirit, but on being anointed (clothed) with the power of God, and using that power in love, in the name of Christ and under the guidance of the Holy Spirit.

On the other hand, it is possible that you could be reading this book and not even know Jesus Christ as your personal Savior. Maybe you think that you do, and that you are going to heaven, but you are not sure. If that is your case, I would encourage you to pause right now and read Appendix A. Get that issue settled, because we ***can*** know for sure, and you need not be in doubt:

13 These things I have written to you who believe in the name of the Son of God, in order that you may know that you have eternal life.

—1 John 5

As you can see from the verse above, it is not a "guess so" or "hope so" situation. We can ***KNOW*** that we have eternal life. If you do not know this, please turn and read Appendix A before recommencing here.

It is possible that you are reading this book and you are not sure that you have been baptized in the Holy Spirit. (That is the first filling of the Holy Spirit, and there can be many subsequent fillings.) If this is your state, please read the next section on being filled with the Holy Spirit carefully and prayerfully.

BEING BAPTIZED WITH THE HOLY SPIRIT

As I mentioned at the beginning of this chapter, the disciples had become Christians at least by John 20, if not before. Yet Jesus told them that they needed something beyond this: they needed to wait to be "baptized with the Holy Spirit" and they would receive power when this happened.

For many people raised in various denominations, even the phrase "baptized with the Holy Spirit" brings visions of fanatical people bouncing off the walls, rolling down the aisles and frothing at the mouth. In some churches, if this subject is broached, and it almost never is, the expression "being filled with the Spirit" is used instead of "being baptized with the Holy Spirit." The phrase "baptized with the Spirit" is almost treated like a dirty word.

I was raised a Methodist and this was my experience growing up. But I came to realize that this is a perfectly good biblical concept, and we need not shy away from any terminology that the Bible itself uses. In talking about Jesus at the very beginning, John the Baptist said this:

> **33 "And I did not recognize Him, but He who sent me to baptize in water said to me, 'He upon whom you see the Spirit descending and remaining upon Him, this is the one who baptizes in the Holy Spirit.'. . ."**
>
> **—John 1**

John said that Christ would baptize us with the Holy Spirit. Right before He ascended into heaven, Jesus Himself said this:

> **5 ". . . for John baptized with water, but you shall be baptized with the Holy Spirit not many days from now."**
>
> **—Acts 1**

Jesus said that these early disciples were to be baptized in the Spirit, which I believe is equated to the first filling of the Holy Spirit. After they were baptized in the Spirit, some of them were filled with the Holy Spirit a number of times subsequently.

It was hard for me to realize that there was something beyond salvation that God wanted to give me—and that was for me to be baptized or filled with the third *person* of the Trinity, the Holy Spirit. One of the places we read about this is in Acts:

> **14 Now when the apostles in Jerusalem heard that Samaria had received the word of God, they sent them Peter and John,**
>
> **15 who came down and prayed for them, that they might receive the Holy Spirit.**
>
> **16 For He had not yet fallen upon any of them; they had simply been baptized in the name of the Lord Jesus.**

17 Then they *began* laying their hands on them, and they were receiving the Holy Spirit.

—Acts 8

These verses tell us that people in Samaria had received Jesus Christ and had been baptized in the name of the Lord Jesus. Evidently, though, there was something they still lacked. Therefore, the disciples in Jerusalem sent Peter and John all the way up to Samaria to help them acquire what they lacked, even though they indeed believed in Christ.

From Jerusalem to Samaria is very rugged terrain. The journey by foot was long and hard, and it must have taken Peter and John at least a couple of days. Yet they were willing to walk all that distance and risk the dangers of traveling through rough countryside in order that the believers in Christ in Samaria might receive the baptism of the Holy Spirit. That is how important it was to Peter and John. They should have known the importance, because they walked, talked and lived with Jesus Christ.

When Peter and John got to Samaria, they prayed for the Christians there and they received the baptism of the Holy Spirit. I believe it is as important for Christians today to be baptized in the Holy Spirit as it was for the Christians in Samaria at that time.

There has been much confusion on the baptism of the Holy Spirit, which there need not be. Perhaps I can clear up some of it, as I share with you the things that God has laid on my heart concerning it.

The first question to arise is this: "How does a Christian know whether or not he has been baptized in the Holy Spirit?" I believe that when a Christian is baptized in the Holy Spirit, something supernatural (unexplainable in human terms) happens to him or through him. The supernatural occurrence might be seeing a vision; it might be praying for someone and he is healed; it might be prophesying, singing in the Spirit, performing a miracle, speaking in tongues or something else. The Holy Spirit will give to each person whatever gift He wants him to have (1 Corinthians 12:1-11). But it will be something miraculous that cannot be explained in human terms. If you have never had something supernatural happen to you or through you, there is a good chance that you have not yet been baptized in the Holy Spirit.

If you think that you might have been baptized in the Holy Spirit but you are unsure, I would encourage you to ask God to give you afresh a supernatural confirmation of your baptism in the Holy Spirit.

If you are a Christian (you have accepted Jesus Christ as your Lord and Savior and have been born again) and you would like to be baptized with the Holy Spirit, the next question is, "How do I receive this?" To help you understand, I would like to relate something that happened to me one time when I was ministering in a church in Minnesota.

Rarely at the end of a message do I feel impressed of the Holy Spirit to give an invitation. Even more rarely do I ask for those who want to be baptized in the Holy Spirit to come forward. But on this particular Sunday, I felt the Lord wanted me to do this. So I asked any of those who would like to receive the baptism of the Holy Spirit to come to the front of the sanctuary. The pastor suggested that they go into a back room, which they did. I stayed out front and prayed with a few people. About ten minutes later I went back and joined them in this room.

What I saw there really grieved my spirit. The man trying to help these people receive the baptism of the Spirit was telling them to drop their jaws, to hold up their hands, not to say anything in English, to make sounds and so forth. I thought, "Oh my! There is no way they are going to receive the baptism of the Holy Spirit this way!" So I asked the man if I could say something. (Since I was the visiting minister, he just about had to say "yes.")

I then related to these precious brothers and sisters how I had initially received the baptism of the Holy Spirit. It had occurred a number of years before when I was flying from Houston to Dallas. This particular plane had a compartment up front with eight seats that was totally isolated from the rest of the cabin. I was the only one in this front compartment and I began to pray, as I frequently do on a flight. As I talked to God, I began to tell Him how wonderful, glorious, magnificent and all-powerful He was and to thank Him because He was so holy, pure and righteous. Pretty soon my human words seemed so inadequate to express what I was feeling toward God. I then began what I call "spiritual humming." (I have only heard one other person do this since then.) As the pitch of my hum went up, it seemed like it touched God and as the pitch of the humming came down, it was as though it touched my heart. I sat there humming from high notes to low notes, to high notes to low notes, communing with God, praising Him, worshiping Him, and adoring Him in a way that was above and beyond what I could do in English words.

After sharing this experience, I encouraged the people who had come forward to get their minds off of the gifts of the Spirit or speaking in tongues and just to begin to worship and praise God. I told them that when English became totally inadequate to express their adoration, God would take over beyond that.

That evening several of these people came up to me stating that they had received the baptism of the Holy Spirit during the afternoon between the morning and the evening services. I particularly remember one young man who came up to me with tears in his eyes. He said that for eight years he had been seeking the baptism of the Holy Spirit and that every time an invitation was given for those who wanted to receive the baptism of the Spirit, he came forward. Evidently he had been forward literally dozens of times during this eight-year period. However, he had never received the baptism of the Holy Spirit.

With tears rolling down his cheeks, he related to me how driving home from church that morning, after I had shared what God had laid on my heart, he began to praise the Lord and, as his words became inadequate, he began to fluently speak and sing in another tongue. He said that he wanted to jump and dance all over the place and had to pull his car to the side of the road and stop, because he was afraid he would have an accident. He then sat at the side of the road for 30 minutes, praising God in this glorious new way. He said that he was so grateful to me for helping him get his eyes off of the gifts of the Spirit and the baptism of the Holy Spirit and helping him to refocus on God and on Jesus Christ.

I might relate one other incident about a friend of mine who was a dedicated Christian but had recently left the church that he had been attending. His daughter started going to an Assembly of God church with a friend of hers. One Sunday morning when he picked her up after church, she had tears in her eyes and she said, "Daddy, this morning I was baptized in the Spirit and spoke in tongues." This really shook up my friend, because he did not believe that those things were for today. He went home and after lunch went into his bedroom alone, knelt down beside the bed and began to talk to God. He said, "God, if this is of You, I want it. I want all that you have for me." As he was praying, a glorious light came upon him and he began to praise God in heavenly singing that was not in English.

I could write an entire book on our relationship with the Holy Spirit. We certainly receive the Holy Spirit when we receive Christ. He comes to indwell us and to seal us (2 Corinthians 1:22; Ephesians 1:13, 14).

However, being baptized with the Holy Spirit is something that ***can*** occur when we receive Christ but frequently occurs later in our Christian life.

If you have invited Jesus Christ into your heart to be your Savior and to take over your life, then you have the Holy Spirit dwelling within you. But, as we have just seen, that does not mean that you have been baptized (the first filling) with the Holy Spirit. If you would like to be baptized with the Holy Spirit, in a moment I am going to suggest a prayer that you might pray. Before I do that, you need to realize that Jesus promised that the Father would not withhold the Holy Spirit from anyone who asked Him for it. Here are the words of Jesus Himself:

> **11 "Now suppose one of you fathers is asked by his son for a fish; he will not give him a snake instead of a fish, will he?**
>
> **12 "Or *if* he is asked for an egg, he will not give him a scorpion, will he?**
>
> **13 "If you then, being evil, know how to give good gifts to your children, how much more shall *your* heavenly Father give the Holy Spirit to those who ask Him?"**
>
> **—Luke 11**

Do you believe that? Do you believe the Heavenly Father will give the Holy Spirit to those who ask? If you believe that, the only thing that remains for you to do is to ask the Father to baptize you with the Holy Spirit, to the glory of Jesus Christ. If this is your desire, you might pray a simple prayer that goes something like this:

Father God, thank You that I know Jesus Christ as my Savior and Lord. I love you so much for sending Your only begotten Son to die for me

> *and for the peace that comes from knowing Him as my Savior. Father, right now I'm asking that You baptize me with your Holy Spirit. I know that You will do this, because You promised that You would not withhold the Spirit from anyone who asked. I trust the Holy Spirit to give me whatever gift He wants me to have. Thank You, Father, that You said Your power would come upon me when I was baptized with the Holy Spirit, and right now I'm receiving that power from You. I want to always use this power only under the guidance and control of the Holy Spirit and only to Your glory and to the glory of Jesus Christ, Your Son and my Savior. It is by faith, in the name of Jesus Christ, that I ask You to do this for me.*

If you just prayed that prayer or a similar one, you may want to put this book aside for a little bit and give God a chance for His Spirit to work His work in you and fill you up to overflowing. Just allow the Holy Spirit to fill you in a glorious way. You may not see stars or flashes of lightning; it may be a very quiet thing, but let Him do His comforting, loving and powerful work in your heart and life.

If you prayed that prayer and truly meant it, I believe God indeed will baptize you with His Holy Spirit, if He has not already done so at this moment. The question naturally arises as to how we can know if we have been baptized in the Holy Spirit. We will tackle that subject next.

THE EVIDENCE OF BEING BAPTIZED WITH THE HOLY SPIRIT

Since being baptized with the Spirit (according to Acts 1:5, 8) appears to be a prerequisite to receiving the power of God, how do we know that we have been baptized with the Spirit? There are some who would say that speaking in tongues is the only valid evidence to ensure that someone has been baptized in the Holy Spirit. The Pentecostal church believes this and also the Full Gospel Businessmen's Fellowship. I am a life member of the Full Gospel Businessmen's Fellowship, and I love them dearly, but that one concept I cannot reconcile with the Scriptures. In Acts 1, according to Jesus, ***the*** evidence of being baptized in the Holy Spirit is that you will receive ***supernatural power***. You won't receive physical or financial power; you will receive supernatural power. The Holy Spirit will give to each Christian the gifts that He wants him to have, through which that supernatural power will be exercised:

> **7 But to each one is given the manifestation of the Spirit for the common good.**
> **8 For to one is given the word of wisdom through the Spirit, and to another the word of knowledge according to the same Spirit;**
> **9 to another faith by the same Spirit, and to another gifts of healing by the one Spirit,**
> **10 and to another the effecting of miracles, and to another prophecy, and to another the distinguishing of spirits, to another *various* kinds of tongues, and to another the interpretation of tongues.**
> **11 But one and the same Spirit works all these things, distributing to each one individually just as He wills.**
>
> **—1 Corinthians 12**

Verse 11 says that the Holy Spirit gives to each one "just as He wills"—just as He chooses. We cannot specify which gift or gifts we are going to have. We can ask God for different gifts, but the Holy Spirit is going to give to each person the gift that He wants him to have. Not everyone will have every one of these gifts.

A passage at the end of that same chapter in Corinthians further supports this:

> **28 And God has appointed in the church, first apostles, second prophets, third teachers, then miracles, then gifts of healings, helps, administrations, *various* kinds of tongues.**
>
> **—1 Corinthians 12**

I would like to present the next two verses in a slightly different form, and then I will repeat them in standard biblical form. The words in parenthesis are the words that the apostle Paul implies by this question. So here are verses 29 and 30 in tabular form:

> **All are not apostles, are they? (No)**
> **All are not prophets, are they? (No)**
> **All are not teachers, are they? (No)**
> **All are not workers of miracles, are they? (No)**
> **All do not have the gifts of healings, do they? (No)**
> **All do not speak in tongues, do they? (No)**
> **All do not interpret, do they? (No)**

Some would try to twist this around to have it apply to just a single meeting which violates all principles of biblical interpretation. Paul is not talking about a meeting here; he is discussing people being prophets, teachers, workers of miracles and so forth. Here Paul clearly teaches us that not everyone is going to speak in tongues.

However, I can say with all clarity and boldness that all who are baptized in the Holy Spirit have supernatural power. They may not use it, but they have it. If they will allow the Holy Spirit to do so, He will demonstrate it through some gift or some other supernatural means.

Let us now review those verses in their normal biblical form:

28 And God has appointed in the church, first apostles, second prophets, third teachers, then miracles, then gifts of healings, helps, administrations, *various* kinds of tongues.

29 All are not apostles, are they? All are not prophets, are they? All are not teachers, are they? All are not *workers* of miracles, are they?

30 All do not have gifts of healings, do they? All do not speak with tongues, do they? All do not interpret, do they?

—1 Corinthians 12

Incidentally, there are five major cases recorded in the book of Acts of people being filled with the Holy Spirit, and in two of these they did not speak in tongues. For example:

31 And when they had prayed, the place where they had gathered together was shaken, and they were all filled with the Holy Spirit, and *began* to speak the word of God with boldness.

—Acts 4

17 And Ananias departed and entered the house, and after laying his hands on him said, "Brother Saul, the Lord Jesus, who appeared to you on the road by which you were coming, has sent me so that you may regain your sight, and be filled with the Holy Spirit."

18 And immediately there fell from his eyes something like scales, and he regained his sight, and he arose and was baptized;

19 and he took food and was strengthened.

—Acts 9

In neither one of these cases was there any biblical evidence that speaking in tongues followed being filled with the Spirit. So the evidence of being baptized with the Holy Spirit is that one has supernatural power. Speaking in tongues is one evidence of supernatural power.

Let me hasten to add that one of the most frequent initial evidences of this supernatural power is speaking in tongues, and I am all for speaking in tongues. I have seen God's supernatural power released through the exercising of that gift many times when prayer in English was just not enough. However, we must accept the fact that there are many beautiful Spirit-baptized Christians who have other gifts of God's power, who do not speak in tongues. James Robison is one. My own wife was baptized in the Holy Spirit for three years before she spoke in tongues.

ANOINTED WITH POWER

We are to be filled with the Holy Spirit, but we are also to receive the power of God. We have had a lot of emphasis on being filled with the Spirit. Now I believe that God is moving us on to emphasize being anointed with the power of God. If we concentrate on the Spirit and almost ignore the power, we will not move in God's power the way He wants us to.

This next thought is a new thought from the Lord and I cannot establish it from the Scriptures as well as I would like. I believe the Lord has shown me that the filling of the Spirit comes from within and the ***power*** pours down on us from the outside, like an anointing oil, such as the oil that was poured over the heads of Aaron, David and others when they were anointed (Exodus 29:7, 30:30; 1 Samuel 16:13). We have already read Acts 10:38, which says that Christ was anointed with the power.

Here are a couple of additional verses that teach this principle:

> **49 "And behold, I am sending forth the promise of My Father upon you; but you are to stay in the city until you are clothed with power from on high."**
>
> **—Luke 24**

> **35 And the angel answered and said to her, "The Holy Spirit will come upon you, and the power of the Most High will overshadow you; and for that reason the holy offspring shall be called the Son of God. . . ."**
>
> **—Luke 1**

> **9 And he said unto me, My grace is sufficient for thee: for my strength is made perfect in weakness. Most gladly therefore will I rather glory in my infirmities, that the power of Christ may rest upon me.**
>
> **—2 Corinthians 12, *KJV***

Did you see in these passages that the power of the Lord "clothes" us, "overshadows" us and "rests upon" us? Once we are baptized (filled) with the Holy Spirit, the Spirit is ***within*** us to perform gifts of the Spirit. But then we also have the power of the Lord resting ***upon*** us.

Please don't get hung up on whether the power is "in" us or "on" us. It is possible that it could be either or both. But for purposes of this book, let us conceptualize the power of God as being upon us.

Another very interesting thing to note is that, for the first twenty-nine years of His life, Jesus Christ did no miracles. During those years He healed no one, He cast out no demons. The first miracle He performed was turning water into wine (John 2:1-10):

11 This beginning of *His* signs Jesus did in Cana of Galilee, and manifested His glory, and His disciples believed in Him.

—John 2

Yet He was the Son of God. Why no miracles for twenty-nine years? The answer is simply that there were no miracles because He did not yet have the power of God resting upon Him.

Something happened when Jesus was thirty that changed all of that. He was baptized with the Holy Spirit. When that happened, the supernatural power of God came down upon Him, and then He could heal the sick, deliver the demon-possessed and perform miracles:

9 And it came about in those days that Jesus came from Nazareth in Galilee, and was baptized by John in the Jordan.

10 And immediately coming up out of the water, He saw the heavens opening, and the Spirit like a dove descending upon Him;

11 and a voice came out of the heavens: "Thou art My beloved Son, in Thee I am well-pleased."

12 And immediately the Spirit impelled Him *to go* out into the wilderness.

13 And He was in the wilderness forty days being tempted by Satan; and He was with the wild beasts, and the angels were ministering to Him.

—Mark 1

Here we see that Jesus was baptized by the Spirit and also received the power and approval of God the Father. That power of God that rested upon Him was there for Him to do healing.

Jesus was so clothed with the power of God that when someone touched Him in faith that individual was healed:

43 And a woman who had a hemorrhage for twelve years, and could not be healed by anyone,

44 came up behind Him, and touched the fringe of His cloak; and immediately her hemorrhage stopped.

45 And Jesus said, "Who is the one who touched Me?" And while all were denying it, Peter said, "Master, the multitudes are crowding and pressing upon You."

46 But Jesus said, "Someone did touch Me, for I was aware that power had gone out of Me."

—Luke 8

This was not only true for this one lady, but for a host of people:

10 for He had healed many, with the result that all those who had afflictions pressed about Him in order to touch Him.

—Mark 3

56 And wherever He entered villages, or cities, or countryside, they were laying the sick in the market places, and entreating Him that they might just touch the fringe of His cloak; and as many as touched it were being cured.

—Mark 6

The power that covered Jesus Christ was almost electric, discharging healing to all who touched Him in faith. In the same way as Jesus, you and I receive power when we are baptized (filled) with the Holy Spirit. We receive the same power that He received. It is there—it may be dormant, but it is there. What will we do with it?

RECHARGEABLE BATTERIES

Consider for a moment electricity as an analogy representative of this supernatural power of God. I am sure that you have all seen exhibited or advertised the batteries that are rechargeable. After they lose their power, you can put them into the recharger, and they will regain full power. You can then put them back into your flashlight or other device, and they discharge their power whenever the switch is turned on.

Car batteries are also rechargeable batteries. However, most people are not aware of it, because the alternator does a continual recharging job as you drive. Actually, you can think of it this way: the car's motor turns a little generator which puts out electricity that recharges your car battery. But, if you cut the wires coming from that generator (alternator) to your battery, very soon it will lose all of its power. Then you will have to go to an outside recharging unit in order to get that battery recharged.

All of these batteries can either be full of power or almost empty of power. If they are empty or depleted, it is wonderful that they can be recharged again, so that they are once more full of power.

I would like to think of you and me, as Christians, as "rechargeable spiritual batteries." We need to be full of the Holy Spirit and also to have our batteries charged with the power of God, the supernatural power of God. We can have both. If we are fully charged with the power of God then, like a good battery, in a controlled way we are able to release that power that is stored within us.

If we are walking around as fully-charged "spiritual batteries," full of the miracle power of God, and we meet someone who is sick, we can lay hands on that person and pray for him and, in Jesus' name, release that supernatural power to do a powerful healing in him. If we are walking clothed with God's power, and we meet somebody who is being harassed by demons, we can release the supernatural power of God to drive those demons away, in the name of Christ and to His glory.

If we are walking, charged with the power of God and we meet someone who is lost without Jesus Christ, who is condemned to an eternity in a burning lake of fire, we can release the supernatural power and present the gospel, not in words only, but in words and in demonstration of the power of God, which is the way Paul presented the gospel.

I trust that by now you have a desire to be a fully-charged spiritual battery, clothed with the power of God, and to be full of the Holy Spirit. As we look at various aspects of this power of God, ways in which He wants to use you, I pray that what I share in this book will help you to operate in the fullness of the miraculous power of God, as He directs and in a way that glorifies Him.

God's supernatural power is for every Christian.

Chapter 4

THE POWER OF GOD

Let us look at something that Jesus said when He told people why they were in error and why they were making mistakes.

> **24 Jesus said to them, "Is this not the reason you are mistaken, that you do not understand the Scriptures, or the power of God? . . ."**
>
> **—Mark 12**

We see in this verse that Jesus said there were two reasons that they were making errors—they did not understand two things:

1. The Scriptures
2. The power of God

This is a very important duo (a dynamite duo); these two things ***must*** go together. If one understands one but not the other, he will be falling far short of all that God wants him to have. There are many good churches today which have a pastor who is a good Bible teacher, and the people there understand the Scriptures, yet the real power of God is not operating in their midst. Understanding the Scriptures is very important. They are our safety net against which to try all things.

However, in this book we will concentrate on understanding the power of God.

Speaking of power, if the Charismatics are honest with themselves, the power that was exhibited in many of their meetings fifteen years ago is really no longer there. Yet I am confident that God wants to exhibit His power whenever Christians gather together, as a major tool in evangelism, and in our individual lives as well.

Oh, that God would give us a burning desire, a deep hunger, to experience the power of God! This is lacking in so many places today. Be asking the Holy Spirit to teach your heart as we learn about the power of God together.

THE POWER OF GOD WAS WITH JESUS

The power of God was with Jesus. One very interesting verse that gives us an insight into this is the following:

> **17 And it came about one day that He was teaching; and there were *some* Pharisees and teachers of the law sitting *there*, who had come from every village of Galilee and Judea and *from* Jerusalem; and the power of the Lord was *present* for Him to perform healing.**
>
> **—Luke 5**

Did you get what that said? Jesus was teaching and, as He was teaching:

THE POWER OF THE LORD WAS PRESENT FOR HIM TO PERFORM HEALING.

For Jesus to perform healing, it was necessary that the power of God be present. Jesus did not use His own power. It was power from God. If that was necessary for Jesus, how much more important it is for us! I have seen many Christians try to perform healings when the power of God simply was not present and, consequently, there were no results.

There were times when Jesus was so engulfed with the power of God that He could sense when some of that power went out from Him:

> **19 And all the multitude were trying to touch Him, for power was coming from Him and healing *them* all.**
>
> **—Luke 6**

The power of God was on Him so much in this passage from Luke 6 that everyone was trying to touch Him, and those who did were healed. This is an example of what happens when the power of God is truly present. In the last chapter, we read about the woman with the hemorrhage from Luke 8. Let's read Mark's account of that same event:

> **25 And a woman who had had a hemorrhage for twelve years,**
>
> **26 and had endured much at the hands of many physicians, and had spent all that she had and was not helped at all, but rather had grown worse,**
>
> **27 after hearing about Jesus, came up in the crowd behind *Him*, and touched His cloak.**
>
> **28 For she thought, "If I just touch His garments, I shall get well."**
>
> **29 And immediately the flow of her blood was dried up; and she felt in her body that she was healed of her affliction.**
>
> **30 And immediately Jesus, perceiving in Himself that the power *proceeding* from Him had gone forth, turned around in the crowd and said, "Who touched My garments?"**

31 And His disciples said to Him, "You see the multitude pressing in on You, and You say, 'Who touched Me?'"
32 And He looked around to see the woman who had done this.
33 But the woman fearing and trembling, aware of what had happened to her, came and fell down before Him, and told Him the whole truth.
34 And He said to her, "Daughter, your faith has made you well; go in peace, and be healed of your affliction."

—Mark 5

If the power of God were really present in a meeting, my next question would be, what did the power of God do? When the power of God was there with Jesus, He did good things—He healed and He set free those who were bound up by Satan.

The people were amazed by the power of God that was with Jesus (emphasis on *power* is the author's):

42 And as he was yet a coming, the devil threw him down, and tare *him*. And Jesus rebuked the unclean spirit, and healed the child, and delivered him again to his father.
43 And they were amazed at the mighty POWER of God. . . .

—Luke 9, *KJV*

36 And amazement came upon them all, and they *began* discussing with one another saying, "What is this message? For with authority and POWER He commands the unclean spirits, and they come out."

—Luke 4

8 But when the multitudes saw *it*, they marvelled, and glorified God, which had given such POWER unto men.

—Matthew 9, *KJV*

Jesus indeed had the power of God on Him, but He was not selfish with it. He acknowledged that it was there and He used it! Power does no good at all unless it is used.

JESUS GAVE THE DISCIPLES POWER

Not only did Jesus Christ have the power of God with Him, He also had the ability and the authority to give this power away to other people:

1 And when he had called unto *him* his twelve disciples, he gave them POWER *against* unclean spirits, to cast them out, and to heal all manner of sickness and all manner of disease.

—Matthew 10, *KJV*

7 And he called *unto him* the twelve, and began to send them forth by two and two; and gave them POWER over unclean spirits; . . .

—Mark 6, *KJV*

19 Behold, I give unto you POWER to tread on serpents and scorpions, and over all the power of the enemy: and nothing shall by any means hurt you.

—Luke 10, *KJV*

The disciples had power "over all the power of Satan"! Not only did He give incredible power to the twelve, but then He extended this gift to the seventy (Luke 10:1, 17-20), and then to many, many believers.

49 "And behold, I am sending forth the promise of My Father upon you; but you are to stay in the city until you are clothed with POWER from on high."
—Luke 24

In this verse from Luke, Jesus does not say anything about the Holy Spirit. He tells them to wait until they are "clothed with POWER." How many Christians that you know would you consider to be "clothed with POWER from on high?" Do you think that He wants us to be clothed with POWER? ***Yes!***

8 but you shall receive POWER when the Holy Spirit has come upon you; and you shall be My witnesses both in Jerusalem, and in all Judea and Samaria, and even to the remotest part of the earth."
—Acts 1

In the two preceding verses, we see that Christ wanted a larger group to remain in Jerusalem until they received power. That was the one thing that Jesus wanted them to have—the power of God. That is very clear from Luke 24:49. Then Acts 1:8 tells us that they would receive this power after the Holy Spirit had come upon them.

I believe that Jesus wants you to have and be clothed with the supernatural power of God. When the supernatural power of God comes upon you, something is going to occur. The power of God never comes just to make itself known and then to leave again. The power of God comes to accomplish something.

1 After these things the Lord appointed other seventy also, and sent them two and two before his face into every city and place, whither he himself would come. . . .

17 And the seventy returned again with joy, saying, Lord, even the devils are subject unto us through thy name.

18 And he said unto them, I beheld Satan as lightning fall from heaven.

19 Behold, I give unto you POWER to tread on serpents and scorpions, and over all the power of the enemy: and nothing shall by any means hurt you.

20 Notwithstanding in this rejoice not, that the spirits are subject unto you; but rather rejoice, because your names are written in heaven.

—Luke 10, *KJV*

We know that this gift of power was extended beyond the initial twelve and the seventy, and ultimately it includes you and me. Once the supernatural power of God comes upon you, then something is going to happen to you that cannot be explained by the human mind. It may be that God will give you a song instantly or you may see a vision; you may lay hands on someone and pray and he is healed; you may speak in an unknown language; you may prophesy or something else. The Holy Spirit gives gifts to men as He chooses, but the common thread that runs through all of these actions is the power of God.

TODAY JESUS GIVES BELIEVERS THE POWER OF GOD

Jesus gave the power of God to the disciples of the first century, and He has also given that same power to all believers of all ages:

17 "And these signs will accompany those who have believed: in My name they will cast out demons, . . .

18 . . . they will lay hands on the sick, and they will recover."

—Mark 16

The fact that this power has been given to every Spirit-filled believer by Jesus Christ is evidenced by the ministries of Peter and Paul, the Gentile Christians and Christians throughout the centuries, including Christians today.

For a discussion of the power of the Holy Spirit, the power of Jesus Christ and the power of God the Father, please see Appendix C. Here we are primarily talking about the power of God the Father. This supernatural power must be used in the name of Jesus Christ and for His glory, under the guidance and control of the Holy Spirit.

POWER IS THE CONFIRMATION OF THE GOSPEL

One of the reasons that God gives this power to us (to perform signs and wonders) is to confirm that what we are speaking is from Him. We find this many places in the Old Testament. Moses is a clear example. Repeatedly, God performed signs and wonders in Egypt which confirmed that Moses was His messenger to Pharaoh to tell him to let the Israelites go. Similarly, with Elijah and others of the prophets, God's power working through them dramatically testified that they were speaking from Him.

Even with Jesus, it was the miracles that He performed that made people accept the words that He was speaking as being from God:

23 Now when He was in Jerusalem at the Passover, during the feast, many believed in His name, beholding His signs which He was doing.

—John 2

In a similar manner, Paul says repeatedly that as he preached the gospel, it was not just with words, but also there was a demonstration of the power of God in signs and wonders along with his preaching, to validate that his preaching was from God:

> **4 And my message and my preaching were not in persuasive words of wisdom, but in demonstration of the Spirit and of power, . . .**
>
> **—1 Corinthians 2**

> **19 But I will come to you soon, if the Lord wills, and I shall find out, not the words of those who are arrogant, but their power.**
> **20 For the kingdom of God does not consist in words, but in power.**
>
> **—1 Corinthians 4**

POWER IN THE EARLY CHURCH

Now let's move on beyond the disciples to the early church. In the excellent magazine, *Christian Life* (now merged with *Charisma*), Peter Wagner, professor at Fuller Seminary, once wrote about the power of the early church. This is what he had to say (October 1985 issue):

> First, I pointed out that many American Christians have difficulty getting in touch with the power of the supernatural in daily life because of the secular humanist world view which permeates so much of our American culture. . . .
>
> This month I want to show how world view played a major role in one of the most astounding historical phenomena ever recorded: the spread of Christianity in the early centuries. It began with 12 in the upper room

around 33 A.D. Within three centuries it had become the predominant religion of the Roman Empire.

What brought this about?

The answer to that question is clearer than it ever has been thanks to Yale University historian Ramsey MacMullen. Just last year his fascinating book, *Christianizing the Roman Empire, A.D. 100-400*, was released by Yale University Press. A great value of this book is MacMullen's perspective. He is not writing as a Christian theologian arguing a point, but simply telling it like it is.

Early in his book, MacMullen raises what he considers a most important question: "What did Christianity present to its audience? For plainly the process of conversion that interests me took place in people's minds on the basis of what they knew, or thought they knew." The answer is deceptively simple. While Christianity was being presented to believe in both word and deed, it was the deed that far exceeded the word in evangelistic effectiveness.

The people of the Roman Empire were not secular humanists. They knew about miracles and took them for granted. "Not to believe in them would have made you seem more than odd, simply irrational, as it would have seemed irrational seriously to suppose that babies are brought by storks," MacMullen says. They expected the gods they believed in to perform miracles, and they did. They healed people, pronounced oracles, made it rain, helped them win wars, and cursed their enemies.

Early Christian missionaries and preachers would not have questioned the miraculous power of pagan gods in the slightest. Their point was that this is the power of the kingdom of darkness, directly caused by demons which the Romans gullibly had been calling "gods." Furthermore, the end result of that power was to bring evil and suffering in the present life, and worst of all, eternal death.

The Christian God, Father of Jesus Christ, was presented first and foremost as a God who works miracles. His power was declared to be greater than the power of the pagan gods. It was a power for good, not evil, and it promised eternal life. MacMullen points out that in the early centuries very few pagans were converted because of Christian doctrine or because of logical presentations of truth. Christianity swept through the Roman empire because the people could see with their own eyes that Jesus did miracles greater than any gods they had known of.

Christian preachers in those days were so sure of the power of God that they did not hesitate to engage in power encounters. They would challenge in public the power of pagan gods with the power of Jesus. MacMullen relates many of these. For instance, he tells how the author of the Acts of Peter provoked a spiritual "shoot-out" in the very forum of the capital. It was done "after a great deal of braggadocio and confrontational theatrics in previous days, and statements for the press, and in the presence of a highly interested crowd."

All this involved "the manhandling of demons—humiliating them, making them howl, beg for mercy, tell their secrets, and depart in a hurry." By the time the Christian preachers got through, no one would want to worship such "nasty, lower powers."

MacMullen tells a story of John the Apostle that is not well-known to Christians because it is not in the Bible. It is told in the Acts of John and takes place in Ephesus. Great acts of healing won many of the people in Ephesus. But the power encounter came in the temple of the god Artemis, apparently the seat of the chief prince of the demons who had jurisdiction over Ephesus.

In the temple, John prayed, "O God . . . at whose name every idol takes flight and every demon and every unclean power, now let the demon that is here take flight in Thy name." As soon as he said that, the altar of Artemis split in pieces, and half of the whole temple fell down.

"We are converted now that we have seen thy marvelous works," the Ephesians said.

When I was in seminary I was taught not to put much stock in these apostolic-times stories which weren't in the Bible. MacMullen disagrees with that. As a respected historian, he believes such stories are reliably reported and can be taken as historically valid. Furthermore, he finds, they were widely used to bring people to conversion to Christianity.

When dramatic events happened like the power encounter in Ephesus, "listeners were and should have been scared half to death," MacMullen affirms. "Divine power had a terrifying, high-voltage quality that split and blinded." He concludes that the supernatural power of God "driving all competition from the field" should be seen as "the chief instrument of conversion" in those first centuries.

For one thing, this remarkable book dispels possible doubts that the supernatural power of God continued after the days of the apostles. Historical research is showing that there never was a time when miracles ceased, particularly on the frontiers where the Gospel of the kingdom was penetrating new people groups.

—Strang Communications
Lake Mary, FL 32746

As you can see from this write-up of the early church, miracles wrought by the power of God were the things that convinced the listeners that the men were speaking words of God.

TODAY THE GOSPEL IS CONFIRMED BY THE POWER OF GOD

In recent history, when the gospel has gone forth with the power of God, it has been tremendously effective. Without this, the results are meager. For example, in the 1700's when the Protestants sent missionaries to China, sometimes they would labor for many years without a single convert. At that same time, the Catholics sent a Spirit-filled Catholic priest to China. The power of God was with him and many were healed and cured of demonic possession, and thousands came to know Christ.

In more recent years, a friend of mine, Dave Clark, was working in Uganda and other African countries. In one year, he and some other brothers established 134 new churches. They would go into a village and gather the people together to preach the gospel to them. The villagers almost inevitably would ask, "What can your God do that ours can't?"

They would then ask them to bring out the worst sick and crippled people. The power of God was with them to heal these people who were sick and crippled. Of course, the place would be packed, providing an excellent opportunity to present the gospel of Jesus Christ. Many accepted Jesus Christ as Savior, as a result of seeing the power of God manifested.

Even today, when Charles and Frances Hunter have one of their "Healing Explosions," a large number of people come to know Christ, as they see the power of God working through healings in an extraordinary way.

A friend of mine from New Zealand has a tremendous ministry of the gospel going out in power. His name is Bill Subritsky (Dove Ministries, P.O. Box 48036, Blockhouse Bay, Auckland, New Zealand). I have seen him pray for a lady in a wheelchair who appeared to be almost dead. After about five minutes of prayer for healing and casting out demons, the lady was able to come out of her wheelchair, walk back and forth, and lift her hands in praise to the Lord.

Terry Calkin, another dear friend of mine, who is a chartered accountant and now lay pastor of Greenlane Christian Centre in Auckland, New Zealand, frequently goes to India on crusades. In one of his crusades, he had a woman who was all bent over come up on stage and he prayed for her healing. Nothing appeared to happen, so he had her just sit there on the stage as he continued to preach and present the gospel of Jesus Christ. Before he had finished preaching, the woman gradually straightened up and when he next turned around to look at her, she was sitting upright in her chair. The entire audience noticed this and the response to Christ was tremendous, both in people being saved and in people being healed.

Where the power of God is, there will be healings. Where healings are, there will be conversions.

If your church or your group has had a lack of people coming to know Jesus Christ as their personal Savior in recent days, months, or even years, then the problem is likely that the power of God is not being used to do the miracles of God.

AUTHORITY AND POWER

There are two other subjects in connection with power that we need to think through together. The first of these is the relationship between authority and power. The reason our government officials can exercise their authority over us is because some place behind them is a man with the power of a gun. If an IRS agent came to audit you and you told him to "get lost" and he could do nothing about it, then his authority would be meaningless, without power behind him.

Similarly, many times there is a military takeover of a country. The military leaders (the junta) will appoint a man to be president. This man has the authority of the presidency, but he does not have any power. The power still rests with the military.

You have likely seen a school monitor or someone who is put in charge (authority) of a group of students but had no power. The students simply mocked him and ignored him. Unfortunately, we put many of our teachers in this position. They have the "authority" over the students, but they do not have very much power over them to back up that authority.

Power and authority really must go hand in hand. ***Authority without power is worthless.***

The Jews sent spies to entrap Jesus, so they could deliver Him to the governor, who had both authority and power:

> **20 So they watched *Him*, and sent spies who pretended to be righteous, that they might seize on His words, in order to deliver Him to the power and the authority of the governor.**
>
> **—Luke 20, *NKJV***

Jesus Himself not only had authority over unclean spirits; He also had the power to force them to come out:

> **36 And amazement came upon them all, and they *began* discussing with one another saying, "What is this message? For with authority and power He commands the unclean spirits, and they come out."**
>
> **—Luke 4**

Jesus did not simply give the disciples authority over disease, demons and so forth; He gave them authority ***and power:***

1 And He called the twelve together, and gave them power and authority over all the demons, and to heal diseases.

—Luke 9

The point of all this is that we do not just have the authority over disease and demonic forces; we also have the *power of God* to actually control them. Jesus did not give us a powerless authority. We need to realize this and to speak in keeping with this power. In dealing with disease or demonic activity, we not only need to say that we are coming in the name and the authority of Jesus Christ. We should also state the fact that Jesus has given us the power of God and that power of God is vastly stronger than the power of those demon forces. We need to command them, with an authoritative voice. We can literally force them out and away by the power of God, through the name of Jesus Christ.

But we can have all of the power and authority in the world and it will do no good, *UNLESS WE USE IT!*

If you are a Spirit-filled Christian, you have the power and authority from Jesus. Now what are you going to do with it? Why not take a chance? Let it flow out. Try utilizing this power in a way that glorifies Jesus, and God will bless your obedience.

FAITH AND POWER

Next, we need to talk about the relationship of power and faith. You can have all of the faith in the world, but if there is not the power of God, little is going to happen. Before you react, let me explain what I mean.

There was a missionary in China who was walking down the road one day and he came across a lady who was kneeling at the roadside in front of an embankment, praying. In front of her were three sticks stuck into the embankment. He stopped and asked her to whom she was praying. She said, "To these three sticks." He asked her who had put the sticks there, to which she replied, "I did." Our faith is only as good as the object in which it is placed.

Many Christians place their faith in many things other than the power of God. They pray and have faith that, "God is going to work everything out alright," or "God will take care of me, regardless what happens." Sometimes they have faith in their positive confessions. We need to have faith that the power of God is there and is able to achieve miraculous things.

It takes both faith and the power of God to achieve miracles for God's glory and the glory of Jesus:

> **8 And Stephen, full of faith and power, did great wonders and miracles among the people.**
>
> **—Acts 6, *KJV***

Here we see that Stephen was full of faith and also full of the power of God, and great miracles were accomplished by him. It takes both faith ***and*** power!

Paul put this even more succinctly when he wrote his second letter to the church at Thessalonica. He told them that they needed to have faith with power:

> **11 To this end also we pray for you always that our God may count you worthy of your calling, and fulfill every desire for goodness and the work of faith with power; . . .**
>
> **—2 Thessalonians 1**

When writing to the church at Corinth, Paul said that he came to them in the power of God (miracles, signs and wonders), so that their faith would not rest on words but on the power of God:

1 And when I came to you, brethren, I did not come with superiority of speech or of wisdom, proclaiming to you the testimony of God.
2 For I determined to know nothing among you except Jesus Christ, and Him crucified.
3 And I was with you in weakness and in fear and in much trembling.
4 And my message and my preaching were not in persuasive words of wisdom, but in demonstration of the Spirit and of power,
5 that your faith should not rest on the wisdom of men, but on the power of God.

—1 Corinthians 2

We might well ask ourselves what our faith rests on. Most of us would say, "The Scriptures and God's promises." That is good, but according to Paul, we need a faith that rests on the power of God.

We need to remind ourselves that a passive faith is no faith at all. As I said earlier, "If there is no risk, there is no faith." The best story I know that exemplifies true faith is one that I heard when I was a young boy. In the story, a man stretched a tightwire across Niagara Falls. He then walked across it and back, and all the crowds were cheering him. Next he got out a wheelbarrow that had the front wheel designed to fit onto the tightwire. He placed the wheelbarrow on the wire and pushed it all the way across Niagara Falls and back. When he returned, the crowd cheered wildly. Then he asked the crowd if they thought he could put someone in the wheelbarrow and push it all the way across and back. With loud enthusiasm, the crowd shouted, "Yes, yes!" Then the man turned to a lady sitting in the first row and said, "Get in." Her cheering quickly subsided.

Up until this point, this lady's faith had been head faith; but now she was faced with the fact that she needed to convert that head faith into real faith. Real faith involves taking an action and taking a risk. Peter exhibited this real faith:

> **2 and a certain man who had been lame from his mother's womb was being carried along, whom they used to set down every day at the gate of the temple which is called Beautiful, in order to beg alms of those who were entering the temple.**
>
> **3 And when he saw Peter and John about to go into the temple, he *began* asking to receive alms.**
>
> **4 And Peter, along with John, fixed his gaze upon him and said, "Look at us!"**
>
> **5 And he *began* to give them his attention, expecting to receive something from them.**
>
> **6 But Peter said, "I do not possess silver and gold, but what I do have I give to you: In the name of Jesus Christ the Nazarene—walk!"**
>
> **7 And seizing him by the right hand, he raised him up; and immediately his feet and his ankles were strengthened.**
>
> **8 And with a leap, he stood upright and *began* to walk; and he entered the temple with them, walking and leaping and praising God.**
>
> —Acts 3

Did you notice verse 7? Peter had real faith; he grabbed this lame man by the hand and pulled him up!

Terry Calkin, whom I mentioned earlier in this chapter, shared with me that the Lord had led him to do a similar thing. In a meeting one time, there was a very emaciated woman in a wheelchair. In this particular meeting, the power of God was healing people left and right. He felt led of the Lord to go over to her, and proclaim her healed in the name of Jesus Christ. He then grabbed hold of her hands and pulled her up out of the wheelchair. At first she was very wobbly and then her legs strengthened more and more, and soon she was running back and forth in front of the platform, praising God and giving glory to Jesus Christ.

Most Christians have had "head faith" about the supernatural power of God, but if it is going to work in their lives to bless them and to bless others, it is going to have to be converted into real faith.

Do you believe this verse?

> **24 "Therefore I say to you, all things for which you pray and ask, believe that you have received them, and they shall be *granted* you."**
>
> **—Mark 11**

Do you believe this with head faith or with real faith?

Do you believe these next two verses?

> **17 "And these signs will accompany those who have believed: in My name they will cast out demons, they will speak with new tongues;**
>
> **18 they will pick up serpents; and if they drink any deadly *poison*, it shall not hurt them; they will lay hands on the sick, and they will recover."**
>
> **—Mark 16**

Here Jesus promises that if we lay hands on the sick, *THEY WILL RECOVER*. Do you believe that? Do you believe it with head faith or with real faith? Satan will try to get us to distrust or have doubts about this promise. Therefore, we are likely to do little, if anything, about healing the sick. Peter had real faith in the promise that Jesus Christ made and he put it to action, when he commanded the lame man to walk in the name of Jesus Christ and ***pulled*** him to his feet.

Some Christians pray for "more power" to meet a particular situation. Other Christians pray for additional power in general. Those prayers are not needed. When we were filled with the Holy Spirit, we received all the power of God that we will ever need. We do not need more power; most Christians simply need the action type of real faith to put to use the power of God that they already have. Remember, "without faith it is impossible to please Him" (Hebrews 11:6).

Faith and fear are opposites, just as light and darkness are opposites. The light switch is ***on*** or ***off***. If the light switch is on, then there is light and we operate in faith. If the light switch is off, then we are in darkness and we operate in fear. When you go to utilize the power that can clothe you, the light switch will either be on or off. Before you pray, turn on the switch of faith and believe the promises of God:

> **20 Now to Him who is able to do exceeding abundantly beyond all that we ask or think, according to the power that works within us, . . .**
>
> **—Ephesians 3**

Do you believe what that verse says—that God is able to do abundantly far beyond ***all*** that you ask or think? How? By giving you additional power? No! It is according to the power that is already within you, working out through faith. I will have more to say about faith later. For now, I hope that I have helped you to desire to move out and begin to operate "according to the power that works within you" (Ephesians 3:20).

MORE ON POWER AND VICTORY

The power of God is such a vast subject with many facets to explore. In the next chapter we will discuss where the power of God comes from, the fact that we, as individuals, can have it operating in our lives, and some current examples of the workings of the power of God.

We each might examine ourselves. When we encounter sickness, disease or demons, can we truthfully say that "the power of God was with me so much that I dealt with them readily?" If we cannot say that, then as individuals, we need to pray that we might walk in such a way that the power of God might be operating in us whenever it is needed.

We also need to begin to ask ourselves if the power of God is really present when we come together as a body of believers. If it is not, no matter how good the preaching, singing and worship might be, we need to earnestly seek that the power of God would be present.

Now that you have the general picture, let's take a closer look at how God's supernatural power can flow through *you*.

God's supernatural power is for every Christian.

Chapter 5

GOD'S POWER THROUGH YOU

God wants to exhibit His supernatural power through every Spirit-filled believer. This is not for just a select few. This is not only for full-time ministers, but equally for laymen. It is not just for the bold, but equally for the shy. It is not just for the strong, but equally for the weak. It is not just for the intellectuals, but equally for the uneducated. It is not just for men, but equally for women; not just for adults, but equally for youth.

GOD WANTS TO USE SUPERNATURAL POWER IN EVERY SPIRIT-FILLED BELIEVER IN JESUS CHRIST

Remember, that is why Jesus wanted the disciples to remain in Jerusalem. He wanted them to have power, and He knew that they would get power—God's supernatural power—when they were filled with (baptized with) the Holy Spirit. If you are a Spirit-filled believer in Jesus Christ, you have this power and you need to begin to use it, under the direction of the Holy Spirit.

Unfortunately, today the Evangelicals, Pentecostals, Charismatics and other Protestants have set up their own false form of "priesthood." If someone in our church or fellowship needs healing, rather than allowing God to let His supernatural power flow through us to do the healing, we encourage that person to go hear brother or sister so-and-so, who has a "tremendous healing ministry."

If someone needs salvation, many Christians would encourage him to hear Billy Graham, James Robison or some other evangelist, rather than presenting the gospel to him ourselves, in the Spirit and in power. We have unknowingly set such people up as a "priesthood"—as someone who stands between us and God. That is wrong. It is not the essence of the New Testament. In the New Testament, every believer is a priest before God and has direct access to the full power of God through Jesus Christ our Savior (1 Peter 2:5,9; Revelation 1:6).

As long as a believer has the view of letting the power of God flow out of somebody else, the power of God will not be exhibited through him, as God wants it to be. We need to realize that God's power can and does flow through housewives, schoolteachers, fishermen, tax attorneys, ditch diggers, young people, old people—any believer who has received the power of God which comes at the filling of the Holy Spirit.

Before you proceed to read the remainder of this chapter, you really need to settle that issue in your own heart. Do you accept the fact that God's power can flow through you? Do you accept that God wants His power to flow through you and that no other believer in Jesus Christ has a preferred access to that power?

Hopefully you have accepted that fact. If you do not hamper it, God's power can and will flow through you.

Remember, in Chapter 3 we drew the analogy of us being rechargeable batteries. As a spiritual battery, one can be fully charged, full of the power of God and ready to go out and do His work, for His glory, or one can be fully discharged, with little or no power, even though he is filled with the Holy Spirit. As we discussed earlier, the power of God and the Holy Spirit are not the same thing. I do not know where you, as a spiritual battery, stand at this point in time, but hopefully you have a strong desire to be a fully-charged battery that can be used by the Lord to meet people's needs and to let His power flow out to heal, deliver, encourage and do miracles, if He so wills.

As I travel and minister at various churches, frequently I will minister in a church where there are about 99 percent "discharged batteries." I believe many of these people have the mistaken idea that if they come to church, they will get charged up. That is not the way it should be. Jesus did not say, "Wait in Jerusalem and keep having meetings and more meetings and in that way you will receive the power of God." Rather, He said, "You will receive the power of God when the Holy Spirit comes upon you" (Acts 1:4-8). The charging of you as a spiritual battery and the receiving of the power of God can happen in your closet. You should come to church fully charged and ready to be used by God. As others come in, you should be praying, "Lord, is this one whom you want your power to touch through me this day?" God will lead you and do glorious things through you.

I do not mean to be facetious or to make light of a serious subject, but perhaps we should form a group called "Batteries for Jesus." Our motto might be:

> *"We are sick and tired of being discharged batteries. We want to be **fully** charged with the power of God, to the glory of Jesus."*

If that is how you feel, you might want to pause now in reading this book and express that to God.

THE AWESOME POWER GIFTS

In the Old Testament, God gave awesome, supernatural power to some of the prophets. He gave them power to do such things as shut up the skies and cause it not to rain and to call down fire from heaven to consume their enemies. In a few pages, I will share with you why I believe these "awesome power gifts" are coming back in abundance at the end of this age. Therefore, they should be very important to us.

Let us first read about an incident when Elijah called down fire from heaven and consumed his enemies:

> **8 And they answered him, "*He was* a hairy man with a leather girdle bound about his loins." And he said, "It is Elijah the Tishbite."**
>
> **9 Then *the king* sent to him a captain of fifty with his fifty. And he went up to him, and behold, he was sitting on the top of the hill. And he said to him, "O man of God, the king says, 'Come down.'"**
>
> **10 And Elijah answered and said to the captain of fifty, "If I am a man of God, let fire come down from heaven and consume you and your fifty." Then fire came down from heaven and consumed him and his fifty.**
>
> **11 So he again sent to him another captain of fifty with his fifty. And he answered and said to him, "O man of God, thus says the king, 'Come down quickly.'"**
>
> **12 And Elijah answered and said to them, "If I am a man of God, let fire come down from heaven and consume you and your fifty." Then the fire of God came down from heaven and consumed him and his fifty.**
>
> **13 So he again sent the captain of a third fifty with his fifty. When the third captain of fifty went up, he came and bowed down on his knees before Elijah, and begged him and said to him, "O man of God, please let my life and the lives of these fifty servants of yours be precious in your sight.**
>
> **14 "Behold fire came down from heaven, and consumed the first two captains of fifty with their fifties; but now let my life be precious in your sight."**

15 And the angel of the LORD said to Elijah, "Go down with him; do not be afraid of him." So he arose and went down with him to the king.

—2 Kings 1

This is a very interesting story. Twice a captain and his fifty men came up after Elijah, and God told Elijah to bring down fire from heaven and destroy them, which he did. Today, with most Christians, had two identical situations occurred and God led them in the same way in both situations, if a third identical situation came up, they would probably respond in the same manner before God could stop them. In this case, they would have called down fire and destroyed their enemies, before God had a chance to give different instructions.

However, Elijah was listening to God in each situation, and on the third occasion, He did not bring down fire from heaven. Elijah was a bondslave of God and he was carefully listening to Him and was obedient to Him. I believe the reason God cannot give this type of power to most Christians today is that He cannot trust them with it. God is going to restore this kind of awesome power only to His bondslaves whom He can trust with it—those whom He knows will only use His power in total obedience and submission to Him.

Before we talk further about what it means to be a bondslave, let us look at a couple of other instances of the power gifts in the Old Testament. I am sure you will remember the dramatic, historic encounter wherein Elijah had a contest with the prophets of Baal and Asherah, 850 of them. Only Elijah was able to bring down fire from heaven to consume his sacrifice:

19 "Now then send *and* gather to me all Israel at Mount Carmel, *together* with 450 prophets of Baal and 400 prophets of the Asherah, who eat at Jezebel's table." . . .

21 And Elijah came near to all the people and said, "How long *will* you hesitate between two opinions? If the LORD is God, follow Him; but if Baal, follow him." But the people did not answer him a word. . . .

35 And the water flowed around the altar, and he also filled the trench with water.

36 Then it came about at the time of the offering of the *evening* sacrifice, that Elijah the prophet came near and said, "O LORD, the God of Abraham, Isaac and Israel, today let it be known that Thou art God in Israel, and that I am Thy servant, and that I have done all these things at Thy word.

37 "Answer me, O LORD, answer me, that this people may know that Thou, O LORD, art God, and *that* Thou hast turned their heart back again."

38 Then the fire of the LORD fell, and consumed the burnt offering and the wood and the stones and the dust, and licked up the water that was in the trench.

39 And when all the people saw it, they fell on their faces; and they said, "The LORD, He is God; the LORD, He is God."

40 Then Elijah said to them, "Seize the prophets of Baal; do not let one of them escape." So they seized them; and Elijah brought them down to the brook Kishon, and slew them there.

—1 Kings 18

It is interesting here that, after Elijah won the contest by bringing the fire down from God, the Lord had him kill all of the 850 false prophets. Most Christians today would love to be able to call down fire from heaven, but they most likely would refuse to obey God if He told them to kill 850 prophets of pagan gods.

The Lord also gave Elijah the power to shut up the heavens so that it would not rain:

1 Now Elijah the Tishbite, who was of the settlers
of Gilead, said to Ahab, "As the LORD, the God of
Israel lives, before whom I stand, surely there shall be
neither dew nor rain these years, except by my
word." . . .

7 And it happened after a while, that the brook
dried up because there was no rain in the land. . . .

—1 Kings 17

1 Now it came about *after* many days, that the
word of the LORD came to Elijah in the third year,
saying, "Go, show yourself to Ahab, and I will send rain
on the face of the earth."
2 So Elijah went to show himself to Ahab. Now the
famine *was* severe in Samaria. . . .

41 Now Elijah said to Ahab, "Go up, eat and drink;
for there is the sound of the roar of a *heavy* shower."
42 So Ahab went up to eat and drink. But Elijah
went up to the top of Carmel; and he crouched down on
the earth, and put his face between his knees.
43 And he said to his servant, "Go up now, look
toward the sea." So he went up and looked and said,
"There is nothing." And he said, "Go back" seven times.
44 And it came about at the seventh *time*, that he
said, "Behold, a cloud as small as a man's hand is
coming up from the sea." And he said, "Go up, say to
Ahab, 'Prepare *your chariot* and go down, so that the
heavy shower does not stop you.'"
45 So it came about in a little while, that the sky
grew black with clouds and wind, and there was a heavy
shower. And Ahab rode and went to Jezreel.
46 Then the hand of the LORD was on Elijah, and
he girded up his loins and outran Ahab to Jezreel.

—1 Kings 18

In this passage, first we see Elijah shutting up the sky so that it would not rain. Then, under God's guidance and direction, three years later Elijah accurately prophesied when the rain would recommence.

THESE AWESOME POWER GIFTS ARE GOING TO RETURN

The book of Revelation lets us know that God is going to restore these awesome power gifts at least to the two witnesses. However, I believe it is possible that the two witnesses of Revelation are not two individuals but two groups of people. Perhaps they are prototypes of the true bondslaves, the overcomers that God is calling forth at the end of the age. Let's read about the power gifts that God is going to restore to them:

> **3 "And I will grant *authority* to my two witnesses, and they will prophesy for twelve hundred and sixty days, clothed in sackcloth."**
>
> **4 These are the two olive trees and the two lampstands that stand before the Lord of the earth.**
>
> **5 And if anyone desires to harm them, fire proceeds out of their mouth and devours their enemies; and if anyone would desire to harm them, in this manner he must be killed.**
>
> **6 These have the power to shut up the sky, in order that rain may not fall during the days of their prophesying; and they have power over the waters to turn them into blood, and to smite the earth with every plague, as often as they desire.**
>
> **—Revelation 11**

If you will notice, verse 5 informs us that the two witnesses will have the ability to call down fire to devour their enemies. In fact, it says that if someone desires to harm them, he "must" be killed by fire that proceeds out of their mouth to devour their enemies. Most Christians would have a difficult time calling down fire from heaven to kill an enemy. Most Christians today would have difficult time doing what Elijah did when He called down fire and consumed the captain and fifty innocent soldiers.

Perhaps the reason that we do not have these awesome power gifts is that we would not use them in the way in which God would instruct us, even if we had them.

If you notice, verse 6 of Revelation 11 says that not only will the two witnesses have the power to shut up the sky so that it does not rain, but they will also be able to turn the waters into blood and to smite the earth with plagues. Could God entrust the average Christian today with such abilities to call down fire from heaven to consume his enemies, to cause it to not rain for years, to turn the waters of our rivers into blood, and to bring down plagues upon people? I think you will agree with me that the majority of Christians could not be entrusted with that type of power.

God could only entrust that kind of power to someone who was continually listening to Him and consistently obedient to what He told him to do. Since God is only going to give this type of power to obedient believers (bondslaves), we need to take a look at the subject of being a bondslave of God.

BE A BONDSLAVE OF GOD

As we begin to explore what it means to be a bondslave of God, we first need to examine the differences between a ***servant*** and a ***slave.*** A servant gets wages, and he can buy with those wages whatever he wants to buy. A servant has days off, during which he can do whatever he wants. A servant can marry whom he wants to marry. He has certain rights. He can quit at anytime because, in a sense, the position is like any job—it is temporary in that it can be terminated by either party at any time.

On the other hand, a slave never has any days off—he is a slave 365 days a year. He does not have any money of his own. Anything that he has, the master gives to him. He may live in relative comfort or even luxury, but if he wants a new chair, he has to ask the master. The master may say, "Yes" or "No," and he may even specify what kind of chair the slave is to have. If he wants to marry, he must marry whom the master tells him to marry. He has no possessions of his own, no time of his own, no rights of his own. He must do whatever his master tells him to do, whether it be to dig ditches, clean the house or fight and die for the master. That describes a ***slave.***

Now, let's look at the Biblical definition of a ***bond-slave.*** A bondslave is a "volunteer permanent slave," as we see in Exodus:

> **2 "If you buy a Hebrew slave, he shall serve for six years; but on the seventh he shall go out as a free man without payment.**
>
> **3 "If he comes alone, he shall go out alone; if he is the husband of a wife, then his wife shall go out with him.**
>
> **4 "If his master gives him a wife, and she bears him sons or daughters, the wife and her children shall belong to her master, and he shall go out alone.**
>
> **5 "But if the slave plainly says, 'I love my master, my wife and my children; I will not go out as a free man,'**
>
> **6 then his master shall bring him to God, then he shall bring him to the door or the doorpost. And his master shall pierce his ear with an awl; and he shall serve him permanently. . . ."**
>
> **—Exodus 21**

According to this passage, after a slave has served his time, he is free to go. But, if he really loves his master, he can choose to decline freedom and instead volunteer to remain as a permanent slave. He will never again be free. He will never again have any money, possessions, time, or rights of his own.

It is interesting to consider that as a slave volunteers to be a permanent bondslave, the master also takes on some obligations. He obligates himself to care and provide for that slave for the rest of his life, assuming that the slave remains obedient to him. So you can see that it is a two-way transaction, wherein both the slave and the master are making a commitment.

God wants us to enter into that type of transaction with Him, whereby we volunteer to become His permanent bondslave. From that moment on, we will have nothing of our own. Yet, since I made that bondslave commitment to the Lord, I have found that He has wonderfully provided for me and taken care of my family and me.

However, let me warn you that if you make a bondslave commitment, God will hold you to it. For example, we had just built a new home on the ranch which is the headquarters for Omega Ministries (the end-times ministry that God has raised up and called us to head). It had a fireplace with a mantel. A few months after the completion of this home, we were in South Africa ministering to various groups there and we saw a beautiful, carved elephant's tusk. I have seen these all over the world but this one was by far the most exquisite one I had ever seen. It was also very reasonably priced. We thought it would look lovely on our mantel, and we could have afforded it. At one time, I would have just bought it, without thinking twice. However, because I had made a commitment to God to be His bondslave, I prayed, "Lord, this is Your money. Can we use some of it to buy this beautiful elephant's tusk?" He said, "No." (So today we have a $6 painted ostrich egg on our mantel instead, as a souvenir of South Africa.) I am His bondslave and it is critical that I learn to walk in obedience to Him in all areas.

I believe that it is only to absolutely obedient bondslaves that God can entrust the incredible power gifts that He is going to give in His next major move here on planet earth. I have authored a book that addresses the three stages of the Christian life: the salvation stage, the baptism of the Spirit stage and the bondslave stage. If you would like to read further on this subject of bondslaves, I would encourage you to get that book, entitled *You Can Overcome,* and read it.

As you have been reading this last section, God already may have been speaking to your heart, urging you that He wants you to make a bondslave commitment to Him. For your convenience, the next to the last page in this book is a bondslave commitment form that you may wish to fill out. If God is speaking to your heart, I would encourage you to pause and turn there. At least read through that commitment and pray about it.

There is one additional point of significance before we leave the subject of bondslaves. At the end of this age, God is going to seal His bondslaves on their foreheads with the seal of the living God:

> **2 And I saw another angel ascending from the rising of the sun, having the seal of the living God; and he cried out with a loud voice to the four angels to whom it was granted to harm the earth and the sea,**
>
> **3 saying, "Do not harm the earth or the sea or the trees, until we have sealed the bond-servants of our God on their foreheads."**
>
> **—Revelation 7**

Some people are worried about the mark of the beast. Let me ask you a question: If God seals you on your forehead with the seal of God for your protection, do you think Satan or anyone else can remove God's seal from your forehead and replace it with the mark of the beast? Of course not! That would be saying that Satan is more powerful than God. Once God seals you for protection, you are protected.

God is raising up an end-time army of bondslaves (also called overcomers) that He is going to use in a very powerful way. He will give them divine protection, just as He divinely protected Daniel and Shadrach, Meshach and Abed-nego, and many others during Biblical days.

I am excited about being a bondslave and ultimately getting divine protection with the seal of God on my forehead. But I am also willing to do anything God wants me to do and I want to be perfectly obedient to Him. I love Him so much. Only then can He can entrust me with "extra-ordinary" power gifts.

Let us now return to the main subject at hand—the fact that God would like every Spirit-filled believer to start using His supernatural power. You may never move in these "awesome power gifts," but I am sure that you want all that God has for you. Right? According to Acts 1:8, you received power when you were first filled with the Holy Spirit. He gave you that supernatural power for a reason. The Bible says that He wants His power to clothe you and to flow through you to others.

THINGS THAT HAMPER GOD'S POWER

God wants you to have His supernatural power and to use it. You need it, and hopefully after reading this far in this book, you earnestly desire to be used in this manner. God wants you, as a spiritual battery, to be fully charged with His power. There is coming upon the earth a new move of God in real power. I know you do not want to miss it. Unfortunately, there are many things that can hamper God's power flowing through you.

For example, do you think that God's power would freely flow through you if you were living in adultery? I believe the answer is *no.*

Do you believe God's power would fill you and freely flow through you if you were obsessed with greed and financial gain and you worked at your job sixteen hours a day, only to obtain wealth? Again, I think the answer is *no.*

If you were a gossip and routinely went around accusing the brethren, do you think God's power would fill you and flow through you to the extent that God would like? Once more, I believe the answer is *no.*

We need to examine some of these hindrances and discuss how to get rid of them, so that our "battery" can be fully charged, ready to be filled afresh with the power of God.

God's supernatural power is for every Christian.

Part II

WHAT HAMPERS GOD'S POWER

Chapter 6

YOUR "DIET" CAN PREVENT POWER

In this chapter, we will be looking at something that can hamper the power of God covering you and flowing out to do His miraculous works. I believe that your "diet" can be a major hindrance to this. In this case, I am not referring to your physical diet, but your ***spiritual diet.*** Just as what goes into your mouth feeds your physical body, what goes into your ***eyes*** and ***ears*** feeds your spirit and soul.

If you have a diet of primarily "spiritual junk food," you are actually harming your soul and spirit and contributing to poor health in those areas. If this is true, the supernatural power of God cannot rest upon you the way God wants it to.

To take an extreme example, let's say that there was a Christian who watched only X-rated movies, whose main reading was pornographic magazines, who watched only the programs containing sex and violence on television, and who rarely read the Bible. Do you think God is going to anoint that type of a person with His supernatural power and use him to perform miracles for the glory of God? I think you would agree with me that the answer is, "No." God would not be able to use that type of a person in a powerful way, because of the daily choices he was making to feed his soul and spirit with unedifying food. To varying degrees, most of us have a less-than-ideal spiritual diet. Although it may not be anywhere close to this extreme case, we may unconsciously be eating a poor diet without even realizing it.

Before looking at our spiritual diet and what it should be, let's take a look at our physical diet, so that we can draw some parallels.

YOU ARE WHAT YOU EAT

The statement that "you are what you eat" applies both to the physical realm and also to the spiritual realm. Almost every professional athletic team has a full-time dietitian. Those professional organizations are willing to spend money on this, because they know that in order to be healthy, vigorous athletes, team members must eat wholesome food. If these professional teams ate nothing but junk food, their stamina, energy and strength would decrease to where they could not perform optimally for the entire game.

There are tennis stars and other individual athletes who have hired their own personal dietitian or nutritionist. They are willing to do this because they know that they will perform better if they eat a better diet. All hospitals have dietitians, because they know that eating right is a major factor in helping patients get well.

In the physical realm, we know that "we are what we eat." This is evidenced by people in Africa and other countries who have a very poor diet and, consequently, become malnourished, weak and easily subject to diseases. In contrast with this are the Olympic athletes, for example. The distance runners eat a very carefully-structured meal the night before a competition and also on the morning of a marathon run, because they know that it makes a difference in their performance. They have healthy bodies that can be pushed to the limit, and they have amazing stamina.

These athletes are willing to sacrifice to get into good physical condition. They train for hours each day, get extra sleep, avoid junk food and give up much of their social lives. What do you think a Christian would be like if he or she made the same sacrifices?

One important point to note here is this: if I have an apple sitting in front of me, I can make a decision to eat it or not. However, if I decide to eat it and I actually chew it up and swallow it, I no longer have a choice. That apple ***will*** become part of me. It ***will*** become part of my blood, my flesh, my organs, my bones and even my brain cells.

Please let that principle soak in. It is only ***before*** I consume a food that I have a choice as to whether or not it is going to become a part of me. After I have eaten it, I have no choice in the matter at all. The reason this principle is so important is that the same thing is true in the spiritual realm.

For example, when Eve was tempted to eat of the tree of the knowledge of good and evil, up until the moment that she took the first bite, she had a choice as to whether or not to eat it—a choice as to whether or not it would become part of her. However, once she had eaten of that fruit, the decision-time was gone and that fruit was destined to become part of her being.

If we watch a movie on television, we think the thoughts of the people on the screen. Before we watch it, we can decide not to partake of it with our eyes and ears. However, after we watch it, it is too late. We have ingested that movie, and it ***will*** become part of us.

One lady I know has bad dreams if she watches any type of horror movie. Recently, she was telling me that she and her husband had watched an eerie science fiction movie with a terrible ending. She said she knew throughout that it was not wholesome or edifying, but she kept watching it anyway because she was "hooked" by the story and kept hoping it would get better.

Afterward she said she felt defiled from watching it. She also felt an irrational anger and irritability that she had picked up from emotions portrayed in the movie. She prayed with her husband before going to bed that God would cleanse their hearts and minds and allow them to have a good sleep. In spite of this, she told me that she was unable to sleep, but just kept seeing "reruns" of scenes from the movie in her mind. Finally, she got up and read her Bible for an hour. Afterward, she was able to sleep peacefully.

"We are what we eat." If we take garbage into our being through our eyes and our ears, it will "bear fruit," so to speak, but it will not be good fruit.

One graphic illustration that helps to communicate this point is the following. If you drive a nail into a fencepost, you can pull the nail out again, but it will leave a hole. There is no denying the imprint that that nail had upon that post. The consequences remain. There are consequences that come with the decisions and choices that we make of what to eat with our eyes and ears. What we choose to take into our being as part of our "spiritual diet" ***will*** become part of us.

An additional thought in the physical eating realm is that most of us do eat good foods. We eat at least some raw fruits and vegetables and other things that are good for our bodies. The problem is not that we do not eat good food, but that, in addition to the good food, we also eat things that harm our bodies, such as cake, ice cream, cookies, sodas and candy. We add junk food to our diet, with rationalizations such as:

"One time won't hurt."
"Everybody else eats things like this."
"I've been doing good; I deserve a binge."

I am sure that you, like me, would like to have a healthy body. However, we may not be so sure that we are willing to pay the price to have a healthy body, by eliminating the bad things from our diets and increasing the proportion of good things that we eat.

These principles in the physical realm apply very directly to the spiritual realm.

YOU ARE WHAT YOU EAT— IN YOUR SOUL, SPIRIT AND MIND

What we take in through the mouth feeds the body. What we take in through our ***eyes*** and ***ears*** feeds our soul and spirit. Just as in the physical realm, wherein what we take in with our mouth determines what we will become, so in the spiritual realm, what we take in with our eyes and ears determines what we will become. Remember, the Bible tells us that as a man thinks in his heart, so is he (Proverbs 23:7a). The thoughts that are deposited in our minds (through our eyes and ears) are what we will become.

We are not talking here about the words and pictures that come in accidently. We are talking about the thoughts (words and pictures) that we choose to take into ourselves, especially those that we "ingest" repeatedly.

Let's take some of the principles that we discussed concerning physical food and apply them in the spiritual realm. Up to the time we have read an article or looked at pictures in a magazine, we can decide whether we are going to spiritually take in what that magazine contains. However, once we have read the article or looked at the pictures, we no longer have a choice. That will become part of us, because what we take in is what we will become. Similarly, we have a choice before we watch a program on television or see a movie as to whether we want to take that into our mind and spirit. However, once we have viewed it, we no longer have that choice. It is part of us and it will, to some degree, determine what we will be.

This is one of the dangers to you (or your children) of sitting and randomly watching television programs. Whether you realize it or not, you have made a passive decision to take into your spirit and mind whatever comes upon the screen and to allow it to become part of you and determine what you will be. That would be the equivalent of going into a restaurant and, rather than ordering something that you want, simply telling them to bring you anything that is edible. They may bring you a nice dinner or they may bring you the discarded lettuce leaves or the potato peelings that have rotten spots in them. You would have abdicated the choice to them, rather than overtly making the decision yourself.

The trouble with believers today is not that we do not take in good spiritual food; most of us do that. The problem is all of the junk that we take in (with our eyes and ears) along with the "good food." If physically I ate 90 percent bad food, and only 10 percent good food, I would not have a healthy body. Likewise, in a given day, if I were to take in fifteen minutes of good, solid spiritual food and three hours of spiritual junk food, I would not wind up healthy on the spiritual level.

If you are overweight and you decide to lose weight and keep it off in order to maintain a healthy body, it means a permanent change in your physical eating habits. If you decide to become really healthy spiritually, in like manner you are looking at a permanent change in your "eating habits" concerning what you feed your mind and spirit. Your spiritual diet can prevent the power of God from flowing through you.

IF YOU WANT CHRIST FORMED IN YOU

As Christ is formed in us, we will stop ingesting spiritual garbage and God can and will fill our clean vessels with His thoughts.

19 My children, with whom I am again in labor until Christ is formed in you—

—Galatians 4

Christ dwells inside every believer, just as He did the believers at Galatia. However, Paul yearned that something even better would happen. He yearned that Christ would be ***formed*** in them. If we would like Christ to be formed in us (if we would like to become like Jesus), then our daily spiritual diet is a real key.

If we want Christ to be formed in us, we ***do not*** achieve this by "eating" the Bible. Satan knows the Bible backwards and forwards, probably better than you or me. In fact, it is possible to use the Bible to make decisions independent of God. The Bible simply must be something that shows us ***Jesus.*** This can easily happen, because He is there on every page.

I highly recommend reading the Scriptures daily. It is so very important to do this. God uses them to speak to us and to reveal Himself to us. A number of years ago, the Lord gave me an exciting plan for reading through the entire Bible in a year in a sequence that really helps the Scriptures to come alive! *The Victory Bible Reading Plan* has had a wide distribution all over the world and there are multiplied thousands of people reading the Scriptures daily, using it as a guide (available through Omega Publications; see last page of this book). However, we want to be careful not to read the Scriptures just for knowledge, or in order to learn the "do's and don't's" of life.

When someone told me that Jesus Christ was on every page, I had just studied through 1 Peter 5. In that chapter, I saw that the elders were not to dominate the flock and that we were supposed to humble ourselves before one another. I had not seen Christ in it at all. So I reread 1 Peter 5, and I saw that the elders were shepherds to the flock of God, and Jesus was the Chief

Shepherd. They should be examples to the flock, as Jesus was our example. Verse 4 really stood out to me. It said that when the Chief Shepherd reappeared, we would receive a crown of glory. As I reexamined the humbling of ourselves to one another, again I saw Christ as our example; He had voluntarily humbled Himself for us. Rather than gritting my teeth and trying to be humble, I saw Jesus and I wanted to be like Him.

We should seek to see Jesus as we read the Bible, and then we will want to be like Him. Psalm 1 says that the man of God meditates in the word of God day and night. As we do so and absorb all the goodness and richness about Jesus (our delicious spiritual food), we ***will*** become like what we eat.

One way to "eat Jesus" is through communion.

> **26 And while they were eating, Jesus took *some* bread, and after a blessing, He broke *it* and gave *it* to the disciples, and said, "Take, eat; this is My body."**
>
> **27 And when He had taken a cup and given thanks, He gave *it* to them, saying, "Drink from it, all of you;**
>
> **28 for this is My blood of the covenant, which is poured out for many for forgiveness of sins. . . ."**
>
> **—Matthew 26**

Christ also told us that as often as we take communion, we should do it "in remembrance of Him" (Luke 22:19). He did not say to do it in remembrance of His death and resurrection. He said to do it in remembrance of ***Him.*** As we take communion, we should remember His preexistence with God, His part in the creation of the universe, His appearances in the Old Testament (such as in the fiery furnace and to Joshua before the battle of Jericho), His humble birth, His life and teachings, His sacrificial death on the cross, His resurrection, His ascension into heaven and His coming powerful return to the earth where He will rule and reign.

There is a beautiful teaching on "eating Christ," based upon the passage wherein Jesus Himself claimed to be the bread of life that came down out of heaven. You may want to read the entire chapter of John 6, but we will look at just a portion of it here:

> **31 "Our fathers ate the manna in the wilderness; as it is written, 'HE GAVE THEM BREAD OUT OF HEAVEN TO EAT.'"**
>
> **32 Jesus therefore said to them, "Truly, truly, I say to you, it is not Moses who has given you the bread out of heaven, but it is My Father who gives you the true bread out of heaven.**
>
> **33 "For the bread of God is that which comes down out of heaven, and gives life to the world."**
>
> **34 They said therefore to Him, "Lord, evermore give us this bread."**
>
> **35 Jesus said to them, "I am the bread of life; he who comes to Me shall not hunger, and he who believes in Me shall never thirst. . . .**
>
> **48 "I am the bread of life.**
>
> **49 "Your fathers ate the manna in the wilderness, and they died.**
>
> **50 "This is the bread which comes down out of heaven, so that one may eat of it and not die.**
>
> **51 "I am the living bread that came down out of heaven; if anyone eats of this bread, he shall live forever; and the bread also which I shall give for the life of the world is My flesh."**
>
> **52 The Jews therefore *began* to argue with one another, saying, "How can this man give us *His* flesh to eat?"**
>
> **53 Jesus therefore said to them, "Truly, truly, I say to you, unless you eat the flesh of the Son of Man and drink His blood, you have no life in yourselves.**

54 "He who eats My flesh and drinks My blood has eternal life, and I will raise him up on the last day.

55 "For My flesh is true food, and My blood is true drink.

56 "He who eats My flesh and drinks My blood abides in Me, and I in him.

57 "As the living Father sent Me, and I live because of the Father, so he who eats Me, he also shall live because of Me.

58 "This is the bread which came down out of heaven; not as the fathers ate, and died, he who eats this bread shall live forever."

—John 6

In verse 51 of this teaching, Jesus says that we must eat the living bread (Himself) if we are to live forever. In verse 56, He tells us that whoever eats His flesh and drinks His blood abides in Him and He in us. If we follow this teaching and actually "eat Jesus," then we will become like Him. He will fill us and satisfy us!

In the Lord's prayer (Matthew 6:11 and Luke 11:3), where we ask God the Father for our daily bread, I have wondered if this is talking about our physical food, or if it is referring to Jesus, the living bread. Perhaps we should pray and ask for both. Jesus was thinking something similar when He said this:

4 But He answered and said, "It is written, 'MAN SHALL NOT LIVE ON BREAD ALONE, BUT ON EVERY WORD THAT PROCEEDS OUT OF THE MOUTH OF GOD.'"

—Matthew 4

Of course, we need physical bread (food) to keep our physical body alive. But we need the words that proceed out of the mouth of God (spiritual bread) to keep our soul and spirit alive, healthy, and operating in the power of God.

In John 4, the disciples went into a town to get something to eat while Jesus talked to the woman at the well. Here is what happened when they came back:

> **31 In the meanwhile the disciples were requesting Him, saying, "Rabbi, eat."**
> **32 But He said to them, "I have food to eat that you do not know about."**
> **33 The disciples therefore were saying to one another, "No one brought Him *anything* to eat, did he?"**
> **34 Jesus said to them, "My food is to do the will of Him who sent Me, and to accomplish His work. . . ."**
>
> **—John 4**

Another piece of spiritual food is to ***do*** God's will and to accomplish God's work, just as Jesus did (John 4:34). However, the main way that we can "eat" an individual is by ingesting His words. We quoted this verse once already, but it is worth repeating:

> **4 But He answered and said, "It is written, 'MAN SHALL NOT LIVE ON BREAD ALONE, BUT ON EVERY WORD THAT PROCEEDS OUT OF THE MOUTH OF GOD.'"**
>
> **—Matthew 4**

It is the words of Jesus, the words of God the Father, that we need to ingest in order to become like Jesus. We want to devour ***every word*** that God speaks.

Sadly, many Christians will never have Jesus formed in them because of their poor spiritual diets. During the lifetime of Christ, many people believed in Him, but did not become His disciples, because they were not willing to pay the price.

Many of us will not have Christ formed in us nor will we become like Jesus, as He would like us to, because of watching so much junk on television. For many of us, television is a primary input into our mind, soul and spirit, and what we take in there is what we are going to become like.

Instead of thinking the thoughts fed to us by television, Paul encourages us to do this:

> **8 Finally, brethren, whatever is true, whatever is honorable, whatever is right, whatever is pure, whatever is lovely, whatever is of good repute, if there is any excellence and if anything worthy of praise, let your mind dwell on these things.**
>
> **—Philippians 4**

What is portrayed on the average network does not match with what we are admonished to do in this verse, does it?

Since the input of television is such a major problem for the majority of those who will read this book, it is worth looking at specifically.

EATING THE TELEVISION OUTPUT

When we talk about "television" in this section, we are not referring to wonderful Christian programs like some of those found on Christian networks and stations. Rather we are talking about the standard network and PBS programming that most families "ingest" all evening long, most nights of the week.

Who produces the standard television programs? Are they Christians? Almost universally the answer is, "no." These are people of the world. Some of them are homosexuals, some of them are involved in the occult, some of them are atheists. With a rare exception, they are of "this world" and not of Jesus.

John tells us what is in the world:

15 Do not love the world, nor the things in the world. If anyone loves the world, the love of the Father is not in him.

16 For all that is in the world, the lust of the flesh and the lust of the eyes and the boastful pride of life, is not from the Father, but is from the world.

—1 John 2

What do you find on network television programming?

1. Lust of the flesh
2. Lust of the eyes
3. Prideful people

The lust of the flesh includes anything that the body craves: sex, drinking, eating, smoking, dope and so forth. The lust of the eyes includes "things": cars, beautiful homes, clothes, jewelry, furniture, stereos and so on. Also, there are many people on television trying to prove that they are the "best" and taking pride in it. Television helps us love the world. (Reread the preceding two verses.) You will find that if anyone loves the world, he does not love the Father.

Remember—we become what we spend our time thinking about. Thus, as we watch network television, if we think about people with loose morals, who are prejudiced or who commit violence, that is how we will become. Most Christians will not lower themselves to read books about many of these things, and yet they spend time each week watching television programs that glorify those same things. They cannot help thinking about those things while they are watching such programs. That is part of their diet of their mind, soul and spirit and, consequently, that is the way they will become.

This may not be as far-fetched as it seems. One Christian girl started living with two guys. When asked why she did it, she replied that after watching "Three's Company" on television, she concluded that it was not such a bad thing after all. Her behavior and morals were influenced and changed by the "diet" that she took in through her eyes and ears.

This takes us to the influence of television on our children. Many parents, even Christian parents, use television as an electronic baby-sitter. They let the kids plop themselves down in front of the television set on a Saturday morning and watch four hours of television. The parents have no idea what is being shown on that set. I recently watched Saturday morning television one day to see what our kids were consuming, and I was shocked to see what was on. There was much violence and murder, stories about the occult which basically glorified the occult, and stories about the supernatural that did anything but glorify God.

My recommendation to a Christian parent is not to let the children watch television unless there is an adult present, so they can either turn off the set if something unwholesome comes on or explain to the children why certain things are not glorifying to God. Parents would probably spank their children if they found them reading books about the very things that are shown on Saturday morning television. As your children think in their hearts, so they will become, and they are thinking about the things that they are watching on television. Once they have ingested those things, they become a permanent part of them.

Some children (and adults too) have nightmares or dreams about the things that they see on television. Would it not be so much better for them to be having dreams about Jesus and things that occurred in the Bible?

Television's impact on the youth is incredible. Several years ago, Michigan State University released their latest findings on a survey conducted to determine how much television American youth watch. The survey showed that children can see their favorite prime-TV characters engage in as many as 40 intimate acts and drink alcohol up to 50 times in a day of viewing. Children in the 4th through 8th grades see most of their favorite shows at night. The survey reports that between 7 and 9 p.m. during a typical week, there are 2.7 instances per hour of intimate sexual behavior between adults and alcoholic drinks are seen about 3.5 times an hour. The number increases to about 4 times during a crime show. The survey shows that children see and hear 7 times more references to sex between unmarried people than between the married. One of those making the survey stated that such relations between married couples hardly exist today on the TV screen.

For some people who are "televisionaholics," the only way to solve the television problem is to go cold turkey and shut it off completely. Following are two examples of people who turned off the television set, and one example of a case where television came to a town that had never had it before.

TV or not TV

> Hats off to Kevin Mitchell! Many people give up in despair on their New Year's resolutions after a short time. This ten-year-old Canadian boy held out in keeping a resolution that would be a challenge even to many adults.
>
> Late in 1984 Kevin read of two American boys who had managed to abstain from television-watching for a year and who had been rewarded by their parents with a computer.

Kevin approached his parents with the proposal that he would refrain from watching television for a year if they were to offer a reward. Since the boy was a virtual TV junkie, they readily agreed.

"It started out as a joke," his mother recalls. "We told him if he carried it through, we would give him a check for $200." They didn't realize how determined their son would be!

The parents noted a marked improvement in Kevin's attitudes after he gave up television watching. He started reading and creating games and puzzles. He joined a neighborhood parks program and won a city-wide award for being the most active participant.

A member of the Cub Scouts, Kevin launched into an ambitious badge-collecting program and soon had more badges than any other member of this pack. Tennis, cross-country skiing, model-building, and roller skating lessons became new interests.

His grade average rose as he became more physically and mentally fit. His parents noted that he also has become more outgoing.

Kevin doesn't pretend that the challenge was easy to meet. His brother refused to join him in the endeavor, so the lure of TV grew even more difficult to resist. But at year end, he had succeeded.

His parents, proud of his determination, readily gave him the check.

When the New Year dawned, however, Kevin announced his first indulgence. "I'm going straight downstairs to watch TV." However, he's pretty well hooked on the new lifestyle he developed and has little time for television now.

Kevin's $200 reward? It almost went for electronic games, but ended up in a savings account.

—*Have a Good Day*, May, 1986
P.O. Box 220, Wheaton, IL 60189

A Community's "Tune-Out" Puts Dent in the TV Habit

A three-day television tune-out last week in the Lower Moreland school district went over so well that it may become an annual event.

"We're thinking about contacting other school districts and inviting them to join us to do it again next January," said William Pezza, a social studies teacher and assistant football coach at Lower Moreland High School. He said he got the idea of trying to kick the television-watching habit during the "smoke-out" last November.

On Friday, Pezza got approval to pursue the idea of having an annual tune-out from Lower Moreland School District Supt. Lawrence Bozomo. Pezza said community response last week was so good that he thought it would be successful.

And going cold turkey from 8 a.m. Wednesday to midnight Friday apparently did help many families in the community get back in touch with one another. A fifth of the 3,000 students in the district participated in the program, according to Pezza.

—*Chicago Sun-Times*, date unknown
Huntington Valley, PA

Invasion of the Mind Snatchers

Before TV came to Essex, California, its citizens had never seen two people playing one guitar at the same time. To get to Essex from L.A. you drive east for about four hours, climbing out of the basin and into the high desert, a region of eccentric rock formations, long stretches of open flatness, recalcitrant soil and sunlight of a consistent and scouring brilliance. The towns are small and far apart. The air is clean, thin and very dry.

A sign on the Needles Freeway marks the exit to Essex. At the end of the offramp is a dusty paved strip, which lapses into disrepair a few miles before it ends, forming a right angle with a second, better-maintained road. At the crossroads there is a tiny Post Office building, and nearby, a half-dozen houses, several parked trailers and two gas stations.

But Essex is a little bit famous. Its notoriety is a creation of television—or, more accurately, the lack of television. For years, Essex has not been in the reception area of any TV station. The "town without television" has been a standby source of human-interest stories for daily newspapers and wire services, stories that invariably quoted the townspeople as saying that they didn't miss TV, that they read, gardened and conversed a lot, that their children were content and studious. Always worth a trip, Essex.

Then, on December 15, 1977, the National Broadcasting Company brought television to the town without television. Through the use of a device called a translator, all the programming of the NBC-TV station in Phoenix, Arizona, can now be seen in Essex. . . .

The present reconsideration of television takes its impetus in large part from Marie Winn's *The Plug-In Drug* published in 1977. A book primarily about the effect of television on children—its disruption of the natural relationship between brain hemispheres; its disastrous reduction of reading skills, attention span and the apprehension of reality—it also defines the essential problem of television watching.

"The very nature of the television experience, as opposed to the contents of the programs, is rarely considered . . . there is a similarity of experience about all television watching. Certain specific physiological mechanisms of the eyes, ears and brain respond to the stimuli emanating from the television screen regardless of the cognitive content of the programs. . . . It is the adverse effect of television viewing on the lives of so many people that defines it as a serious addiction. The television habit distorts the sense of time. It renders other experiences vague and curiously unreal while taking on a greater reality for itself. It weakens relationships by reducing and sometimes eliminating normal opportunities for talking, for communicating."

Harsh as Winn's analysis was, it seems mild in comparison to that advanced by Jerry Mander in *Four Arguments For The Elimination Of Television.* Mander hits the medium from every angle—physiological (the deleterious effects of continually and unconsciously forming an image from the flickering dots of light on the screen), economic (television and advertising as partners in sustaining the grand illusion that acquisition is the key to personal happiness), political (television recreates people's understanding of life in a way ideally suited to dictatorial control). TV, he contends, is a technology with certain inherent biases, owing to its cost, its picture quality, the people who predominate in its hierarchy and its commercial use. "Violence is better TV than non-violence . . . superficiality is easier than depth . . . feelings of conflict, and their embodiment in actions, work better on television than feelings of agreement and their embodiment in calm and unity . . . competition is inherently more televisable than cooperation . . . materialism, acquisitiveness and ambition . . . work better than spirituality, non-seeking, openness and yielding. The medium cannot deal with ambiguity, subtlety or diversity . . ."

—*New Times,* date unknown
P.O. Box 2474, Boulder, CO 80322

Television: Corrupter and Time Waster

Would Satan like to get you corrupted? Would he like to have your morals at least softened up a little bit? Would he like to see you waste away your time rather than growing spiritually and doing the work of the kingdom of God? The answer to all of those questions is "yes." He seems to have chosen television as the vehicle to accomplish these goals very effectively.

It is not that I am against television. It is that I am *for* "having Christ formed in us." I am for each Christian being clothed with the supernatural power of God. Anything that slows down that process or prevents it, I believe should be discarded or controlled severely.

IMPROVING YOUR SPIRITUAL DIET

Many people will not become trim and attractive physically, because they do not want to change their diet. They want to indulge themselves. Likewise, many people will not see Jesus formed in them, because they do not want to change the diet taken in by their eyes and ears. They want to indulge themselves.

If you are serious about wanting to have Christ formed in you so that you can see the supernatural power that He has given you put to use, here are some practical suggestions concerning your spiritual and mental "diet":

1. Reduce your television watching to one evening a week. Pray carefully and then pre-choose what you will watch, so that it will be something that will help Christ to be formed in you. If you cannot find this on the network television programs, then watch one of the good Christian networks, or rent a Christian movie at your local video store.
2. If you have a VCR, purchase video tapes of Christian teachings, Christian singing groups, Bible or Christian-oriented movies and things of this nature, so that your family will be uplifted when they watch them and will be drawn closer to Christ.

3. Make your home an education center, instead of an entertainment center. Teaching your children the good things of life is not the responsibility of the church or even of Christian schools; it is the responsibility of the parents. Spend an evening reading books to your children and discussing the issues of the day. Adults, as well, could profit by spending two evenings a week reading good, solid, uplifting books.
4. Spend one evening a week visiting hospitals, prisons, helping the poor, or witnessing to those who do not know Jesus Christ (Matthew 25:31-46).
5. Keep track for a month of how many hours a day you spend taking in good spiritual food and how many hours a day you spend taking in junk and bad spiritual food (such as television). Once you know what your percentage of good food is, ask the Lord if He wants you to make any changes in it.
6. Spend extra time in prayer and reading the Scriptures, seeking to know Jesus better, so that you can become more like Him.
7. Buy a cassette album of the Bible or the New Testament, and put that on in the background while you are cleaning house, eating dinner and so forth.
8. Get good Christian music cassette albums to play as background music.
9. Read the Bible before you read the paper.
10. Read the book *Become Like Jesus* (see the last page of this book).
11. Use the *Victory Bible Reading Plan* as a guide to read through the Bible in a year.
12. If you are really serious about wanting Jesus formed in you, then resolve that you are

willing to pay the price, even if the cost means that you are going to have to change your evening routine and what you do with your time in general.

May God bless you as you pray about your spiritual diet. My heart yearns that you will change your intake to the extent that Jesus Christ can be formed in you. Sadly, television alone will be the culprit that keeps many people from becoming like Jesus Christ and having the spiritual power that He wants them to have.

A bad physical diet can cause you to be out of shape to the extent that you do not have the physical power to do some of the things you would like to do. A bad spiritual diet can cause you to be in such a spiritual condition that God's power is limited in you and you cannot achieve all of the things that God wants you to accomplish.

God's supernatural power is for every Christian.

Chapter 7

BUSYNESS CAN PREVENT POWER

Some people are so involved in numerous activities that they are like a whirling dervish. They have PTA meetings, Little League practices and games, meetings of the local environment committee and of the anti-abortion group, evening church services, choir practice, church all day Sunday, church committee meetings, and so on.

I am sure that you have known this type of person or perhaps you even are one yourself. You seem to be running at a full gallop continually, without even a chance to pause and catch your breath.

Suppose God wanted that type of individual to go over to the hospital some evening to pray for somebody who was sick, because He wanted to release His power through him to heal that person. Would that hurried, hassled, busy Christian have time to squeeze it into his busy schedule?

Unfortunately, this type of person tends to ignore those quiet promptings of the Lord. All of this "busyness" may well prevent the miraculous, supernatural power of God from clothing him and flowing through him.

We like to think that "all men are created equal." However, observation says that this is not true (other than in God's eyes regarding salvation—we must all come to God through His righteous provision, Jesus Christ, His Son). Men are created with different talents, different gifts, different financial and religious family heritages and so forth. Yet there is one way in which we are truly created equal, and that is with regard to "time." No matter what background we have, how rich or poor we might be, or how talented we are, each of us has twenty-four hours each day—no more and no less. We are ***all*** exactly equal in the amount of time that we have in each day.

If you show me how a man spends his time, I can tell you where his heart is. If you show me how a man spends his time, I can tell you what he holds most important in life. If you show me how a man spends his time, I can show you what he worships. (Far more people have idols today than they would like to think.)

There is a story in the Bible that I thought might help you in regard to how you spend your time.

BUSY HERE AND THERE

We find this interesting story in 1 Kings. Through one of the prophets, God had told the king of Israel that the king of Aram was going to come up against Israel and that the king of Israel was to destroy this enemy king. Unfortunately, the king of Israel disobeyed God and let the king of Aram live. This is what subsequently happened:

> **35 Now a certain man of the sons of the prophets said to another by the word of the LORD, "Please strike me." But the man refused to strike him.**
>
> **36 Then he said to him, "Because you have not listened to the voice of the LORD, behold, as soon as you have departed from me, a lion will kill you." And as**

soon as he had departed from him a lion found him, and killed him.

37 Then he found another man and said, "Please strike me." And the man struck him, wounding him.

38 So the prophet departed and waited for the king by the way, and disguised himself with a bandage over his eyes.

39 And as the king passed by, he cried to the king and said, "Your servant went out into the midst of the battle; and behold, a man turned aside and brought a man to me and said, 'Guard this man; if for any reason he is missing, then your life shall be for his life, or else you shall pay a talent of silver.'

40 "And while your servant was busy here and there, he was gone." And the king of Israel said to him, "So shall your judgment be; you yourself have decided *it*."

41 Then he hastily took the bandage away from his eyes, and the king of Israel recognized him that he was of the prophets.

42 And he said to him, "Thus says the LORD, 'Because you have let go out of *your* hand the man whom I had devoted to destruction, therefore your life shall go for his life, and your people for his people.'"

—1 Kings 20

Verses 35 and 36 are interesting in that the consequences of disobeying God, when He speaks through one of His prophets, can be very disastrous. However, that is not the thing that we are primarily interested in here.

We see in verse 38 that the prophet disguised himself. As the king passed by, the prophet told the king a story. The story goes something like this. A servant was out in the battle area and someone brought him a very important prisoner and told him to guard this prisoner. If for any reason he let the prisoner escape, his life was going to have to pay for the life of the prisoner.

Then in verse 40 we read a very sad thing. It says that the prisoner escaped. He escaped while the servant was ***"busy here and there,"*** leaving undone the most important thing—the guarding of the prisoner.

Then the king realized that the prophet was telling him the story to show him what was going to happen to him.

The Story Within the Story

I would like to look in detail at the story that the prophet told to the king. Perhaps we could cast it in today's terms. Suppose we pass by a soldier standing guard over a man in a jail cell, and we ask him what he is doing. He tells us that he is guarding this very important prisoner and that he is dedicated to that task.

A few days later, we come back looking for our friend who was guarding the important prisoner. He is not there. Someone else is in his place. We ask the new guard where our friend is. He says that he is in the cell, because the important prisoner got away.

We feel great remorse for the soldier, so we go over to talk to him. We ask him, "What happened? Did a group of commandos or a swat team come up and, with their strategy and higher fire power, force you to let the prisoner go?" The young soldier, who is now the prisoner, answers sadly, "No."

We say, "Did someone sneak up behind you, hit you over the head and knock you out and take the prisoner from you?" Again, he sadly answers, "No, it did not happen that way." We then ask, "Did huge numbers of soldiers from the enemy come up and overpower you with their overwhelming numbers, as you fought valiantly to protect the prisoner?" Again, the young soldier sadly hangs his head and says, "No."

So we say, "Well then, what in the world happened?" He says, "I was out shining my shoes, cleaning my rifle, looking at the sunset, taking a walk and watching television, and when I wandered back over here to the jail cell, the prisoner was just gone."

We suddenly have a change of heart; we no longer feel sorry for this young soldier, but we think how stupid he was to be just "busy here and there" and thus to neglect his primary responsibility. He was doing things that were good—they were not evil or bad—but they were not the most important things and they were not the things that he should have been doing when he was entrusted to guard that prisoner. Inwardly, we may think that he is reaping what he deserves.

Are We Busy Here and There?

Before we are too quick to condemn the young soldier in our preceding story, perhaps we should turn our eyes inward for a moment to take a look at ourselves. Perhaps this last year there were times when we have just been busy doing good things—perhaps worthwhile things and not evil things—but we let the most important things of life go undone. What are the more important things in life that we might have left undone? Some of them might be such things as:

1. Reading the Bible and praying every day
2. Reading at least one good Christian book every month
3. Visiting sick people in the hospital regularly
4. Visiting people in prisons regularly
5. Learning a new language
6. Learning a new skill
7. Spending time reading to our children
8. Spending time with our spouse
9. Writing letters to people we care about
10. Phoning people we care about

Of course, the list could go on. The main thing is to pray and find out from God if we are spending our time the way He wants us to. There are so very many things that could easily keep us from doing the important tasks—things such as: watching television too much, spending too much time with a hobby, working too much, sleeping too much, spending time worrying, and wasting time in idle chitchat.

We may not have included your favorite ways to waste time in this brief enumeration, but you might want to think back through this last year and guess just how many hours were spent being "busy here and there" in an average week. Perhaps it averaged two or three hours per day or even more. Then, of course, weekends are even worse for most of us. If you are typical, most likely you wasted twenty to thirty hours each week. Just think what you could have achieved if you had used that time productively for the Lord.

You cannot do anything about last year, but you *can* make a decision to stop being "busy here and there" during this year. You can choose to use those twenty to thirty hours each week to do some productive things, of course *under God's guidance.*

THE SUPER IMPORTANT PLACE OF WORKS

As I said earlier, the works that we do and how we choose to spend our time reflects where our heart is. Works have an important role in our lives and the Scriptures indicate that God expects good works of us. As we determine not to be "busy here and there," it may be wise to reexamine how God may be wanting us to spend our time and how good works fit in.

There are some churches that preach a salvation by works. Most truly born-again Christians realize that they cannot be saved by works, because of what the Bible has to say on this:

16 nevertheless knowing that a man is not justified by the works of the Law but through faith in Christ Jesus, even we have believed in Christ Jesus, that we may be justified by faith in Christ, and not by the works of the Law; since by the works of the Law shall no flesh be justified.

—Galatians 2

8 For by grace you have been saved through faith; and that not of yourselves, *it is* the gift of God;
9 not as a result of works, that no one should boast.

—Ephesians 2

Unfortunately, to keep from preaching salvation by works, many Christians, including pastors and leaders, go to the other extreme and almost ignore or belittle works, neglecting their importance. What these Christians do not realize is that the moment we are born again, by receiving Jesus Christ as our personal Savior, the situation concerning "works" flips 180 degrees and our works (deeds) become very important. In fact, they are the major thing on which we will be judged when we stand before the judgment seat of Christ.

Many people, including myself, are excited about Jesus Christ returning to the earth. But when asked what the first thing is that Christ will do after He returns, most Christians have no idea. After He returns to the earth, having destroyed His enemies at the battle of Armageddon, the Bible tells us clearly what He will do. Let's look at the answer the Scriptures give and an analysis of it, as recorded on pages 232 through 241 of my book, *The Future Revealed*:

31 "But when the Son of Man comes in His glory, and all the angels with Him, then He will sit on His glorious throne.

32 "And all the nations will be gathered before Him; and He will separate them from one another, as the shepherd separates the sheep from the goats;

33 and He will put the sheep on His right, and the goats on the left.

34 "Then the King will say to those on His right, 'Come, you who are blessed of My Father, inherit the kingdom prepared for you from the foundation of the world.

35 'For I was hungry, and you gave Me *something* to eat; I was thirsty, and you gave Me drink; I was a stranger, and you invited Me in;

36 naked, and you clothed Me; I was sick, and you visited Me; I was in prison, and you came to Me.'

37 "Then the righteous will answer Him, saying, 'Lord, when did we see You hungry, and feed You, or thirsty, and give You drink?

38 'And when did we see You a stranger, and invite You in, or naked, and clothe You?

39 'And when did we see You sick, or in prison, and come to You?'

40 "And the King will answer and say to them, 'Truly I say to you, to the extent that you did it to one of these brothers of Mine, *even* the least *of them*, you did it to Me.'

41 "Then He will also say to those on His left, 'Depart from Me, accursed ones, into the eternal fire which has been prepared for the devil and his angels;

42 for I was hungry, and you gave Me *nothing* to eat; I was thirsty, and you gave Me nothing to drink;

43 I was a stranger, and you did not invite Me in; naked, and you did not clothe Me; sick, and in prison, and you did not visit Me.'

44 "Then they themselves also will answer, saying, 'Lord, when did we see You hungry, or thirsty, or a stranger, or naked, or sick, or in prison, and did not take care of You?'

45 "Then He will answer them, saying, 'Truly I say to you, to the extent that you did not do it to one of the least of these, you did not do it to Me.'
46 "And these will go away into eternal punishment, but the righteous into eternal life."

—Matthew 25

Verse 31 of the preceding passage tells us that, when Christ comes in glory with His angels, He will sit on His glorious throne. Verse 32 tells us the first thing that He is going to do. He will gather all of the nations before Him and He will judge them. This is what the Bible calls "the judgment seat of Christ."

One question we need to ask ourselves is who is gathered before Jesus at His throne? Is it only Christians or is it the saved and the unsaved? Since we know that "the nations" will be gathered before Christ (verse 32), this tells us that all of the non-Christians will not be killed at the battle of Armageddon. There will still be many alive on the earth and Christ will gather those together for judgment, evidently along with the Christians, because verse 46 tells us that the righteous are destined for eternal life.

There will be a great white throne judgment (Revelation 20:11-15), when all people will stand before God the Father, but that comes much later. When Christians stand before the judgment seat of God the Father, we will be wrapped in the robe of the righteousness of Christ and He will see us as perfect. However, when Christians stand before the judgment seat of Christ, they will stand clothed only in the deeds that they have done. The Holy Spirit told Paul about this judgment seat of Christ, and he passed it on to the Corinthians:

10 For we must all appear before the judgment seat of Christ, that each one may be recompensed for his

deeds in the body, according to what he has done, whether good or bad.

—2 Corinthians 5

Paul is writing to the Christians in Corinth and he says that we must all appear before the judgment seat of Christ. That means every Christian is going to appear before the judgment seat of Christ.

The second half of this verse tells us what we are going to receive as we stand before the judgment seat of Christ. It says we are going to be recompensed (paid back) for what we did when we were in our natural bodies. We will be rewarded, either good or bad, depending on our deeds.

This is a significant point. What are we going to be judged on when we stand before the judgment seat of Christ? We will *not* be judged on whether or not we have received Christ as Savior; that question will be determined by God the Father at the great white throne judgment. If that is not what we are judged on, on what are we judged when we stand before the judgment seat of Christ? The Bible clearly tells us in 2 Corinthians 5:10 that we will be judged on our deeds, on what we have done. Did we walk in the Spirit? Did we live holy and righteous lives? Did we help the needy? Did we preach the gospel? The list could go on to include our family relationships, whether or not we cheated on our taxes, and every other area of our lives.

The Bible says that if we have done bad things, we are going to receive retribution for those bad things; if we have done good things, we will receive good payment in return. Living a holy and righteous life is all-important. If you lead someone to Christ, you have a responsibility to help that new Christian to grow up into righteousness.

We find more details about the judgment seat of Christ in Paul's first letter to the Corinthians:

10 According to the grace of God which was given to me, as a wise master builder I laid a foundation, and another is building upon it. But let each man be careful how he builds upon it.

11 For no man can lay a foundation other than the one which is laid, which is Jesus Christ.

12 Now if any man builds upon the foundation with gold, silver, precious stones, wood, hay, straw,

13 each man's work will become evident; for the day will show it, because it is *to be* revealed with fire; and the fire itself will test the quality of each man's work.

14 If any man's work which he has built upon it remains, he shall receive a reward.

15 If any man's work is burned up, he shall suffer loss; but he himself shall be saved, yet so as through fire.

—1 Corinthians 3

In this passage of Scripture, we see that when we become Christians, Jesus Christ is our foundation, and the foundation is empty. After we have received Christ as our Savior, we each build our own building on the precious foundation of Jesus Christ. Verse 13 tells us that it is our "work" that determines what we build on that foundation.

When we stand before the judgment seat of Christ, He is going to apply fire to the building that we have built on His foundation. The good things that we have done, represented by gold and silver, will not be burned up, but will remain. Verse 14 tells us that we will receive a reward for those things. However, the bad things that we have done, or even the neutral things ("busy here and there"), will be burned up, and we will "suffer loss" for those things. We do not know what that loss or negative payment will be, but I assure you that it is something that we will not want.

In verse 15 of 1 Corinthians 3, we see that if the work that a man has built upon the foundation of Christ is totally burned up, he will be saved "yet so as through fire." In other words, he will be saved but it will be equivalent to him going through fire. That is not something that we would like at all.

Christ yearns that each Christian build on His precious foundation a valuable building composed of good works. If you are not interested in good works now, believe me, you will be when you stand before the judgment seat of Christ. I would encourage you to really pray about this and to ask God to help you emphasize good works, holiness, and righteousness in your personal life.

Jesus Himself told you in no uncertain terms on what basis He was going to judge you. He said that He was going to pay back (recompense) every man according to his deeds:

> **27 "For the Son of Man is going to come in the glory of His Father with His angels; and WILL THEN RECOMPENSE EVERY MAN ACCORDING TO HIS DEEDS. . . ."**
>
> **—Matthew 16**

We need to be highly concerned about our deeds. Would your neighbors classify you as a man or woman of good works and good deeds? Not all Christians would be classified that way by their neighbors. Are you concerned for the victims when a natural disaster hits? Are you concerned for the survivors of the families of those who are killed when war breaks out? Are you concerned for the poor and the needy in your community? Are you eager to take the gospel of the kingdom to everyone in your community and to help others take it places where you cannot go? Many Evangelicals and Charismatics are eager to share the gospel, but they are really not very concerned about their deeds or their good works.

A number of years ago, there was a professor at Dallas Theological Seminary who was also pastor of a church in the suburbs of Dallas. There was a Methodist preacher right down the street and this good pastor had disdain toward the Methodist preacher, because he was not really preaching "the gospel."

Then one afternoon there was a tornado alert there in Dallas. Our good evangelical pastor shut down the church office and rushed home to take care of his family. A few days later he found out that while he was home hiding under the kitchen table, the Methodist pastor was calling his parishioners and telling them to bring canned food, blankets and clothing to the church so they could distribute these things to the victims of the tornado when they found out where it had hit. This evangelical pastor confessed that God really clobbered him about his lack of concern for other people's needs.

Let me ask you a question. Assuming that both of these men knew Christ as their Savior, when each of them stands before the judgment seat of Christ, which one's works do you think will be gold and silver, in this specific instance? I believe it will be the deeds of the Methodist pastor.

This judgment seat of Christ is no light thing. Christ had this to say about it:

> **35 "Be dressed in readiness, and *keep* your lamps alight.**
>
> **36 "And be like men who are waiting for their master when he returns from the wedding feast, so that they may immediately open *the door* to him when he comes and knocks.**
>
> **37 "Blessed are those slaves whom the master shall find on the alert when he comes; truly I say to you, that**

he will gird himself *to serve*, and have them recline *at the table*, and will come up and wait on them.

38 "Whether he comes in the second watch, or even in the third, and finds *them* so, blessed are those *slaves*.

39 "And be sure of this, that if the head of the house had known at what hour the thief was coming, he would not have allowed his house to be broken into.

40 "You too, be ready; for the Son of Man is coming at an hour that you do not expect."

41 And Peter said, "Lord, are You addressing this parable to us, or to everyone *else* as well?"

42 And the Lord said, "Who then is the faithful and sensible steward, whom his master will put in charge of his servants, to give them their rations at the proper time?

43 "Blessed is that slave whom his master finds so doing when he comes.

44 "Truly I say to you, that he will put him in charge of all his possessions.

45 "But if that slave says in his heart, 'My master will be a long time in coming,' and begins to beat the slaves, *both* men and women, and to eat and drink and get drunk;

46 the master of that slave will come on a day when he does not expect *him*, and at an hour he does not know, and will cut him in pieces, and assign him a place with the unbelievers.

47 "And that slave who knew his master's will and did not get ready or act in accord with his will, shall receive many lashes,

48 but the one who did not know *it*, and committed deeds worthy of a flogging, will receive but few. And from everyone who has been given much shall much be required; and to whom they entrusted much, of him they will ask all the more. . . . "

—Luke 12

Verse 40 of this passage makes it obvious that this is talking about what happens right after Christ comes back. But did you notice verse 46? This parable about the slaves of the master who returns unexpectedly is a depiction of what things will be like when Christ, our Master, returns. If a Christian is not truly following Christ, it says that Christ will "assign him a place with the unbelievers." (I did not say that—Jesus did.) That is very strong, and we certainly would not want to be found in that category, so it behooves us to be ready for the Lord's return and to be doing the Father's will.

Do you see what I am trying to say in this section? I am not trying to put anybody under the law or in bondage. I am encouraging you to become like Jesus. Jesus' heart went out to those who were sick and to those who were hungry, and He reached out to meet their needs. If we want to be like Him, we should do this also. I would encourage you to pause for a moment and imagine yourself standing before the judgment seat of Christ. If your works from just this last year were under consideration and Christ applied fire to them, how would they fare? Would most of your works remain or would most of them be burned up? How much time were you just "busy here and there"?

Looking forward to this next year, you can determine what kind of deeds you are going to do during the next twelve months. Forgetting what lies behind and looking toward what lies ahead, let us press on to full maturity in the Lord. May all of your deeds and mine this next year be glorifying to God and to Christ. May they be gold, silver, and precious stones, built upon the foundation of Jesus.

The Lord encourages us to live the Christian life just one day at a time. One thing that I have found helpful is to ask the Lord, at the end of every day, what I have done that day that He would consider to be building with gold, silver, and precious stones. After He shows me, I ask Him to help me do more of those things the following day. Then I ask Him to show me what I have done that day that is wood, hay, and straw. I ask Him to show me the careless words that I have spoken and the times when I was not glorifying Him. I ask Him to show me when I was just "busy here and there." After He shows me and I repent of those things, I pray earnestly not to be guilty of doing those things during the next day. By taking it a day at a time, the task of building something beautiful on the foundation of Jesus Christ becomes much more attainable. (This ends the extraction from *The Future Revealed.*)

TYRANNY OF THE URGENT

Many years ago I read a booklet entitled *Tyranny of the Urgent!* (by Charles E. Hummel, InterVarsity Christian Fellowship, P.O. Box 1400, Downers Grove, IL 60515). Its basic thesis was that the urgent things in life keep us from doing the important things in life.

For example, taking a course in learning a second language does not have a deadline. Reading your Bible does not have a deadline. Visiting people in the hospital does not have a deadline. However, there are a whole host of things that do have deadlines, such as cooking meals, shopping, putting out a report at work, organizing a new company, and so on. These "urgent" things all too often tend to prevent us from doing the important things in life.

One time I was speaking to a group of the top executives of the Blue Cross Insurance Company, and I made this point by asking them if they should spend more time *creating* or *reacting*. They all said, "Creating." I then asked them what they *did* spend more time doing. Almost all of them said they spent all of their time reacting. One Blue Cross president said that he was going to go back to his office after he got home and set aside an hour a day for creating, and if that was the only thing he had learned from me, the entire trip would have been worth it.

We too periodically need to pause and evaluate, to see if the urgent things in our lives are crowding out the important things. One of the important things that could be getting crowded out by the urgent things in our lives is having enough free time first to be anointed with the power of God, then to go out into the highways and byways and other places where God would direct you and to let this supernatural power flow out to the sick, the possessed, the hungry, the homeless and the needy.

It may even be that we are being caught up doing "good things," but not that which is God's perfect will for us. One time I accepted the job of teaching the single young adults in the Beverly Hills Baptist Church. When I took this position, however, I told the pastor that I was only obligating myself to be at Sunday school, not even at Sunday morning church. He agreed to this. About 99 percent of the time, I did stay for church, and I got to know those precious people.

After the people began to get to know me, one Sunday morning this rather short, plump, sweet lady came up to me and said, "Oh, Brother McKeever, we missed you at our prayer meeting Wednesday night." This was really her way of pressuring me to come. My reply was that she should not have missed me, because if God had wanted me to be there, I would have been there. I told her that God had wanted me to be someplace else, and I would not plan on being there until such time as God directed me to come. I let this sweet lady know that, in the meantime, she should not miss me at all. I am sure that she was a bit shocked by this reply, for she assumed that God would want all members to be at every Wednesday night meeting.

WE MUST SPEND OUR TIME WHERE GOD WANTS US TO BE.

I am all for the local church. God has used it through the centuries and I think He will mightily use it in the end of this age. However, we can get so caught up in church activities that all of our friends are members of the church and the power of God cannot really flow through us to help others, aside from possibly those within the church circle. It is my opinion that many "churchaholics," would have a hard time hearing and obeying God if some Wednesday evening He wanted them not to go to their Wednesday prayer meeting, but to go down to the local hospital, instead. Suppose He wanted them to let Him guide them to a room in order to pray for the person in that room because He wanted to heal and deliver him. There are many Christians who would have their "hearing aid" turned off, because they are so entrenched in their religious traditions that they would not hear, nor obey, God. The power of God cannot fully be utilized in a person who does everything by schedule and rote, rather than every day and every evening asking God what He wants him to do.

Our schedules and our efforts to meet the urgent needs in life can have us so booked up that we cannot really be the vessels of supernatural power that God wants us to be. I would urge you to take a fresh look at your life and your schedule. Be sure that you are not just "busy here and there" or bogged down by the "urgent" matters in life, allowing those to crowd out some really important things that God may have for you. He wants His supernatural power to flow through to bring healing, deliverance and help to others. Do not be so "busy" that you really do not take the time to spend hours quietly alone with Him to recharge your spiritual-power battery. Do not allow "busyness" to rob you of the time for Him to lead you to people who need a miracle, and who are not likely to be at one of your church meetings. God wants to use you in a mighty way, if you will make time for Him in your schedule.

God's supernatural power is for every Christian.

Chapter 8

YOUR WORDS CAN QUENCH THE POWER

Suppose there was a Christian who went around cursing and using foul language, telling one dirty joke after another and gossiping. Suppose he was constantly bad-mouthing people, especially other Christians, and verbally stabbing people in the back. Do you think the supernatural power of God would clothe such a Christian and overflow to do miracles? I doubt it very seriously.

Our words are so very important. In this chapter, we will be looking at the importance of our words, especially in connection with accusing other Christians. Unfortunately, Christians accusing other Christians is something that is too prevalent in the body of Christ today.

Do you realize how important the words of your mouth are? When you stand before the judgment seat of Christ, one of the major questions Jesus Christ is going to ask you is about your words:

> **36 "And I say to you, that every careless word that men shall speak, they shall render account for it in the day of judgment.**
>
> **37 "For by your words you shall be justified, and by your words you shall be condemned."**
>
> **—Matthew 12**

According to these two verses, we are not only going to have to give account for every bad word we have said, but even for every careless word that we speak.

Since our words are going to determine a great deal about how we fare at the judgment seat of Christ, think about what He would have to say to you if you used your words in a way that was totally contrary to His instructions. That would be a very serious affair. We will have more to say about that in just a moment, but first we need to look at Satan's role in all of this.

SATAN'S PRIMARY JOB

Satan right now spends the majority of his time before the throne of God doing something dreadful. Let's see what the Bible says he is doing right now:

> **9 And the great dragon was thrown down, the serpent of old who is called the devil and Satan, who deceives the whole world; he was thrown down to the earth, and his angels were thrown down with him.**
>
> **10 And I heard a loud voice in heaven, saying,**
>
> **"Now the salvation, and the power, and the kingdom of our God and the authority of His Christ have come, for the accuser of our brethren has been thrown down, who accuses them before our God day and night. . . ."**
>
> **—Revelation 12**

From this, we learn that, as of the time of Revelation 12, Satan is standing before God accusing the brethren—that is, accusing Christians. One time I heard Pat Robertson asked where Satan was. His answer was that he is before the throne of God, accusing the brethren.

If someone says something like "Brother X used to be really godly, but now he's gone modern, has his own jet airplane and . . . ," what is he doing? He is accusing the brethren. Whose team is he playing on when he accuses the brethren? He is playing on Satan's team.

When a Christian says something like, "Brother Y has really lost it now. He shouldn't be preaching . . . ," what is he doing? He is accusing the brethren. Whose team is he playing on when he does that? Right. He is playing on Satan's team.

Likewise, when a Christian says of himself, "I'm no good, I'm rotten, I'm worthless" or any of the other things that people commonly think when they are having their own pity party, what is he doing? He is accusing the brethren, because he is one of the brothers. Of course, when he is doing that, he is playing on Satan's team.

Just as an aside, if self-condemnation is a problem that you have, this verse is a good one to remember:

> **14 I will give thanks to Thee, for I am**
> **fearfully and wonderfully made;**
> **Wonderful are Thy works,**
> **And my soul knows it very well.**
>
> **—Psalm 139**

If you get nothing else of value out of this chapter, I would encourage you to breathe a little prayer right now asking the Lord to forgive you for times past when you have accused the brethren. Resolve in your heart never again to accuse the brethren and, by so doing, never again to help Satan out in his task.

GO DIRECTLY TO YOUR BROTHER

A legitimate question arises as to what a Christian should do when another brother has done something, or is reported to have done something, or is teaching something that offends him. Jesus Christ clearly gave us the answer to that question:

15 "And if your brother sins, go and reprove him in private; if he listens to you, you have won your brother.

16 "But if he does not listen *to you*, take one or two more with you, so that BY THE MOUTH OF TWO OR THREE WITNESSES EVERY FACT MAY BE CONFIRMED.

17 "And if he refuses to listen to them, tell it to the church; and if he refuses to listen even to the church, let him be to you as a Gentile and a tax-gatherer. . . ."

—Matthew 18

There is much I would like to say about these verses, but let me first point out that this is the *only* instruction that Christ gave the church (ekklesia) on how to operate in the future after He was gone. He could have told the church how to organize, how to conduct their services, what to do about music, how to handle their finances and many other items. However, He left the church just *one instruction* as to how to operate in the future. Therefore, that must have been the very most important thing for the church to do. That one instruction is contained in the three verses that we just read.

However, if one were to tour all of the churches in the average city, he would find out that this one instruction of Christ's is probably the very thing that they do rarely, if ever. In His single instruction to the church, Christ outlined three steps.

STEP ONE: If your brother sins (the *New International Version* says, "If your brother sins against you"), you are to go to him. You do not "pass Go"; you do not collect $200—you go directly to him. You do not tell your pastor, you do not tell your wife (or husband); you go directly to him. This is what Jesus commanded you to do. If you do anything else, it is sin.

In practicing this over the years, I have found out that the majority of the times there has simply been a misunderstanding, and it can be cleared up in two or three minutes. Other times, when going to a brother who has offended me, I have found that I was really the one in the wrong or in error. Practicing Christ's exhortation from Matthew 18 gives us an opportunity for a face-to-face air clearing.

Some Christians may try to use an excuse such as, "His personality is too strong for me; I couldn't go to him," or "He is a national figure and I could never go to him." As far as I'm concerned, those are flimsy excuses, to rationalize why you are not obeying Christ. If you do not obey Him, remember, it is sin.

Once you go to a brother who has offended you and he "listens," then you have won your brother. It does not say that he has to change. My definition of "listen" is that he is willing to prayerfully and sincerely consider the matter before the Lord.

For example, it may be that you do not believe in drinking wine and you saw your brother drinking wine. You go to him and express your concern. He gives you his biblical reasons why he thinks that wine drinking is okay, but he says that he is willing to hold it up before the Lord and is perfectly willing to stop drinking wine if God tells him to do so. The two of you can then have sweet fellowship in Christ, even if you ultimately do not agree on a given subject, such as drinking wine.

On the other hand, if that brother refuses to "listen"—to prayerfully consider the matter before the Lord—then you are to go on to the next step.

STEP TWO: You then take one or two brothers with you and you go back to the brother who has offended you. It is very likely, with the added influence of the other individuals, that the brother will listen and, if he is living in overt sin, it is likely that he will repent and turn from it. On the other hand, if he throws you out and/or refuses to listen, then you go to the final step.

STEP THREE: You bring that brother to the entire church. If he still refuses to "listen," then you treat him like a non-Christian.

You might ask yourself whether or not you and others in your church follow this three-step program that Christ instituted. If you perceive that someone in your church, or a national Christian leader, is involved in sin or error, what do you do? You have four choices:

1. You can tell someone else (gossip), which is accusing the brethren and is a vile sin.
2. You can keep it bottled up inside (mentally accusing that person).
3. You can just totally forgive and forget.
4. You can obey Christ and go to that individual.

1 Corinthians Versus 2 Corinthians

In his first letter to the church at Corinth, Paul amplifies on Christ's three-step process by which the church is to operate:

> **9 I wrote you in my letter not to associate with immoral people;**
>
> **10 I *did* not at all *mean* with the immoral people of this world, or with the covetous and swindlers, or with idolaters; for then you would have to go out of the world.**
>
> **11 But actually, I wrote to you not to associate with any so-called brother if he should be an immoral person, or covetous, or an idolater, or a reviler, or a drunkard, or a swindler—not even to eat with such a one.**
>
> **12 For what have I to do with judging outsiders? Do you not judge those who are within *the church?***
>
> **13 But those who are outside, God judges. REMOVE THE WICKED MAN FROM AMONG YOURSELVES.**
>
> **—1 Corinthians 5**

In this passage, Paul clearly points out that if a person claims to be a brother and is immoral, covetous, a drunkard or a swindler, we are not even to eat with such a one. You should not even have lunch with him. (Incidentally, it also says in these verses that we are to righteously judge Christians, but not those outside the church.)

God uses the three-step procedure set forth by Christ as a means to keep the church pure and holy. This was brought back to me very vividly a couple of years after I graduated from college. There was a young lady in a Bible study that I was leading. She had a non-Christian boyfriend that she was sleeping with and this was common knowledge among the group. After a year or so, she broke up with this young man, and not long after that we studied Matthew 18 and 1 Corinthians 5.

When we were studying the process that the Bible outlines as the way to deal with conflicts, the young lady said, with tears in her eyes, "How I wish you had applied that to me." She said that as long as she could have both her Christian friends and Bible study, and also her non-Christian boyfriend, she would take both. She further stated that if she had had to choose between her Christian friends or her activities with her non-Christian boyfriend, she would have chosen her Christian friends.

God is calling His people to be holy, pure and clean. He is preparing a bride without spot or blemish. I believe the day is here when we need to practice this instruction that Jesus gave to the church.

If a brother or sister is sinning, we are to go to that person. If he listens, praise God! We have helped our brother to turn from sin. If he refuses to listen, then we should go through the other steps. If he refuses to listen even when taken before the church, we are to cast him out and have nothing to do with him.

But that is not the end of the story. We cannot practice 1 Corinthians without also practicing 2 Corinthians. In 1 Corinthians, Paul says that if a brother insists on living in sin, have nothing to do with him. However, in 2 Corinthians, Paul says that if such a brother repents, then we are to forgive him and restore him to full fellowship.

> **6 Sufficient for such a one is this punishment which was *inflicted by* the majority,**
> **7 so that on the contrary you should rather forgive and comfort *him,* lest somehow such a one be overwhelmed by excessive sorrow.**
> **8 Wherefore I urge you to reaffirm *your* love for him.**
>
> **—2 Corinthians 2**

The beautiful spirit of restoration also was shared by Paul as he was writing to the church at Galatia:

> **1 Brethren, even if a man is caught in any trespass, you who are spiritual, restore such a one in a spirit of gentleness; *each one* looking to yourself, lest you too be tempted.**
> **2 Bear one another's burdens, and thus fulfill the law of Christ.**
>
> **—Galatians 6**

We should be far more eager to restore someone than we are to put someone out of our fellowship. In a battle, such as in World War II, if a soldier is wounded, one of his buddies will risk his own life to crawl over and drag him to safety. We call that soldier a hero.

In our spiritual battles, if one of our fellow Christian soldiers gets wounded, sadly, many Christians today will crawl over and "pour salt in his wound" by the words that they speak, rather than helping him to safety. *We need each other.* Just like a good military soldier, we should be willing to do anything to help save and restore a wounded fellow soldier in Christ's army. Jesus said:

> **35 By this all men will know that you are my disciples, if you have love one for another.**
>
> **—John 13, *RSV***

We need to show real love and concern for a wounded soldier in this spiritual war.

Similarly, through the parable of the prodigal son, Christ pointed out that if a brother goes and wallows with the pigs for a season, but then repents and comes home, we should restore that brother to full fellowship and/or ministry without reservation. (God forgave us; who are we to do less?)

Simon Peter committed a sin as bad as any. He, who had lived so closely with Jesus, denied Him three times. Did Christ "put him on the shelf" for five years (or one year) and refuse to trust him or use him again until he had "proved himself"? No. Fifty days later, the Lord powerfully used him on Pentecost. This "penalty box" mentality is not something that I find in the Scriptures.

David also sinned (murder and adultery), but God did not remove him from being king. The man who sins must repent (turn from that sin); then God restores, and so must we.

ALL GOSSIP IS MALICIOUS

While we are on the subject of our words, we need to take a look at the horrible sin of gossip:

> **2 For men will be lovers of self, lovers of money, boastful, arrogant, revilers, disobedient to parents, ungrateful, unholy,**
>
> **3 unloving, irreconcilable, malicious gossips, without self-control, brutal, haters of good,**

> **4 treacherous, reckless, conceited, lovers of pleasure rather than lovers of God; . . .**
>
> **—2 Timothy 3**

As you can see here, gossips—really malicious gossips—are classified with the unholy and the treacherous. Gossips are part of Satan's "accuser chain letter." They are taking things they have heard and are passing them on to other people. We know that God hates gossip; the book of Romans even groups it with murder:

> **29 being filled with all unrighteousness, wickedness, greed, evil; full of envy, murder, strife, deceit, malice; *they are* gossips,**
>
> **30 slanderers, haters of God, insolent, arrogant, boastful, inventors of evil, disobedient to parents, . . .**
>
> **—Romans 1**

One of the reasons that gossip is so malicious and vicious is that through gossip one can essentially murder a person's reputation and that individual has no chance to defend himself. In all likelihood, what a person is passing on is not the complete truth anyway, because things have a way of getting distorted in Satan's "rumor mill" (accuser mill). Thus, one would likely also be guilty of bearing false witness against a brother.

Anytime someone comes to me with something negative to say about a brother or sister in Christ, my first question is, "Have you gone to that brother?" If he has not, then I say that I am not interested even in listening. I am not going to help that individual perpetuate his sin. I feel that God wants me to point him in the right direction. If he has heard something negative about a brother, he either needs to forget it and never share it with anyone else or go directly to that brother. If he passes it on, he is involved in malicious gossip and he is accusing one of the brethren. He may indeed be passing on a little handful of salt to pour into that person's wounds.

If God gives you a heart of caring and a desire to help restore a brother, then go to him, and God will bless you for your efforts. You may even come out of it with a better relationship than you have ever had before with that brother.

One of the difficulties with gossip is that it is very deceptive (Satan's main characteristic). It usually comes from someone you know who is genuinely concerned about your spiritual well-being. This person may even be a pastor or a Christian leader in whom you have a great deal of confidence. However, even your close friends, pastors and Christian leaders are sometimes mistaken, and you certainly would not want to be guilty of perpetuating an error that they are making. If someone is bringing something to you about another Christian brother that he has not personally tried to rectify with that brother, then no matter how well-intentioned he may be, he is gossiping and accusing one of the brethren.

There is a spirit of accusation and gossip running rampant through the body of Christ today and, as the spiritual war heats up, it will get worse. We need to resist gossip and certainly not participate in it. The Holy Spirit's job is to build up the individual members in the body of Christ and Satan's goal is to tear them down. Gossip only tears down and never builds up.

IF THEY PREACH CHRIST, REJOICE

Years ago, I was president of a Christian Businessmen's Luncheon in Dallas, Texas, that met at the First Baptist Church there. I usually invited in a guest speaker, but there began to be friction among some of the folks about water baptism, the baptism of the Holy Spirit and other issues. I thought the Lord wanted me to address this friction and He led me to speak out of Philippians:

> **15 Some, to be sure, are preaching Christ even from envy and strife, but some also from good will;**
> **16 the latter *do it* out of love, knowing that I am appointed for the defense of the gospel;**
> **17 the former proclaim Christ out of selfish ambition, rather than from pure motives, thinking to cause me distress in my imprisonment.**
> **18 What then? Only that in every way, whether in pretense or in truth, Christ is proclaimed; and in this I rejoice, yes, and I will rejoice.**
>
> **—Philippians 1**

In this passage, Paul pointed out that some people were preaching Christ out of envy of Paul; others were preaching Christ to try to create strife among the believers; and still others, out of selfish ambition. Some were doing it out of a pure heart. But look at verse 18! Paul said that it really did not matter. The wonderful thing was that Christ was being preached, and he rejoiced in this and would continue to rejoice in it.

If we are going to be fellow soldiers for Christ, we are not going to agree on everything. For example, Hal Lindsey and I do not agree on the timing of the rapture nor on who Israel is. However, he preaches Jesus Christ and thousands of people have come to know Christ as their personal Savior from reading his books. As long as he preaches Christ as the only begotten Son of God and the only way to heaven, he is my brother, and I will rejoice in his ministry. In fact, if I were pastor of a church, Hal Lindsey, Chuck Smith, and many others who do not agree with me on certain subjects would be more than welcome to speak there. The Holy Spirit is the guardian of the truth in people's hearts.

This was brought home to me very clearly when the Lord first started a Bible study on Catalina Island which later grew into a church. We had a Baptist couple, an Episcopal couple, a Pentecostal couple, and one of just about every label imaginable. I asked the Lord what I should do when someone disagreed with me on a subject, for I was sure that was bound to happen. The Lord told me to let him have his complete say and then I should share with the group why I did not agree, but He said that I could only do that one time. If the person were to come back with a "rebuttal," I was to keep silent.

The Lord told me that the Holy Spirit would witness to the people's hearts and spirits about what was really truth. I believe that many pastors today are trying to do the Holy Spirit's job for Him. They want to keep away from their people any literature or speakers who do not agree 100 percent with their theology. That is really sad, because if the Holy Spirit wanted to do a new thing in their church, they would have Him so bound up that it would be difficult for Him to break through their restrictions and structure.

We need to remind ourselves that our fellowship is not around the form of water baptism, our views on eternal security, the gifts of the Spirit, the timing of the rapture, who Israel is or any other doctrinal subject. Our fellowship is around the living person of Jesus Christ. As long as any brother loves Christ with all his heart, soul, mind and strength and is open and teachable, we get along beautifully.

Let us resolve never to play on Satan's team again by accusing a brother, any brother (including ourselves). We need to stop accusing and start loving, forgiving and building. This is the "Jesus way."

KEEPING YOUR WORD

There are many specific things that we could discuss as to how your words can prevent the power of God from freely flowing through you. One in particular that I would like to mention is keeping your word. I have had more Christians break their word to me, including major Christian leaders, than you could possibly imagine.

This is contrary to the way that I was raised and the way the Bible tells us we should be. I was raised as a southern gentleman, with the teaching from my father that my word was as good as my bond. In other words, if I told somebody I was going to do something or be somewhere, regardless of what it cost me (unless I was in an accident and physically prevented), I was to follow through on my word.

Jesus said the same thing. He said that when we say "yes," it had better really mean *yes*; and when we say "no," it should really mean *no*:

> **37 "But let your statement be, 'Yes, Yes' *or* 'No, no'; and anything beyond these is of evil. . . ."**
>
> **—Matthew 5**

Most of us would like to dwell on the holy hill (Mount Zion) with Jesus during the millennium. Evidently, there will be Christians scattered out across the earth even during the millennium, but some small group will have the privilege of dwelling with Jesus on His holy hill. As we read the requirements of those who are going to dwell on His holy hill, notice how much of it involves your words:

> **1 O LORD, who may abide in Thy tent?**
> **Who may dwell on Thy holy hill?**

2 He who walks with integrity, and
works righteousness,
And speaks truth in his heart.
3 He does not slander with his tongue,
Nor does evil to his neighbor,
Nor takes up a reproach against his friend;
4 In whose eyes a reprobate is despised,
But who honors those who fear the LORD;
He swears to his own hurt, and does not
change; . . .

—Psalm 15

The one aspect that I especially would like to call your attention to is the last phrase in verse 4. The one who is going to dwell on the holy hill with Jesus is a man who "swears to his own hurt, and does not change."

In the early days of our country, a man's word was as good as his bond—just as though he had put up $5,000. For example, two men might shake hands in the evening in agreement over the sale of a horse to be picked up in the morning, stating that the sale was completed. If the horse died during the night, the buyer would pay the seller for the horse anyhow, because he had given his word. His word was as good as a written contract.

Psalm 15 says that a righteous man swears to his own hurt and yet will not change. In our example of the man buying the horse, he would not go back on his word, even though it meant financial loss to himself. Keeping your word, and letting your "yes" really mean *yes* and your "no" really mean *no*, glorifies the Lord and will stand you in good stead when you give an account of your words before the judgment seat of Christ.

HOW WILL YOU USE YOUR WORDS?

We know that words can be very creative or very destructive. Words can build up or they can tear down.

You can decide whether or not your words will become sin and tear down others, and likewise yourself, or if they will build up and help others. You can choose whether or not you will be involved in accusing brothers, gossiping, or speaking discouragement rather than encouragement. You can also make the decision that you do *not* want to be known as someone who does not keep his word. You can decide to let your words be used by God as one of the major vehicles by which the power of God flows out to other people.

We have seen that the words which we speak have great importance in God's sight—every word. With our lips we can speak life or we can quench the Spirit and the power of God from flowing through us. This is a critical area to bring into submission to God, as we are seeking to use His supernatural power to His utmost glory.

God's supernatural power is for every Christian.

Chapter 9

OTHER HINDRANCES TO GOD'S POWER

We have looked at three major things that can hamper the power of God from working in us and through us.

1. A poor spiritual diet (what we eat with our eyes and ears)
2. Spending our time our way (busy here and there)
3. Speaking words that do not glorify God (plus idle words)

Of course, there are other things that can also hamper the power of God. Some of these would be equally important as the ones that I have chosen to discuss in the previous three chapters. However, rather than trying to cover all of the possible hindrances extensively, which would take volumes, we will list some of these and trust that the Holy Spirit will quicken to you any that apply to your life. Other possible hindrances include:

1. Bitterness
2. Unforgiveness
3. Anger

4. Immorality (adultery or even lust)
5. Unholy behavior
6. Unrighteousness
7. Impurity
8. Pride
9. Idolatry
10. Lack of faith ("God could never use me")
11. Rebellion
12. Preconceived ideas
13. Comparing yourself to others (envy)
14. Unbelief ("Miracles were for the Bible days, but they are not for today")
15. Lack of teaching on the subject (ignorance)

Many of these are self-explanatory, to a large degree. Harboring bitterness, unforgiveness and anger inside can be very destructive and certainly can cause spiritual blockages to God's power. All impurity and unholiness can definitely hamper the Lord from being able to entrust you as an ambassador of His power and might, as He wishes you to be.

Although these things hamper God's power from flowing through you, they might not prevent it altogether. Think of it this way: When the air filter in your automobile or home heating or air conditioning system is clean, the air (wind) can flow through it freely. The dirtier the filter gets, the less air that can flow through. If it gets really dirty, almost no air can flow through. Or think of it like an automobile radiator, which gets so clogged with bugs that inadequate air can flow through to cool the engine water. So it is with the hindrances in our lives—the little sins, careless words, lack of faith, wasting time, unforgiveness, spiritual junk food, passing on accusing information about a brother, and so on; these things are the "bugs and the dirt" that clog up our "power filter" and prevent the power of God from flowing through us freely.

Everyone need not do this, but I like to think of the power of God like a small ball of light on top of my head that could expand and flow down over me like an invisible stream. Underneath this "ball," I envisage this "power filter." The power must flow down through this filter in order to clothe my body with incredible power. My hands are the primary high voltage conduits to pass this power on to others. But if the filter is clogged up, the power will not flow down like it could.

Pride is one of the dirty things that hampers the flow. It can take numerous forms. For example, you may have believed for years, and even taught others, that miracles are not for today, and your pride would be offended if you had to change your theology. Your pride may take the form of fear; perhaps you are afraid of looking foolish as you try to step out in God's power and have some "failures." (What is a failure in your eyes may not be in God's view.)

Maybe you have preconceived ideas about how God's power should be used, and you need to allow Him to speak to you afresh as you read the remainder of this book. Perhaps you are so busy looking at the way God uses others that you forget that God works with each of us individually. The way He chooses to use you may be totally different than the way He uses an evangelist, or your pastor or your spouse. But God *does* want His supernatural power to flow through each one of us.

For many people, simply a lack of Bible-based teaching on the subject of God's supernatural power can be a block. For one thing, it can lead to a false belief that God's power is for other people, but not for you.

The list of things that can block the transmission of the power of God could be a very long one. Let's turn to see what the Scriptures have to say about some of these:

> **9 Or do you not know that the unrighteous shall not inherit the kingdom of God? Do not be deceived; neither fornicators, nor idolaters, nor adulterers, nor effeminate, nor homosexuals,**
>
> **10 nor thieves, nor *the* covetous, nor drunkards, nor revilers, nor swindlers, shall inherit the kingdom of God.**
>
> **—1 Corinthians 6**

As you can see from these verses, adulterers, fornicators, effeminate, thieves and covetous people will ***not*** inherit the kingdom of God. They are not going to have the power of God. This is not my list; this is the Lord's list. In writing to the Galatians, Paul added things to this list, such as sensuality, strife and jealously:

> **19 Now the deeds of the flesh are evident, which are: immorality, impurity, sensuality,**
>
> **20 idolatry, sorcery, enmities, strife, jealousy, outbursts of anger, disputes, dissensions, factions,**
>
> **21 envying, drunkenness, carousing, and things like these, of which I forewarn you just as I have forewarned you that those who practice such things shall not inherit the kingdom of God.**
>
> **—Galatians 5**

Did you notice that if we are jealous, we are ***not*** going to inherit the kingdom of God? If we create strife, have disputes, cause dissensions or have impurity or immorality in our lives, we will not inherit the kingdom of God. This is a very hard teaching, but it is straight from the Scriptures. My task is only to refresh these things to your memory; the Holy Spirit will speak to your heart what you need to hear. These are all things that clog up our spiritual filter.

The Bible lists similar things other places and says that the people who are involved in these things will inherit the wrath of God. It is unlikely that God would grant power to those with whom He is angry.

> **5 Therefore consider the members of your earthly body as dead to immorality, impurity, passion, evil desire, and greed, which amounts to idolatry.**
> **6 For it is on account of these things that the wrath of God will come, . . .**
>
> **—Colossians 3**

CLEAN UP YOUR ACT FIRST, THEN THE POWER

I have a video teaching tape entitled *"Judgment Upon America."* It is based on this well-known Scripture:

> **13 "If I shut up the heavens so that there is no rain, or if I command the locust to devour the land, or if I send pestilence among My people,**
> **14 and My people who are called by My name humble themselves and pray, and seek My face and turn from their wicked ways, then I will hear from heaven, will forgive their sin, and will heal their land. . . ."**
>
> **—2 Chronicles 7**

I believe that the message of this passage is vital for us today. It does not say anything about what the non-Christians should do, but God says, "If ***My people*** who are called by My name" (Christians) do four things, then He will hear from heaven and heal their land. The four things that He lists are these:

1. Humble themselves
2. Pray (continuously)
3. Seek His face
4. Turn from their wicked ways

The basic reason that Christians at large are not following this verse today and having their land healed is because they do not acknowledge that they have any wicked ways. They are not going to turn from them until they first acknowledge that they have wicked ways. They go to the church meetings, prayer and praise meetings, conventions and conferences, and they come away feeling wonderfully righteous and holy. Unfortunately, this "righteousness" is in their eyes and not necessarily in the eyes of God. Acknowledging sin and wickedness in our lives is the first step to repenting or turning from our wicked ways.

God is calling us to a life of purity and holiness. Following what God outlines in 2 Chronicles 7:14 is an essential step, if we are going to have the supernatural power of God.

I would like to look in more depth at one passage of Scripture that deals with defilement (and this includes defilement of Christians). This is Jesus Himself talking:

> **20 And He was saying, "That which proceeds out of the man, that is what defiles the man.**
>
> **21 "For from within, out of the heart of men, proceed the evil thoughts, fornications, thefts, murders, adulteries,**
>
> **22 deeds of coveting *and* wickedness, *as well as* deceit, sensuality, envy, slander, pride *and* foolishness.**
>
> **23 "All these evil things proceed from within and defile the man."**
>
> **—Mark 7**

As we stated earlier, God is not going to pour out His power miraculously through a defiled person. Look at the things that Jesus said would defile a man:

1. Evil thoughts
2. Fornications

3. Thefts
4. Murders
5. Adulteries
6. Deeds of coveting
7. Deeds of wickedness
8. Deceit
9. Sensuality
10. Envy
11. Slander
12. Pride
13. Foolishness

Offhand, you may not think that you or any of your fellow Christians in your church or fellowship have any of these things in your lives, and are thus defiled. But let's examine them a little more closely, one at a time. As we look at my definition of these, please pray and ask God to show you if any of these things are in your life.

1. ***Evil Thoughts:*** Have you ever wished that something bad would happen to someone? Have you ever thought something along the line of: "I forgive you, but God will get you." These are just two minor examples of evil thoughts that many Christians have often.

2. ***Fornications:*** The term "*fornications*" is a much broader term than *adultery*. It involves any type of sexual abuse, including—but not limited to—sex between two single people. One can commit fornication within a marriage. For instance, a wife can be cold toward her husband, and that is a form of fornication. A husband can rape his wife and that is fornication. One can be having sex with his spouse and be thinking of someone else, and that too is fornication.

3. ***Thefts:*** Have you ever taken a yellow pad, a pencil or a pen from the office? Have you ever used stamps at the office to mail your personal letters? Have you ever made a personal long-distance telephone call on a company telephone? Those are all acts of theft or stealing—taking something that belongs to someone else if you did not have permission, and our consciences are so seared that it doesn't even bother us. If someone pays them $50 in cash for doing something that helped him, many Christians do not report that on their income tax. That is stealing from the government.
4. ***Murders:*** The Lord referred to the Old Testament passage that said, "You shall not commit murder" and "whoever commits murder shall be liable to the court." He then proceeded to outline an even stricter measure of conduct. He said that anyone who is even "angry with his brother shall be guilty before the court" and if he calls him, "You fool," he shall be guilty enough to go into the fiery hell (Matthew 5:21,22).
5. ***Adulteries:*** Jesus said that if we even lust after a woman in our heart, we have committed adultery (Matthew 5:27,28).
6. ***Coveting:*** This is wanting the things that someone else has. It may be that we covet someone else's car, house, or clothes. We could covet another person's wife or husband.
7. ***Deeds of wickedness:*** There are some people who are just plain ornery and mean; they seem to enjoy picking on others. In a church setting, they may be the ones who seem to delight in picking on the pastor or some national Christian leader, for example.

8. ***Deceit:*** When they are in their office but do not wish to take a call, some Christian bosses tell their secretaries to tell a caller that they are "not in." That is lying and it is deceitful. Telling only half of the truth can be very deceitful. Sometimes children do this with parents or husbands and wives with each other, when they are trying to hide something or cover up a portion of the truth.

9. ***Sensuality:*** People, including Christians, can dress sensually, wink sensually, give hugs at church sensually, and they can make sensuous remarks. Sensuality is anything that will stimulate the sexual interest of someone of the opposite sex other than your spouse.

10. ***Envy:*** This is the green-eyed monster. Jealousy is part of envy. Envy causes us not to be able to rejoice when one of our friends has some good fortune or wins a contest or a prize. Sometimes we envy that person, and it crowds out being able to honestly rejoice and celebrate with him or her. We can envy someone their position or status in the church or community. We can be envious of another person's lifestyle.

11. ***Slander:*** This is one of the worst of all of these defiling deeds. When we slander someone, we are killing that person's reputation, without him being there to defend himself. As we saw earlier, the Bible says that Satan is the "accuser of the brethren" (Revelation 12:9, 10). When we slander, we are playing on Satan's team. We can slander people in our church, in our community, and even in our own family. We may be guilty of having slandered national Christian leaders, particularly those who get into difficulties.

12. ***Pride:*** God is opposed to the proud and He gives grace to the humble (James 4:6). God will tear down the house of the proud (Proverbs 15:25). There is so much pride in the body of Christ today that it is pathetic and disgraceful. Pride is ***you*** taking the glory rather than giving God the glory. You need to remember that you are like the flea on the back of the elephant that walked across a swinging bridge; when they got to the other side, the flea said, "Boy, we really shook it, didn't we?" We are nothing, and God is everything. We are simply a flea. Don't let your pride cause you to claim that you are worth anything. Learn of Jesus, for He was meek and lowly (Matthew 11:29, *KJV).* How many television preachers would you consider to be "meek and lowly"? Perhaps there is pride in their lives instead.

13. ***Foolishness:*** The Bible mentions silly and foolish talk. If you were at the average Christian potluck, what would you hear? The answer is much "foolishness." Most of the talk would be about anything but the things of the Lord. The early believers in Jesus Christ were called "Christians" because the name that was heard most often from their lips was *Christ*. If someone were to eavesdrop on some of our church potlucks and social dinners today, we might be called "Baby-ans," "footballians," "cosmeticians" or "new homeians." When we get together, so often we talk about almost everything, except Jesus Christ, who should be the central focus of our lives. Much of our idle chatter could well be considered foolishness and fluff.

We could use a "John the Baptist" today who would call the body of Christ to repentance. Christians need to repent of the things that defile them, but so many are oblivious to the fact that they even have evil ways. Therefore, they don't acknowledge them. Neither do they acknowledge that they are defiled. Therefore, they do not repent and turn from the things that defile them.

If you are going to have the supernatural power of God working in your life, you are going to need to face the things we have just discussed, examining them in the light of God's word rather than "television morality." When God reveals an area of defilement in your life to you, repent and turn from it. As you cease to be defiled, you will be able to present yourself to God as a cleansed vessel, ready for the power of God to flow through you.

The Lord may be convicting you in regard to some of the things discussed in this chapter or the previous three chapters. He may want to clean your spiritual power filter right now. Confess and turn from these sins, misdeeds, lacks and defilements, and He will cleanse you.

> **6 If we say that we have fellowship with Him and *yet* walk in the darkness, we lie and do not practice the truth;**
>
> **7 but if we walk in the light as He Himself is in the light, we have fellowship with one another, and the blood of Jesus His Son cleanses us from all sin.**
>
> **8 If we say that we have no sin, we are deceiving ourselves, and the truth is not in us.**
>
> **—1 John 1**

Praise God—after we confess (repent of) all our sins and shortcomings and turn away from them, He will not only cleanse us of those, but of ***all*** unrighteousness:

> **9 If we confess our sins, He is faithful and righteous to forgive us our sins and to cleanse us from all unrighteousness.**
>
> **—1 John 1**

Repentance and the blood of Jesus can make our power filter totally clean!

The things discussed in this chapter are extremely serious. Regardless of our theology about eternal security, we are talking about things that can defile you and even keep you from inheriting the kingdom of God. We are talking about some very important matters. I would encourage you to just take some time and let the Holy Spirit do a cleansing work in your heart.

Hopefully, you have taken the time to get many of these things cleared up with God and you stand pure before Him, cleansed of all unrighteousness, not because you deserve it, but because of His mercy and grace and the precious blood of Jesus Christ. If you have done that, then right now, your spiritual "air filter" is clean and the power of God can flow through you.

In this and the previous three chapters, we have looked at some of the things that can hamper you from really being clothed with God's miracle power and being used as His tool or messenger to go where the supernatural power of God is needed to overflow to others. Before discussing some details on how you can have that power and use it, I feel the Lord wants us first to get a clear understanding of some of the major reasons why God wants you to have His supernatural power and why you will need it both now and in the days that lie ahead. His supernatural power is and will be needed in some very vital areas.

God's supernatural power is for every Christian.

Part III

USE OF THE POWER

Chapter 10

POWER TO PRESENT THE GOSPEL

Why do we need supernatural power? There are a number of things for which God's power is essential, both in the present time and during the end times. One of these is spreading the gospel.

In the vast majority of cases, as the gospel is presented today, it is primarily presented in words. This is certainly true of the way the gospel is presented over the radio or television. It is also true in the majority of our churches in America today. I suspect that it is also true the majority of the time in individual witnessing.

We have become good at getting people down the aisle and persuading them with our words to come to Jesus Christ. As we read earlier in this book, it was not by persuasive words that Paul presented the gospel:

> **4 And my message and my preaching were not in persuasive words of wisdom, but in demonstration of the Spirit and of power,**
>
> **5 that your faith should not rest on the wisdom of men, but on the power of God.**
>
> **—1 Corinthians 2**

This says that Paul presented the gospel ***"in demonstration"*** of the power and the Spirit of God. He wanted their faith to rest on the demonstrated power of God, and not on man's wisdom or intellect. "In demonstration" means that actual miraculous events were occurring.

I am not talking about "powerful" preaching here. I am speaking of actual demonstration of the supernatural power of God in miracles, signs and wonders. No one will be saved by the demonstration of power alone; the gospel must also be presented. To be most effective, it takes both.

Before we proceed to look at sending out the gospel today in power, let's review how people in the Old Testament knew that a prophet or a teacher's words were really from God.

OLD TESTAMENT VALIDATION

I have some favorite prophets in the Old Testament. One of these is Jeremiah, who had it pretty rough. One instance I would like us to recall together is when Jeremiah was talking to Zedekiah the king, telling him about something that had happened:

> **6 And Jeremiah said, "The word of the LORD came to me, saying,**
>
> **7 'Behold, Hanamel the son of Shallum your uncle is coming to you, saying, "Buy for yourself my field which is at Anathoth, for you have the right of redemption to buy *it*."'**
>
> **8 "Then Hanamel my uncle's son came to me in the court of the guard according to the word of the LORD, and said to me, 'Buy my field, please, that is at Anathoth, which is in the land of Benjamin; for you have the right of possession and the redemption is yours; buy *it* for yourself.' Then I knew that this was the word of the LORD. . . ."**
>
> **—Jeremiah 32**

It was because of the miraculous revelation to Jeremiah of what was going to happen that others knew that he was speaking the words of God. The supernatural power of God let them know that this message was indeed from God.

As you know, Elijah was an incredibly powerful prophet who performed many wonders because God's hand was on him. His protégé or understudy was Elisha. When Elijah was taken up in the fiery chariot, his mantle and a double portion of Elijah's spirit was transferred to Elisha. Right after this occurred, Elisha was coming back to the prophets:

> **14 And he took the mantle of Elijah that fell from him, and struck the waters and said, "Where is the LORD the God of Elijah?" And when he also had struck the waters, they were divided here and there; and Elisha crossed over.**
>
> **15 Now when the sons of the prophets who *were* at Jericho opposite him saw him, they said, "The spirit of Elijah rests on Elisha." And they came to meet him and bowed themselves to the ground before him.**
>
> **—2 Kings 2**

Do you see that because the supernatural power of God was working through Elisha, the other prophets acknowledged and honored him? It was not his words, but the power of God that convinced them that the spirit of Elijah rested on him.

Not only was that principle true in the Old Testament and with Paul; it was even true with Jesus Christ. You may not realize it, but most of the people who believed in Him, believed not because of His words, but because of the miracles that He did. Let us see some examples.

PEOPLE BELIEVED BECAUSE OF THE MIRACLES

If Jesus Christ could not, or would not, use persuasive words to convince people that He was the Son of God, why should we even try? As I have just stated, people believed in Him primarily because of the miracles that He did. This subject could easily be a book in itself. We will just take a few examples out of the Gospel of John.

Why did Nicodemus, a very good man and a ruler of the Jews, come to Jesus? Why did he think that Jesus had come from God?

> **1 Now there was a man of the Pharisees, named Nicodemus, a ruler of the Jews;**
>
> **2 this man came to Him by night, and said to Him, "Rabbi, we know that You have come from God *as* a teacher; for no one can do these signs that You do unless God is with him."**
>
> **—John 3**

Nicodemus believed that Jesus had come from God, not because of the words that Jesus spoke, as wonderful as they were, but because of the signs (attesting miracles) that He did. Not only Nicodemus, but the disciples themselves believed in Jesus because of His signs:

> **11 This beginning of *His* signs Jesus did in Cana of Galilee, and manifested His glory, and His disciples believed in Him.**
>
> **—John 2**

After turning water into wine at Cana, Jesus went to Jerusalem for the Passover. This is what happened there:

23 Now when He was in Jerusalem at the Passover, during the feast, many believed in His name, beholding His signs which He was doing.

—John 2

Why were many believing in His name, according to this verse? It was because of the signs that He was doing which were a demonstration of the supernatural power of God working through Him.

Even though some of the Pharisees did not believe Jesus, in spite of the signs, there were others who were convinced because of them:

16 Therefore some of the Pharisees were saying, "This man is not from God, because He does not keep the Sabbath." But others were saying, "How can a man who is a sinner perform such signs?" And there was a division among them.

—John 9

It is also interesting to note that the reason many of the Jews believed in Jesus was that He raised Lazarus from the dead.

9 The great multitude therefore of the Jews learned that He was there; and they came, not for Jesus' sake only, but that they might also see Lazarus, whom He raised from the dead.

10 But the chief priests took counsel that they might put Lazarus to death also;

11 because on account of him many of the Jews were going away, and were believing in Jesus.

—John 12

Many believed that Jesus' words were words from God, not because of His persuasiveness, His logical arguments or His good teaching outlines; it was because of the signs, wonders and miracles that He did. It was in this manner that Jesus preached the gospel, not only in words, but in demonstration of the power of God. If we are to become like Jesus, we definitely should spread the gospel in the same way.

THE TWELVE APOSTLES AND POWER

There is absolutely no doubt in the mind of anyone who has read the New Testament that, after the ascension of Jesus back into heaven, the disciples spread the gospel with power. Although acts of healing and deliverance were an exciting part of it, that was not all that occurred. After the outpouring of the Holy Spirit in Chapter 2 of Acts, we see the supernatural power of God working through Peter in the very next chapter. There was a miracle, which got everyone's attention, and after the miracle, the gospel was presented. The rest of Acts 3 contains the remaining part of Peter's sermon, but here is enough for you to get an idea of what was happening:

> **1 Now Peter and John were going up to the temple at the ninth *hour*, the hour of prayer.**
>
> **2 And a certain man who had been lame from his mother's womb was being carried along, whom they used to set down every day at the gate of the temple which is called Beautiful, in order to beg alms of those who were entering the temple.**
>
> **3 And when he saw Peter and John about to go into the temple, he *began* asking to receive alms.**
>
> **4 And Peter, along with John, fixed his gaze upon him and said, "Look at us!"**
>
> **5 And he *began* to give them his attention, expecting to receive something from them.**

6 But Peter said, "I do not possess silver and gold, but what I do have I give to you: In the name of Jesus Christ the Nazarene—walk!"

7 And seizing him by the right hand, he raised him up; and immediately his feet and his ankles were strengthened.

8 And with a leap, he stood upright and *began* to walk; and he entered the temple with them, walking and leaping and praising God.

9 And all the people saw him walking and praising God;

10 and they were taking note of him as being the one who used to sit at the Beautiful Gate of the temple to *beg* alms, and they were filled with wonder and amazement at what had happened to him.

11 And while he was clinging to Peter and John, all the people ran together to them at the so-called portico of Solomon, full of amazement.

12 But when Peter saw *this*, he replied to the people, "Men of Israel, why do you marvel at this, or why do you gaze at us, as if by our own power or piety we had made him walk?

13 "The God of Abraham, Isaac, and Jacob, the God of our fathers, has glorified His servant Jesus, *the one* whom you delivered up, and disowned in the presence of Pilate, when he had decided to release Him.

14 "But you disowned the Holy and Righteous One, and asked for a murderer to be granted to you,

15 but put to death the Prince of life, *the one* whom God raised from the dead, *a fact* to which we are witnesses.

16 "And on the basis of faith in His name, *it is* the name of Jesus which has strengthened this man whom you see and know; and the faith which *comes* through Him has given him this perfect health in the presence of you all. . . ."

—Acts 3

We see in this passage that the power of God was upon Peter and overflowed to this man crippled from birth. But remember, Peter grabbed the lame man's right hand and pulled him up. It is faith in action that releases the power of God. It was not Peter's piety (verse 12); it was his:

FAITH IN ACTION

So we learn that Peter, like Paul, did not present the gospel primarily with words, but also in demonstration of the miraculous power of God.

Evidently the signs and the wonders occurring through the apostles were so numerous that Luke could not even enumerate them all, as he was writing the book of Acts:

> **12 And at the hands of the apostles many signs and wonders were taking place among the people; and they were all with one accord in Solomon's portico.**
>
> **13 But none of the rest dared to associate with them; however, the people held them in high esteem.**
>
> **14 And all the more believers in the Lord, multitudes of men and women, were constantly added to *their number*;**
>
> **15 to such an extent that they even carried the sick out into the streets, and laid them on cots and pallets, so that when Peter came by, at least his shadow might fall on any one of them.**
>
> **16 And also the people from the cities in the vicinity of Jerusalem were coming together, bringing people who were sick or afflicted with unclean spirits; and they were all being healed.**
>
> **—Acts 5**

During Jesus' ministry, people had brought the sick from the surrounding area to the place where He was going to be, so that they could be healed and delivered. As we see in these verses from Acts 5, the same thing was happening with these believers of the first century who were endowed with supernatural power.

Continuing in that same chapter of Acts, let's read what occurred next:

> **17 But the high priest rose up, along with all his associates (that is the sect of the Sadducees), and they were filled with jealousy;**
>
> **18 and they laid hands on the apostles, and put them in a public jail.**
>
> **19 But an angel of the Lord during the night opened the gates of the prison, and taking them out he said,**
>
> **20 "Go your way, stand and speak to the people in the temple the whole message of this Life."**
>
> **21 And upon hearing *this*, they entered into the temple about daybreak, and *began* to teach. Now when the high priest and his associates had come, they called the Council together, even all the Senate of the sons of Israel, and sent *orders* to the prison house for them to be brought.**
>
> **22 But the officers who came did not find them in the prison; and they returned, and reported back,**
>
> **23 saying, "We found the prison house locked quite securely and the guards standing at the doors; but when we had opened up, we found no one inside."**
>
> **24 Now when the captain of the temple *guard* and the chief priests heard these words, they were greatly perplexed about them as to what would come of this.**
>
> **25 But someone came and reported to them, "Behold, the men whom you put in prison are standing in the temple and teaching the people!"**
>
> **—Acts 5**

Here we see that the power of God delivered the apostles from jail. In this particular case, the Lord used an angel to exhibit His power. Nonetheless, the gospel was going out, not just in words, but in demonstration of the supernatural power of God.

Now let's turn our attention from Peter to Paul. As Paul went over to Macedonia to present the gospel, he was not going to present it just in words, but also in demonstration of the power of God:

> **16 And it happened that as we were going to the place of prayer, a certain slave-girl having a spirit of divination met us, who was bringing her masters much profit by fortunetelling.**
>
> **17 Following after Paul and us, she kept crying out, saying, "These men are bond-servants of the Most High God, who are proclaiming to you the way of salvation."**
>
> **18 And she continued doing this for many days. But Paul was greatly annoyed, and turned and said to the spirit, "I command you in the name of Jesus Christ to come out of her!" And it came out at that very moment.**
>
> **19 But when her masters saw that their hope of profit was gone, they seized Paul and Silas and dragged them into the market place before the authorities,**
>
> **20 and when they had brought them to the chief magistrates, they said, "These men are throwing our city into confusion, being Jews,**
>
> **21 and are proclaiming customs which it is not lawful for us to accept or to observe, being Romans."**
>
> **22 And the crowd rose up together against them, and the chief magistrates tore their robes off them, and proceeded to order *them* to be beaten with rods.**
>
> **23 And when they had inflicted many blows upon them, they threw them into prison, commanding the jailer to guard them securely;**

24 and he, having received such a command, threw them into the inner prison, and fastened their feet in the stocks.

—Acts 16

Early in this passage, we see Paul instantly casting a demon out of this girl, in a demonstration of the supernatural power of God. As a result, he wound up in jail. Let us now proceed with the story to see what happened:

25 But about midnight Paul and Silas were praying and singing hymns of praise to God, and the prisoners were listening to them;

26 and suddenly there came a great earthquake, so that the foundations of the prison house were shaken; and immediately all the doors were opened, and everyone's chains were unfastened.

27 And when the jailer had been roused out of sleep and had seen the prison doors opened, he drew his sword and was about to kill himself, supposing that the prisoners had escaped.

28 But Paul cried out with a loud voice, saying, "Do yourself no harm, for we are all here!"

29 And he called for lights and rushed in and, trembling with fear, he fell down before Paul and Silas,

30 and after he brought them out, he said, "Sirs, what must I do to be saved?"

31 And they said, "Believe in the Lord Jesus, and you shall be saved, you and your household."

—Acts 16

Which came first—the miracle or the message? Again, in this case the miracle preceded the message. The miraculous demonstration of God's power got the jailer's undivided attention, after which he was totally open to the presentation of the gospel.

On his way to Rome near the end of his life, Paul had a shipwreck and landed on an island. This is what occurred there:

> **2 And the natives showed us extraordinary kindness; for because of the rain that had set in and because of the cold, they kindled a fire and received us all.**
>
> **3 But when Paul had gathered a bundle of sticks and laid them on the fire, a viper came out because of the heat, and fastened on his hand.**
>
> **4 And when the natives saw the creature hanging from his hand, they *began* saying to one another, "Undoubtedly this man is a murderer, and though he has been saved from the sea, justice has not allowed him to live."**
>
> **5 However he shook the creature off into the fire and suffered no harm.**
>
> **6 But they were expecting that he was about to swell up or suddenly fall down dead. But after they had waited a long time and had seen nothing unusual happen to him, they changed their minds and *began* to say that he was a god.**
>
> **7 Now in the neighborhood of that place were lands belonging to the leading man of the island, named Publius, who welcomed us and entertained us courteously three days.**
>
> **8 And it came about that the father of Publius was lying *in bed* afflicted with *recurrent* fever and dysentery; and Paul went in *to see* him and after he had prayed, he laid his hands on him and healed him.**
>
> **9 And after this had happened, the rest of the people on the island who had diseases were coming to him and getting cured.**
>
> **10 And they also honored us with many marks of respect; and when we were setting sail, they supplied *us* with all we needed.**
>
> **—Acts 28**

In this passage, Paul did not present the gospel to the leading men of the island in words only, but also in demonstration of supernatural power. I am sure that he also spoke the gospel to those whom he healed. Again, the miracles came before the message. The gospel was going out not in just words, but in actual demonstrable acts of the power of God. It takes both to do the best job.

Acts 14:1 tells us that when Paul and Barnabas entered the synagogue of the Jews in Iconium, they spoke in such a manner that a great multitude of Jews and Gentiles believed. Continuing in the chapter, we read this:

> **3 Therefore they spent a long time *there* speaking boldly *with reliance* upon the Lord, who was bearing witness to the word of His grace, granting that signs and wonders be done by their hands.**
>
> **—Acts 14**

God confirmed the words that they were boldly speaking by granting that many signs and wonders be accomplished by their hands. Again, we see that their message was presented in demonstration of the power of God, and not in words alone.

In the following passage, we see that Paul not only spoke out boldly about the kingdom of God, but in addition the word of the Lord was confirmed by the extraordinary miracles that God was performing through him:

> **8 And he entered the synagogue and continued speaking out boldly for three months, reasoning and persuading *them* about the kingdom of God. . . .**
>
> **10 And this took place for two years, so that all who lived in Asia heard the word of the Lord, both Jews and Greeks.**

11 And God was performing extraordinary miracles by the hands of Paul,

12 so that handkerchiefs or aprons were even carried from his body to the sick, and the diseases left them and the evil spirits went out.

—Acts 19

Perhaps you can now better appreciate what Paul meant when he wrote to the church of Corinth the two verses that we looked at earlier:

4 And my message and my preaching were not in persuasive words of wisdom, but in demonstration of the Spirit and of power,

5 that your faith should not rest on the wisdom of men, but on the power of God.

—1 Corinthians 2

We have seen that the power of God was with the apostles for healing in a dramatic way. Other times, the demonstration of the power of God had the opposite effect from healing:

3 But Peter said, "Ananias, why has Satan filled your heart to lie to the Holy Spirit, and to keep back *some* of the price of the land?

4 "While it remained *unsold*, did it not remain your own? And after it was sold, was it not under your control? Why is it that you have conceived this deed in your heart? You have not lied to men, but to God."

5 And as he heard these words, Ananias fell down and breathed his last; and great fear came upon all who heard of it.

6 And the young men arose and covered him up, and after carrying him out, they buried him.

—Acts 5

If you are familiar with this story in Acts, you know that this man's wife came in shortly afterward and the same thing occurred to her. So in this case, we see the power of God striking down a couple who lied to God and to the church.

In a similar way, we see the power of God being used by Paul to strike a man blind:

> **6 And when they had gone through the whole island as far as Paphos, they found a certain magician, a Jewish false prophet whose name was Bar-Jesus,**
>
> **7 who was with the proconsul, Sergius Paulus, a man of intelligence. This man summoned Barnabas and Saul and sought to hear the word of God.**
>
> **8 But Elymas the magician (for thus his name is translated) was opposing them, seeking to turn the proconsul away from the faith.**
>
> **9 But Saul, who was also *known* as Paul, filled with the Holy Spirit, fixed his gaze upon him,**
>
> **10 and said, "You who are full of all deceit and fraud, you son of the devil, you enemy of all righteousness, will you not cease to make crooked the straight ways of the Lord?**
>
> **11 "And now, behold, the hand of the Lord is upon you, and you will be blind and not see the sun for a time." And immediately a mist and a darkness fell upon him, and he went about seeking those who would lead him by the hand.**
>
> **12 Then the proconsul believed when he saw what had happened, being amazed at the teaching of the Lord.**
>
> **—Acts 13**

We have read about the demonstration of the power of God for healing, for deliverance, for protection from vipers, for release from prison and even for judgment on sin. The power of God was so great on the early disciples that there was even the raising of the dead:

> **7 And on the first day of the week, when we were gathered together to break bread, Paul *began* talking to them, intending to depart the next day, and he prolonged his message until midnight.**
>
> **8 And there were many lamps in the upper room where we were gathered together.**
>
> **9 And there was a certain young man named Eutychus sitting on the window sill, sinking into a deep sleep; and as Paul kept on talking, he was overcome by sleep and fell down from the third floor, and was picked up dead.**
>
> **10 But Paul went down and fell upon him and after embracing him, he said, "Do not be troubled, for his life is in him."**
>
> **11 And when he had gone *back* up, and had broken the bread and eaten, he talked with them a long while, until daybreak, and so departed.**
>
> **12 And they took away the boy alive, and were greatly comforted.**
>
> **—Acts 20**

This incident occurred when Paul was in Troas. We read that a young man was killed when he fell three stories out of a window, and then the power of God working through Paul brought him back to life.

You may think that the power of God was just for the first century or that today it is just for Christian "big wigs." I do not believe this is so. But don't take my word for it—listen to what Jesus had to say on the subject. Before we read this next passage, let me ask you a question. Have you believed in Jesus? If you answer "yes" to that, Jesus told you what signs would accompany *you*:

15 And He said to them, "Go into all the world and preach the gospel to all creation.

16 "He who has believed and has been baptized shall be saved; but he who has disbelieved shall be condemned.

17 "And these signs will accompany those who have believed: in My name they will cast out demons, they will speak with new tongues;

18 they will pick up serpents, and if they drink any deadly *poison*, it shall not hurt them; they will lay hands on the sick, and they will recover."

—Mark 16

In these verses, Jesus says that those who believe in Him ***will*** have His miracle power. I believe Jesus when He says this. To see that it is true, let's look at some examples of the exhibition of the power of God in evangelism that have occurred since the first century.

THE GOSPEL IN POWER IN THE PHILIPPINES

In his booklet entitled *The Believer Takes Authority*, Maurice Martin shares something that happened one time when he was conducting a crusade in the Philippines:

> I was conducting a crusade in the city of Bacolod in the Philippines. One day I passed a desk at the hotel where I was staying. The lady at the desk had been very friendly, so to encourage her to come I told her about a little deaf mute girl who had been healed the night before. There was another young lady with her and she started telling me about having tonsillitis and a real sore throat. I touched her throat and said "In the name of Jesus I command all soreness to go!" Then I said now swallow, when she swallowed I said to her "did some-

thing happen?" She exclaimed, "it is gone." I went on up town and after lunch there came a knock on the hotel door. There was a whole group of people there wanting me to minister to them also. One girl had infection in her feet. They looked terrible, both of them completely black with big running sores. She said they had been this way for over two years and the doctors could do nothing. The next step would be to amputate both feet. She could hardly walk, the pain was so severe. I told the family I wanted them to come to the crusade, that it would be easier to receive, but that I would minister to the girl for pain so she would not be in such discomfort.

Then I told her to relax. I said, "you don't have to pray. All you have to do is receive." I touched her on the forehead and said, "In Jesus name I command all pain and soreness to go." Then I had her to walk asking, "did something happen?" She said, "yes, it doesn't hurt anymore." The man that was with the group was going deaf but I told him that it would be easier for him to receive if he would come to the crusade, so that night the whole family came. I ministered to them, commanding healing in Jesus' name. The next day I met this man's son who was the owner of the hotel. He told me the girl's feet were getting well and his father was able to hear well since he was ministered to, there were two whole families who came to the Lord because a girl's sore throat disappeared.

—Miracles Now Evangelistic Assoc., pp. 12-13

THE GOSPEL IN POWER TO AFRICA

When we were ministering in South Africa, we met a precious couple there, Dave and Mary Clark. They had been missionaries in Uganda under Idi Amin and had suffered severe persecution during that time. In fact, Dave had had his head slashed opened by a machete in one frightening incident, but God protected them through many miracles. They shared about numerous such happenings with us as we stayed in their home in South Africa at that time, and we have remained close ever since.

I mentioned the following report in Chapter 4 briefly, but it bears repeating here as it relates to the subject of presenting the gospel in the demonstration of the power of God.

One day, as Dave and I were talking, he casually mentioned that he and some other brothers had started 134 churches in a single year in Uganda. My mouth fell open; I could not believe what I was hearing. I said, "Dave, how in the world did you start so many churches in a year?" The reply from this gentle, humble man was that they would go to a village where the gospel had not been preached and tell the people in that village that they would like to tell them about their God. The people in the village would ask what the Christian God could do that their gods could not. Dave and the brothers with him would then tell the people to bring out all the sick and crippled people in the village. As they laid hands on them, the power of God that was all over them flowed out to touch these people and heal them all. Of course, following such a miraculous event, the entire village would turn out that night to the big meeting where the gospel was presented. A vast majority of the villagers would receive Christ as their Savior.

Here again, we see the pattern that we have seen before. There were miracles, and following that, the gospel of the kingdom was presented. The gospel did not go out just in words; it also went out in demonstration of the supernatural power of God.

Peter Wagner, a professor at Fuller Theological Seminary, received a report from Terrie Lillie, a student who documented a miraculous event that occurred in a small village in Kenya. Here is what was reported to Peter Wagner:

A child was deadly sick in the same house after the end of the second week. She had malaria and surely she was dying. We were awakened at night by a big cry. We all ran to the direction of my grandmother's house. Kavili was crying, and Mbulu and the old woman, Kanini, the child born recently, was dying. She had changed her color and her eyes had turned completely white. There was no blinking.

Many more people were there and a lot more were coming. I got inside. Here was the people who did not know what to do and how to do it. I was as they were in the middle of the night, with no car or anything which could help anyone. No medicine was available at that time. Something had to be done. I thought it would be a good idea to pray and see what we would do next.

I asked to be given the child. I put her under my arms and called my wife to come near. I told everyone to come in that we may pray for the dying child. They came in but some feared that the child was going to die and so they did not go inside the house with a dead child. Then I had all of them sit. I began to pray. I did not make a long prayer. I said very few words. I simply asked the Lord to heal the child in the name of Jesus. Then I gave the child back to the mother.

The moment I gave it back, she was well. She was now breathing. She began to cry, she was nursed and she was well. Everyone took time to praise the name of the Lord. I could not really understand what was happening but I felt the power of God proceed out of me, and for a moment I did not want to say a lot of things. This was a big issue which made everyone present wonder to see how the Lord worked so quickly.

As a result of this instant, [sic] the whole village became Christians.

—*Power Evangelism*
Harper & Row Publishers, pp. 18-19

THE GOSPEL IN POWER IN AMERICA

A traveling evangelist who spoke at Faith Bible Center, a church here in Medford, Oregon, shared an incident that had happened to him. He had presented the gospel to a man who was in a wheelchair. The man seemed interested and open, but there was still a hesitancy on his part to receive Christ.

This evangelist then asked him, "If God healed you and you got up out of that wheelchair, would you receive Christ as your Savior?" The man replied that of course he would. So this evangelist placed his hand on the head of this crippled person, and said, "In the name of Jesus Christ, be healed." Then he told him to stand up, which he did, and he found that he was totally healed.

Weeping and rejoicing all at the same time, the man then knelt and prayed to receive Christ as his Savior. What a time of rejoicing he had! He was transferred from the kingdom of Satan into the kingdom of God. He now had eternal life instead of eternal death, and he also could get rid of the wheelchair that had been his prison for so many years. This is an example of the gospel going out in power, not just in words.

THE POWER OF GOD IN THE VINEYARD

I had already dictated this book when I began to read John Wimber's book *Power Evangelism*. Evidently, the Lord has led both of us to almost the identical conclusion, but from totally separate paths.

In his book, *Power Evangelism*, John shares an example of personal evangelism where supernatural power was involved:

It was the end of a long day of ministry and I was exhausted. I had just completed a teaching conference in Chicago and was flying off to another speaking engagement in New York. I was looking forward to the plane ride as a chance to relax for a few hours before plunging back into teaching. But it was not to be the quiet, uneventful trip I had hoped for.

Shortly after takeoff, I pushed back the reclining seat and readjusted the seat belt, preparing to relax. My eyes wandered around the cabin, not looking at anything in particular. Seated across the aisle from me was a middle-aged man, a business man, to judge from his appearance, but there was nothing unusual or noteworthy about him. But in the split second that my eyes happened to be cast in his direction, I saw something that startled me.

Written across his face in very clear and distinct letters I thought I saw the word "adultery." I blinked, rubbed my eyes, and looked again. It was still there. "Adultery." I was seeing it not with my eyes, but in my mind's eye. No one else on the plane, I am sure, saw it. It was the Spirit of God communicating to me. The fact that it was a spiritual phenomenon made it no less real.

By now the man had become aware that I was looking at him ("gaping at him" might be a more accurate description).

"What do you want?" he snapped.

As he spoke, a woman's name came clearly to mind. This was more familiar to me; I had become accustomed to the Holy Spirit bringing things to my awareness through these kinds of promptings.

Somewhat nervously, I leaned across the aisle and asked, "Does the name Jane [not her real name] mean anything to you?"

His face turned ashen. "We've got to talk," he stammered.

The plane we were on was a jumbo jet, the kind with a small upstairs cocktail lounge. As I followed him up the stairs to the lounge, I sensed the Spirit speaking to me yet again. "Tell him if he doesn't turn from his adultery, I'm going to take him."

Terrific. All I had wanted was a nice, peaceful plane ride to New York. Now here I was, sitting in an airplane cocktail lounge with a man I had never seen before, whose name I didn't even know, about to tell him God was going to take his life if he didn't stop his affair with some woman.

We sat down in strained silence. He looked at me suspiciously for a moment, then asked, "Who told you that name?"

"God told me," I blurted out. I was too rattled to think of a way to ease into the topic more gracefully.

"*God* told you?" He almost shouted the question, he was so shocked by what I had said.

"Yes," I answered, taking a deep breath. "He also told me to tell you . . . that unless you turn from this adulterous relationship, he is going to take your life."

I braced myself for what I was sure would be an angry, defensive reaction, but to my relief the instant I spoke to him, his defensiveness crumbled and his heart melted. In a choked, desperate voice he asked me, "What should I do?"

At last I was back on familiar ground. I explained to him what it meant to repent and trust Christ and invited him to pray with me. With hands folded and head bowed, I began to lead him in a quiet prayer. "O God . . ."

That was as far as I got. The conviction of sin that had built up inside him seemed virtually to explode. Bursting into tears, he cried out, "O *God*, I'm so *sorry*" and launched into the most heartrending repentance I had ever heard.

It was impossible, in such cramped quarters, to keep hidden what was happening. Before long everyone in the cocktail lounge was intimately acquainted with this man's past sinfulness and present contrition. The flight attendants were even weeping right along with him.

When he finished praying and regained his composure, we talked for a while about what had happened to him.

"The reason I was so upset when you first mentioned that name to me," he explained, "was that my wife was sitting in the seat right next to me. I didn't want her to hear."

I knew he wasn't going to like what I said to him next.

"You're going to have to tell her."

"I am?" he responded weakly. "When?"

"Better do it right now," I said gently.

The prospect of confessing to his wife was, understandably, somewhat intimidating, but he could see there was no other way. So again I followed him, down the stairs and back to our seats.

I couldn't hear the conversation over the noise of the plane, but I could see his wife's stunned reaction, not only to his confession of infidelity, but also to his account of how the stranger sitting across the aisle had been sent by God to warn him of the consequences of his sin. Eyes wide with amazement (and probably terror!), she stared first at her husband, then at me, then back at her husband, then back at me, as the amazing story unfolded. In the end the man led his wife to accept Christ, right there on the airplane.

There was little time to talk when we got off the airplane in New York. They didn't own a Bible, so I gave them mine. Then we went our separate ways.

This might seem like an unusual, if not bizarre, event, yet I could write hundreds of other accounts like it—both from my own experience and from that of others

> I know. I call this type of encounter *power evangelism*, and I believe it was one of the most effective means of evangelism in the early church. Further, power evangelism appears to have been present during periods of great missionary expansion and renewal throughout church history.
>
> —Harper & Row Publishers, pp. 32-34

John Wimber had been seeking the power of God to work in his own life and in his church for a good while, and finally it came. Out of this has grown the Vineyard churches. I praise God for the emphasis that John has brought to the body of Christ that signs and wonders are for today. In fact, he taught a course entitled, "Signs and Wonders are for Today" at Fuller Seminary. I pray that more churches will get into a condition to use the supernatural power of God in their evangelism.

I don't mean to imply that John Wimber is the only one or even the main one using miracles as a regular part of presenting the gospel. Many excellent examples may be found, for instance, Harald Bredesen's book *Need A Miracle?* (Harrison House Publishers).

Lester Sumrall is another man of God who moves in this way. In fact, he tells the young men who graduate from his schools, located in various countries, not to go out and try to raise support. He tells them simply to go to a new city and start knocking on doors. He says that you knock on the first door and ask if there is anyone there who is sick or in need. You tell them that you would like to pray for them to get well and that it is free; there is no obligation. Very likely there will be someone in that house who is sick or has some type of pain. You pray for that individual and he receives his healing.

Then Lester says to go to the next house and do the same thing. Keep it up, one house at a time and, certainly by noon, someone will have invited you to have lunch. If you keep that up all afternoon, before the day is over someone will have invited you to stay for supper and spend the night.

You get up and start the same process the next day, with people getting healed and hearing the gospel. If you repeat this day after day, after a couple of weeks, you will have led quite a number of people to the Lord. They will be wanting to meet regularly, so they can learn more about what is happening to them and how to help others. A church will be formed and there will be enough support for you to live on.

Lester encourages young ministers to get their minds focused on spreading the gospel in demonstration of the power and then the support will come, rather than concentrating on the support and hoping that the demonstration of the power of God will come. I would certainly agree with my good brother in that.

Unfortunately, it is far easier to do this in a Third World country than it is in America, Europe, Japan or any nation where the degree of education and scientific learning has risen to a fairly high level. The Third World countries believe in the supernatural. They do not try to figure it out. If you tell them, "I am going to pray for you, as you receive Jesus Christ, and not only will your sins be forgiven, but you will also be healed," they absolutely believe it, with pure, childlike faith. If you were to do that same thing in America, there would be skeptics standing around thinking, "What if nothing happens?" Even a sick person who has just been converted or is about to be converted may get distracted, wondering how the molecules in his twisted spine can be straightened, trying to figure it out logically. We immediately begin to approach it from a scientific perspective rather than believing in faith.

Oh, how I wish that the church in America would return to a solid belief in the supernatural and would begin to exercise supernatural power. If we believe it strongly enough, and it begins to be demonstrated, then even the skeptical non-Christians are going to begin to believe in supernatural power.

THE GOSPEL IN POWER IN INDIA

In Chapter 4, I mentioned Terry Calkin, a chartered accountant in New Zealand and also lay pastor of Greenlane Christian Fellowship. He recently shared with me how a healing started a revival in India. Here is the story in his own words:

> A group of us went to Vijayawada in India, to hold meetings in four different areas. The meeting I was conducting was in Minvillivilli. The first night only about 30 people showed up at my meeting in this very large area. That night the leaders of the various teams met back together and one had had 5,000 people out to the meeting, another 4,000 and another about the same size. I was a bit ashamed to report that I had only 30 people.
>
> The second night there were about 150 there and I said, "Lord, what do I have to do?" And He said, "Do what the disciples did. It's miracles that the people want to see." So I had the word of God. God showed me that there was a woman with a bad back condition. So I called up someone who had a bad back condition, and this woman came up. When she came up, she had had this condition for about ten years. She had a degenerative hip which caused her to be bent over double. She couldn't stand up and she was in constant pain, and everybody in the village knew her.
>
> So I laid hands on her and prayed for her, in front of everybody, and absolutely nothing happened—*nothing.* I wished the stage would open up and swallow me and

leave the rest of the team sitting there with the problem, while I went back to New Zealand. I really felt terrible. It was a terrible let down and a difficult situation to be in.

I hadn't preached at that point, so I said to her, "Just sit in my chair over there, while I preach, because I believe that God showed me He was going to heal you, and He is going to heal you." So, I stood up to preach and when I finished, I turned around to see how she was. I couldn't talk to her directly. I had to ask through an interpreter. When I turned around to her, I could tell by the look on her face—she was just beaming from ear to ear. She stood up and gave her testimony, that while I was preaching, God had healed her and she was able to stand up straight and had no pain. She bent over and touched her toes and the whole place erupted.

As a result of that, the next night there were 6,000 there, and we ended up with a very successful campaign with hundreds coming to know Jesus.

—Greenlane Christian Fellowship
17 Marewa Rd., Greenlane
Auckland, New Zealand

GLASSES IN THE GARBAGE CAN

Remember, we are looking at the gospel going out in power, not just in words. What do you think would happen if some Sunday evening, in one of the churches in your area, one of the people prayed for all those who were wearing glasses and the eyesight of all of them was instantly healed? Imagine that they were healed instantly, so that they were able to make use of the garbage can placed at the exit, where everybody could throw their unneeded glasses.

Suppose this individual announced that he felt he should do it again the following Sunday night. What do you think would happen? Probably everyone in the surrounding area who wore glasses would be there. There would probably be standing room only. The miracles get the attention in order that the gospel can be presented. If churches today were presenting the gospel in power, they would continually have to be subdividing, because their facilities would not be big enough to hold the crowds.

There are those who talk about a great revival coming during the end of this age. I believe that this is true, but it is not going to come by the gospel being spread in words only. It will only come when the gospel goes out in demonstration of the supernatural power of God.

SUMMARY AND CONCLUSION

Even back in Old Testament times, the way people knew that a prophet was a man of God and spoke the words of God was through the miraculous signs and wonders that God's power performed through him. This was true even of Jesus Christ in the New Testament days. Many of the people believed in Him because of the signs that He did, the miracles that the power of God caused to happen through Him.

Peter certainly took the gospel out in power. The Lord used that power to heal the sick, as well as to cause a man and his wife to die, among other things.

The Lord used the apostle Paul to raise the dead, to heal the sick and to deliver people from demonic forces. God also had Paul use that divine power to cause an evil man to go blind. In addition, the power of God protected Paul, when an extremely poisonous viper bit him.

I am sure that if you had been around either Peter or Paul, you could have felt the power of God in them. They were like charged up, rechargeable batteries, ready to discharge God's power wherever and whenever God said to let it help someone.

We have seen that this power of God was not just for the Old Testament times, for Jesus' day or for the early disciples, but it is even for today. It is for you and for me. Jesus wants to give us His power. In Acts 1:8, He said that we would get His power when the Holy Spirit came upon us. If you have been filled with the Holy Spirit, you have that power resting upon you. We need to get a lot of crud out of our lives, clean up our act, and dedicate ourselves totally to Jesus Christ, so that our battery can become fully charged with the miraculous, supernatural power of God.

In this chapter, we have looked at the gospel going out in power. In the last chapter of this book, we will deal with how you can personally share the gospel, not only in words, but also in demonstration of the power of God.

Before we get to that, there are some other exciting things that we need to discuss. God wants you to use the supernatural power that He has given to you for many other things other than spreading the gospel in demonstration of the power of God.

God's supernatural power is for every Christian.

Chapter 11

POWER TO HEAL

One of the gifts of the Holy Spirit is healing. There are people to whom the Spirit seems to give a special "gift of healing," such as Kathryn Kuhlman, Oral Roberts, Aimee Semple McPherson, Smith Wigglesworth and many others whom we could name, both through past centuries and those living today. We have no control over whom the Holy Spirit gives this gift to, because it is a gift from Him. ***But***, there is a healing power that is for every Spirit-filled Christian. Just as "giving" is also a special gift of the Spirit that some have in greater measure, and yet all Christians are to give, we should all be used of God to heal.

Let's remind ourselves of two verses that we have used before to help us see that this is so, from the authority of the Scriptures. As we review these Scriptures, we need to ask ourselves afresh whether we believe in Jesus. Hopefully, the answer is *yes*. If that is true, then this is what Jesus Himself said we would do:

> **12 "Truly, truly, I say to you, he who believes in Me, the works that I do shall he do also; and greater *works* than these shall he do; because I go to the Father. . . ."**
>
> **—John 14**

Jesus is talking about an individual here, not a group of Christians. He did not say that the "church" or a group of Christians who believe in Him will do the works that He did. He said, "*He* who believes in Me, the works that I do shall he do also." If you have believed in Jesus, then the works that He did, you will (can) do also.

Then the question arises as to what the works of Jesus were. Let's turn again to the Scriptures to find out:

> **38 "*You know of* Jesus of Nazareth, how God anointed Him with the Holy Spirit and with power, and *how* He went about doing good, and healing all who were oppressed by the devil; for God was with Him. . . ."**
>
> **—Acts 10**

In this verse, we clearly see that the works of Jesus were doing good and also healing all who were oppressed by the devil. If we want to exert a godly, Christlike character, then we will be doing good and helping people out, and we also will be ***healing.***

You may recall the instance wherein John the Baptist sent two of his disciples to ask Jesus whether or not He was the Expected One. Here is Jesus' answer to them—His answer as to what His works were:

> **22 And He answered and said to them, "Go and report to John what you have seen and heard: *the* BLIND RECEIVE SIGHT, *the* lame walk, *the* lepers are cleansed, and *the* deaf hear, *the* dead are raised up, *the* POOR HAVE THE GOSPEL PREACHED TO THEM. . . ."**
>
> **—Luke 7**

In this verse from Luke, we see that Jesus defined His works as healing even the blind, crippled, lepers and deaf, as well as raising the dead and preaching the gospel to the poor (who could not afford offerings to the preacher). These are the works of Jesus that He said we would do if we believed in Him.

The other significant passage that we looked at earlier is found in the Gospel according to Mark:

> **16 "He who has believed and has been baptized shall be saved; but he who has disbelieved shall be condemned.**
>
> **17 "And these signs will accompany those who have believed: in My name they will cast out demons, they will speak with new tongues;**
>
> **18 . . . they will lay hands on the sick and they will recover."**
>
> **—Mark 16**

Jesus said these things not just to first-century disciples, not just to preachers and evangelists, not just to those with the gift of healing, but to all those "who have believed." He said that he who has believed ***"will lay hands on the sick and they will recover,"*** as well as casting out demons and other things that we will talk about later. In this chapter, however, we want to concentrate on the portion that states that we will lay hands on the sick and they ***will*** recover.

Let me ask you once again: "Have you believed in Jesus? Have you been filled with the Holy Spirit?" If so, this healing power has come upon you, and God wants you to be clothed in it. He wants you to pray for the sick and they will recover.

This is something that you need to get settled in your own mind, before we look at some biblical aspects of healing and some practical suggestions. ***Do you think that the intention of Jesus Christ was for you to lay hands on the sick and they would be healed and recover?***

If your answer to that was "no," then go back and reread the first part of this chapter over and over again, until your answer is "yes." All I am asking here is whether you think it was the ***intention*** of Jesus for you to heal the sick. Have you believed? What was the intention of Jesus for everyone who has believed?

HEALING OF CHRISTIANS

Up to now, we have been primarily talking about healing in connection with the gospel going out or healing of unbelievers, either right before they accepted Christ or right afterwards. We do want to continue with that thought, but we need first to address the question of Christians themselves being healed.

Many Christians may not realize this, but the Bible outlines the normal way in which Christians should be healed:

> **14 Is anyone among you sick? Let him call for the elders of the church, and let them pray over him, anointing him with oil in the name of the Lord;**
> **15 and the prayer offered in faith will restore the one who is sick, and the Lord will raise him up, and if he has committed sins, they will be forgiven him.**
> **16 Therefore, confess your sins to one another, and pray for one another, so that you may be healed. The effective prayer of a righteous man can accomplish much.**
>
> **—James 5**

If any Christian is sick and wants to have the miraculous power of God heal him, he is to go straight to the elders of his church and ask them to pray for him. This is God's way and His command. Other avenues of healing should be investigated only ***after*** the elders of the church have prayed for the sick believer. But remember, those elders have no power to heal anyone.

They must have the miracle-working power of God flowing through them in the name of Jesus Christ.

However, an integral part of this type of healing is found in verse 16 which says that there is to be confession of sins to one another with the prayer, so that you may be healed. The reason that many people do not want to go to the elders or, in some cases, the elders do not want to pray for a sick person, is because they do not want to get involved in confessing their sins to each other. What this means is that their "air filter" (power filter) is all clogged up, and the healing power of God normally will not flow through until this confession has taken place, and the filter is clean.

If the anointing with oil by the elders, confessing of sins, and praying in faith does not raise up the sick person, then other avenues can be sought for the healing. But, I believe that it pleases God for a Christian to try this way first—that is, for a sick Christian to go to the elders. If you do not belong to a church that has elders who will pray for the sick, then you should ask God if He would have you move to another fellowship which does have elders who will pray for the sick in their church and see the results of God. Certainly you would want to pray for your pastor and elders that they would obey the Bible and do this for you and others.

HEALINGS BY "AVERAGE CHRISTIANS"

We already read of a number of healings in the Bible in Chapter 10, where we discussed how the apostles shared the gospel both in word and in demonstration of the power of God. I would like to take just one more here from the Scriptures in order to orient our thinking on the subject of supernatural healing. Let's read about something that happened to Philip:

> **5 And Philip went down to the city of Samaria and *began* proclaiming Christ to them.**

6 And the multitudes with one accord were giving attention to what was said by Philip, as they heard and saw the signs which he was performing.

7 For *in the case of* many who had unclean spirits, they were coming out *of them* shouting with a loud voice; and many who had been paralyzed and lame were healed.

8 And there was much rejoicing in that city. . . .

12 But when they believed Philip preaching the good news about the kingdom of God and the name of Jesus Christ, they were being baptized, men and women alike.

13 And even Simon himself believed; and after being baptized he continued on with Philip; and as he observed signs and great miracles taking place, he was constantly amazed.

—Acts 8

Here we see Philip performing great signs and wonders. As a result of the miracles and his message about the kingdom of God through Jesus Christ, many believed. You might think that Philip was some sort of a high-powered evangelist. Not so—he was simply a deacon, as the Bible tells us. If you read Acts 6:1-4, you will see that, as the number of disciples of Jesus were increasing, the apostles were needing helpers to tend to the oversight of daily tasks, so that they could devote themselves to prayer and the ministry of the word. This is what happened when the first "deacons" (as we call them today) were chosen:

5 And the statement found approval with the whole congregation; and they chose Stephen, a man full of faith and of the Holy Spirit, and Philip, Prochorus, Nicanor, Timon, Parmenas and Nicolas, a proselyte from Antioch.

—Acts 6

Even as a young Christian, I would acknowledge that there were miraculous healings in Bible times, even by deacons such as Philip. However, as a scientist (in my undergraduate work), I was extremely skeptical about any contemporary miraculous healings. In my mind, I placed almost all of them in the category of psychosomatic illnesses that were temporarily healed by prayer and positive thought. This was essentially my attitude until, as I mentioned earlier in this book, my own lower wisdom teeth were dissolved, removed by a miracle of God. The hard, cold facts brought me to a realization that healings were indeed for today.

God can and will use anyone, regardless of age or occupation, to do His healing work. It is the right and the heritage of every believer. In fact it seems as though the people whom God is using mightily in healing today frequently do not have a theological background. For example, several I know personally include a retired attorney in New Zealand, Bill Subritzky; an ex-chartered accountant who now pastors a church in New Zealand (without salary), Terry Calkin; and an ex-businessman in Australia, Stuart Gramenz. These, and thousands of men like them, simply were willing to take a chance, be bold and let the power that God had placed on them when they were baptized with the Holy Spirit work through them to heal people.

I would have to put myself in this "layman" category. After I graduated from college, I was in the oil business for five years. Then I was with IBM for ten years. I had my own consulting firm for five years and I have worked as an economist for the last fifteen. Though a businessman by background, God has seen fit to let His power flow through me to do His healing work.

HEALING AND THE GIFT OF KNOWLEDGE

In my own ministry, the primary way that healings have occurred are in connection with what are called "words of knowledge," one of the gifts of the Spirit listed in 1 Corinthians 12 (verse 8). For example, the Lord may show me that someone's hip is being healed or someone's heart is being healed. If this occurs in a group meeting or service, I simply announce that to the people. I am not the one doing the healing—God is doing it. I am simply letting the people know what God is doing, as He reveals it to me.

I could give hundreds of examples of this. One such incident happened while I was ministering in a church in Hawaii. As God revealed it to me, I simply said that God was touching someone's elbow, and it was being healed. Afterward, a man went back to the book table where Jeani was, excitedly bending his arm back and forth. He exclaimed, "Look I can bend my arm!" Jeani wondered why this was a big deal, until he shared that he had only been able to bend it from a straight position up just about three inches. He also shared that he was a missionary, and the very next day he was returning to the mission field where he really needed to have full use of that arm. Praise God! The supernatural power of God healed this brother's arm, and we were able to rejoice together.

One time we were having a meeting that was attended by a pastor and his wife from a local church whom I knew very well. At one point during the meeting, the Lord had me ask anyone present who needed prayer for physical healing to hold up his hand. This pastor's wife raised her hand. She said that she needed healing for some fever blisters on her lips that normally lasted several weeks (these wound up lasting only three days). As I was praying for her lips, the Lord told me to pray for her right leg, so I began to pray, "Lord, heal her leg, touch it and make it whole." While I was praying this, I was thinking, "There is nothing wrong with her leg. Why am I praying this?"

I then went on to pray for the next person, and she turned to her husband, and said, "Did you tell him anything about my leg?" He replied, "No." It turned out that that very afternoon she had hurt her leg while out water-skiing. God not only revealed to me that there was a problem, but that His miraculous power was flowing into her to heal not only her lips, but also her leg. I give Jesus all the glory, for I obviously did not heal her leg; He did. I was not even smart enough to know that her leg was hurting. In a supernatural way God revealed this to me and used my hands simply as transmission lines to provide the healing power for this precious lady.

A similar situation happened at one of our conferences. I was praying for another lady for her legs. All of a sudden, the Lord told me to pray for her left kidney. I laid my hand on the left side of her lower back and prayed for her left kidney. Later, in joyous exclamations, she shared that she just found out that very day that she had problems with her left kidney. No one knew about it except her and her doctor, and she certainly had not said anything about it to anyone. God had chosen to allow His supernatural power to flow to her to heal her kidney as well, and He had revealed to me that specific problem, so that we could acknowledge His divine intervention and give Him the glory. Praise be to the Lord who reveals these things and then heals by His supernatural power!

I would like to share with you one other instance that is really exciting to me. We were having one of our Omega Conferences in Medford, Oregon and Jimmy Smith and I were ministering together. The Lord showed Jimmy that there was someone in the back of the room who wore a catheter (a tube into the bladder to drain urine when the bladder is not functioning properly). When no one came forward in response to this word of knowledge, the Lord revealed to him specifically who it was—a lady in a blue dress on the back row whom I had known for years. He asked her to come forward. It turned out that not only did she have a catheter (which I had not known), but she was also a severe diabetic. We prayed for healing in both of these areas. She was very skeptical about healing but allowed us to pray for her anyhow.

That night, at about 2:30 a.m., she woke up in pain so intense that she went to the emergency ward of the hospital. The doctor on duty asked her why she had in a catheter. She replied that it was because her bladder did not work. He told her that her bladder was now functioning normally, he removed the catheter and he told her that the pain would be eliminated if she would simply go use the bathroom. She did so and the pain left immediately. For fourteen years, this woman had not been able to take a bath or go swimming and now that the catheter was removed, she could do all of these things normally.

She then thought, "If God healed me from that, He also must have healed me from my diabetes." At that time, she was on the maximum allowable dosage of insulin and she had to check her blood every four hours. "Cold-turkey" she stopped taking her insulin injections. Had I known, I would not have advised her to do this, but this was her independent decision. She did not tell anyone about it until weeks later. I kept track of this young lady for several years, and for at least the next four years, she did not have a single drop of insulin injected. She was totally healed of her diabetes and of the need for a catheter.

A psychosomatic healing may occur when someone is anxious and has a headache, and someone prays for him and the headache goes away. This could be explained by many different methods. However, a supernatural healing is one in which there is no logical explanation whatsoever, other than the power of God touching an individual and making him whole.

In another case, a young lady who was a receptionist for Omega Ministries had fallen asleep at the wheel while driving. She went off the road, rolled the car and totalled it completely. God miraculously protected her from any major injuries and she didn't even miss a day's work. However, at lunchtime a couple of days after the accident, she began crying because she was in so much pain in her back and shoulders. We laid hands on her and began praying for release of the pain. Within about 15 minutes, the pain left her. She was a very young Christian and this was a tremendous witness to her of the miraculous power of God.

We have seen that true healings from God, beyond the body's normal healing processes, may come by the elders praying, in response to prayer following a word of knowledge or even in the midst of worship as the powerful presence of the Lord is made manifest. Whether by these or any other method, they all require that the supernatural power of God be on us and with us to be utilized by Him in the lives of others in need.

Recently, Bill and Pat Subritzsky, some friends of ours in New Zealand, wrote us with this exciting report of how God had been blessing their crusades in the South Pacific countries with wonderful miracles of healing. This is a portion of what they described in their December 1989 newsletter (22 Tropicana Drive, Hillsborough, Auckland 4):

> We have seen many marvelous miracles of healing and deliverance. One of the areas in which the Lord seems to have really blessed the ministry this year has been the gift of miracles in the meetings. The Lord spoke to us earlier this year concerning the anointing

> which flows from true worship. As a result of the leading of the Lord, we put together a bracket of worship songs which have been sung at the beginning of our meetings, thus leading the public meetings into true worship before God. Then the sovereign power of God has begun to fall in the meetings and we have seen mighty miracles of instantaneous healings. About three months ago in Wellington, a lady was instantly healed of blindness. . . . Similarly there have been many instantaneous miracles of healing of eyesight, straightening of limbs, disappearance of tumors and lumps. At each meeting we have asked those who can specifically say publicly that they have had a definite instantaneous healing in the meeting to either raise their hand or stand up. It has been common to see upwards of 100 people stand. This has truly been the sovereign work of God and we are truly grateful to Him!

In years gone by, Jim Spillman, a friend and an outstanding man of God, was one of the pastors at Melodyland Church, across from Disneyland in Southern California. One time a young lady whom he knew came up to him before a service and said, "Pastor, I think this is my day." He noticed that one of her eyes was a little irregular and they did not move together.

After the service, during a time of healing, he prayed for her and she went down in the Spirit and was laid down on the carpet with her head up the aisle and her feet lower down the slanted aisle.

Later he saw her excitedly pointing at various objects, reading distant letters and exclaiming about colors and things that she was seeing. She had her hand over her left eye. Her right hand was closed except for the index finger, with which she was zealously pointing at things. Jim felt this was a little unusual and he had her come back up onto the platform to tell him what was happening. He had assumed that she had simply had a wandering eye and that the Lord had healed it, so that her two eyes would track together. She moved her left hand and he saw two beautiful brown eyes staring at him. But then she opened her other hand and there was a glass eye!

It turned out that she had not had an eye in that empty socket from birth. While she was lying down under the power of God, one of the ushers saw the glass eye come out of the right socket and begin to roll down the aisle. He retrieved it and put it in her right hand. He then noted some white, swirling substance in her right eye socket and saw an eye being formed under her eyelid.

This is well documented and was reported on Channel 9 in Los Angeles (1972), including testimonies by her parents and her doctor.

Isn't it exciting that God can do incredibly wonderful things if we trust Him? All Jim did was to pray a simple prayer, "Lord, make her eye perfect."

Jim currently has a traveling ministry and can be contacted at this address:

Jim Spillman
P.O. Box 1207
Apple Valley, CA 92307

SOME PRACTICAL CONSIDERATIONS

When considering the subject of healing, we first must acknowledge the sovereignty of God. It is God who is doing the healing. He will heal whom He wants to heal, when He wants to heal and how He wants to heal. We can never "demand" that God heal someone.

In my book *Believe It Or Not . . . It's In The Bible*, I had discussed at some length (an entire chapter) the fact that there are numerous cases recorded in the Bible in which God made someone sick. The Bible does not say that "God permitted these people to become sick," or that "God allowed Satan to make them sick." It says that God Himself made them sick. He can do that, because He is sovereign. I would not dare to contradict the Bible, as some popular Christian teachings have done in saying that God would never make anyone sick. Here are just a few of the Scriptures.

> **10 Then Moses said to the LORD, "Please, Lord, I have never been eloquent, neither recently nor in time past, nor since Thou hast spoken to Thy servant; for I am slow of speech and slow of tongue."**
>
> **11 And the LORD said to him, "Who has made man's mouth? Or who makes *him* dumb or deaf, or seeing or blind? Is it not I, the LORD? . . ."**
>
> **—Exodus 4**

> **22 "The LORD will smite you with consumption and with fever and with inflammation and with fiery heat and with the sword and with blight and with mildew, and they shall pursue you until you perish. . . ."**
>
> **27 "The LORD will smite you with the boils of Egypt and with tumors and with the scab and with the itch, from which you cannot be healed.**
>
> **28 "The LORD will smite you with madness and with blindness and with bewilderment of heart;**
>
> **29 and you shall grope at noon, as the blind man gropes in darkness, and you shall not prosper in your ways; but you shall only be oppressed and robbed continually, with none to save you. . . ."**
>
> **—Deuteronomy 28**

> **17 Therefore the Lord will afflict the scalp of the**
> **daughters of Zion with scabs,**
> **And the LORD will make their foreheads bare."**
>
> **—Isaiah 3**

5 And the LORD struck the king, so that he was a leper to the day of his death. And he lived in a separate house, while Jotham the king's son was over the household, judging the people of the land.

—2 Kings 15

27 Therefore whoever eats the bread or drinks the cup of the Lord in an unworthy manner, shall be guilty of the body and the blood of the Lord.
28 But let a man examine himself, and so let him eat of the bread and drink of the cup.
29 For he who eats and drinks, eats and drinks judgment to himself, if he does not judge the body rightly.
30 For this reason many among you are weak and sick, and a number sleep.
31 But if we judged ourselves rightly, we should not be judged.
32 But when we are judged, we are disciplined by the Lord in order that we may not be condemned along with the world.

—1 Corinthians 11

You can see that the Scriptures clearly teach that God can and does make people sick at times. If God has made someone sick for a reason or wants him sick for a reason, you can pray until you are blue in the face, and that individual will not be healed. You can repeat your prayers over and over, and you can anoint the person with a bucket of oil, and nothing is going to happen, if it is not God's will. In fact, if God has made that individual sick, and wants him sick, and you are praying for him to be healed, you may be praying contrary to God's purposes.

Because healing is purely in the hands of a sovereign God, we must be careful to fit in with His will and to pray for those people for whom He leads us to pray.

As each opportunity presents itself, be sure to ask the Lord if this is someone you should pray for to be healed.

For whatever reason, only a certain percentage of the people that you pray for will recover. This is true of an evangelist anointed with the gift of healing. It will also be true of Mary Jane, a sweet housewife. Even Christ was not able to heal many in His hometown because of their lack of faith.

Stuart Gramenz, whom I mentioned earlier in this chapter, has real success in praying for people with leprosy. He has consistently seen about 90 percent of the lepers he has prayed for healed, many of them instantly. Should he stop praying for the 90 percent, because the 10 percent do not get healed? Of course not! He should be obedient to God; it is up to God which ones that he prays for actually get healed. However, if you are seeking God, following His scriptural principles concerning prayer and healing, and flowing in His will with a clean "power filter," then your percentage is not going to be zero.

However, it is important to realize that you will never "walk on the water" as long as you are still "sitting in the boat." In order for Peter to have the amazing experience of walking to Jesus on water, he had to *step out of the boat* (Matthew 14:25-33). Remember what we said earlier: ***"If there is no risk, there is no faith."*** We must move out, be bold and begin to exercise the power that God has given to us.

I know one brother, a truck driver, who was convinced of this truth. One day his small son twisted his ankle and the ankle was beginning to swell up substantially, about double its normal size. He put his hands around that ankle and said simply, "Be healed, in Jesus' name." By the time he took his hands away, the ankle was back to normal. He acted on his faith, and God blessed. If you act on your faith, God will bless you as well.

GENERALS FOR JESUS

Generals have authority to command, and when they command they expect their orders to be carried out. Earlier in this book we discussed the authority that we have in Jesus Christ, as believers in Him.

One thing we need to realize is that when we command someone to do something, we tend to raise the volume of our voice. If we suggest something to our children, our tone may be soft. However, if we command them to go to their room, our voice usually will rise in volume, sometimes substantially. The same thing is true when the troops are called to attention for a general: the command to come to attention is given in a loud voice. We need to use an authoritative voice when we are involved in healing, miracles or deliverances. We see that Jesus used a loud voice at times. For example:

> **43 And when He had said these things, He cried out with a loud voice, "Lazarus, come forth."**
>
> **—John 11**

The same is true of Paul. He used a loud voice when healing a lame man:

> **8 And at Lystra there was sitting a certain man, without strength in his feet, lame from his mother's womb, who had never walked.**
>
> **9 This man was listening to Paul as he spoke, who, when he had fixed his gaze upon him, and had seen that he had faith to be made well,**
>
> **10 said with a loud voice, "Stand upright on your feet." And he leaped up and *began* to walk.**
>
> **—Acts 14**

We are not talking about screaming, yelling or shouting. We are talking about the loud tone of voice that generals use to command their troops. Jesus has given us that authority. We are generals for Jesus and we can command illnesses (and spirits that cause illnesses) to leave people, in His name.

Won't a Quiet Prayer Do?

In his book *How to Heal the Sick (*available from Omega Ministries, P.O. Box 1788, Medford, Oregon 97501) Stuart Gramenz had this to say about a time when he tried to pray quietly rather than in commanding manner.

> Oh, I have wished on many occasions that a quiet prayer would be enough to heal! I have ministered in conservative churches where people are not used to healing services and the principle of commanding. It would be so much "nicer" if we did not have to be loud at times. In my earlier ministry at one particular church, I asked the Lord: "Can't we have it nice and quiet today please Jesus? I want them to embrace this healing message and perhaps commanding could upset them."
>
> After preaching and calling for the sick to come forward, the first man to come out had a pain in his lower back. Naturally, wanting to raise faith in the other people, I was believing for him to be healed instantly. I prayed a beautiful soft prayer. I am sure all the congregation were suitably impressed. "He is not some radical," they would probably have thought. "He obviously has a lot of love in him!" I stood back rather saintly and asked how he was. "Nothing happened," he shot back at me. I prayed another equally nice prayer, then another. Still nothing happened.
>
> I could feel the faith of the congregation falling through the floor.

What was I to do? I suppose I could have said: "God is healing you, and you will get better, sometime."

I knew however, that this particular congregation would be thinking: "It can't be God's will to heal him at all," as they knew little about divine healing. I screamed from my mind: "What's going wrong Lord?"

The Lord said to me: "Do you want him healed or do you want to keep up those nice prayers?"

"I want him healed!" I said, somewhat taken back.

"Then command it!"

"Spirit of infirmity," I cried in a loud voice, "come out of him, in the Name of Jesus Christ!"

I am sure everyone jumped up twelve inches from their pews, but by the time they had landed, the man was instantly healed and we continued to see many MORE MIRACLES.

—pp. 122-124

WE MUST USE THE NAME OF JESUS CHRIST

Since this power and authority does not come from us, we must use the name of Jesus Christ. We find this throughout the Scriptures:

33 And there he found a certain man named Aeneas, who had been bedridden eight years, for he was paralyzed.

34 And Peter said to him, "Aeneas, Jesus Christ heals you; arise, and make your bed." And immediately he arose.

—Acts 9

6 But Peter said, "I do not possess silver and gold, but what I do have I give to you: In the name of Jesus Christ the Nazarene—walk!"

> **7 And seizing him by the right hand, he raised him up; and immediately his feet and his ankles were strengthened.**
>
> **—Acts 3**

It is essential that we pray for healing ***in the name of Jesus Christ.*** That does not mean simply saying the words; that also involves faith in the name of Jesus Christ. Then, verse 7 implies that we must act—we must step out, we must take a risk, for "if there is no risk, there is no faith." Peter seized the lame man by the right hand and pulled him up. In so doing, Peter took a chance.

TWO CAUSES FOR ILLNESS

We need to realize that, according to the Scriptures, there are two basic causes of illness:

1. Physical
2. Spiritual

If a person has a broken arm, it is fairly clear that he has a condition that has a physical cause. Therefore, the prayer for healing or the command to be healed needs to be directed to the physical cause or problem.

On the other hand, the Bible clearly tells us that demons have caused sicknesses. Let's take a look at a couple examples of this. This first one evidently was something like epilepsy, which caused this man's son to fall into the water or the fire; evidently the source of it was purely a demon:

> **14 And when they came to the multitude, a man came up to Him, falling on his knees before Him, and saying,**

15 "Lord, have mercy on my son, for he is a lunatic, and is very ill; for he often falls into the fire, and often into the water.

16 "And I brought him to Your disciples, and they could not cure him."

17 And Jesus answered and said, "O unbelieving and perverted generation, how long shall I be with you? How long shall I put up with you? Bring him here to Me."

18 And Jesus rebuked him, and the demon came out of him, and the boy was cured at once.

—Matthew 17

In a similar situation, Jesus cast a "deaf and dumb" spirit out of a boy:

25 And when Jesus saw that a crowd was rapidly gathering, He rebuked the unclean spirit, saying to it, "You deaf and dumb spirit, I command you, come out of him and do not enter him again."

—Mark 9

On another occasion, we see Jesus casting out a demon so that a dumb man could speak:

32 And as they were going out, behold, a dumb man, demon-possessed, was brought to Him.

33 And after the demon was cast out, the dumb man spoke; and the multitudes marveled, saying, "Nothing like this was ever seen in Israel."

—Matthew 9

We will take just one other example, but I am sure you are beginning to get the picture that according to Jesus, many illnesses and diseases were caused by evil spirits. In this instance, there was a woman who was bent double, who could not even straighten up:

11 And behold, there was a woman who for eighteen years had had a sickness caused by a spirit; and she was bent double, and could not straighten up at all.

12 And when Jesus saw her, He called her over and said to her, "Woman, you are freed from your sickness."

13 And He laid His hands upon her; and immediately she was made erect again, and *began* glorifying God.

—Luke 13

As you begin to be bold, to "step out of the boat" and take action based on your faith, the Lord will begin to use you in healing people. Sometimes He will give you the gift of discernment, so that you can discern whether an illness is caused by a demon or is purely from physical causes. As we will see later, you should approach these differently.

If the Lord does not show you what the root cause of the illness is, then I believe it is wise to pray for that illness first as though it were demon-caused and then to follow that by praying as though the cause were physical. However, we need to remember that the Lord honors our faith. As we step out and pray for the sick to be healed, even if we pray the wrong type of prayer, the Lord is going to honor our obedience and heal the sick.

The sovereignty of God allows healing to occur anytime, any place that He wants it to occur. It can be in a parking lot, in someone's home or at a gathering of believers in Jesus Christ. I know one girl who had chronic bronchitis and also the Chronic Fatigue Syndrome (Epstein-Barr virus). This condition had dragged on for months and months and it was sapping all of her energy and strength. One night she was totally healed as she was taking communion. She did not realize that she had been healed then until she was driving home and she felt a renewed energy. She then realized that she had been healed as she was worshiping Jesus. Her healing has remained until this day.

Since it is up to God who gets healed, when they get healed and where they get healed, we always need to pray to be sure that we are moving in His will as we lay hands on the sick in order to pray for their recovery.

As a general rule, you lay hands on those who are sick (those with an illness caused by a physical problem) and you speak to the spirit in those who have a demon causing an illness, but you do not lay hands on them. If you will examine the ministry of Jesus, this is the basic approach that He took. But God can and will honor your obedience if you do otherwise. The important thing is to be in His will doing what He tells you to do.

GAIN FAITH AS YOU GO

If the Lord is going to use you to heal people, at some point you have to begin. You have to step out of the boat. You have to be bold and take a risk. As you begin to pray for the sick in obedience to the Lord, God will cause your faith to grow as you begin to see results. He wants you to be a transmitter of His supernatural power to touch the lives of others around you who are in need. Remember, it is not more power that you need; rather, you need to begin to use what God has already given to you. As you do so, you will gain the faith to do more.

I would also like to suggest another couple of things to you. I have mentioned Stuart Gramenz, a man of God from Australia who has a powerful healing ministry. A number of years ago, God told him that he could continue in his personal healing ministry and gain worldwide recognition, but that would be God's second best. God told him that His very best would be for Stuart to change direction and start training others to do the same. He didn't want him to go into "the promised land" alone, but to take thousands of people in with him, like an army.

Stuart conducts "JESUS HEALS" campaigns in India, the Philippines and Indonesia. He trains laymen and clergy alike, and then they actually go out and have hands-on experience. He also has a more lengthy course which is just for full-time ministries. If you are interested, you can write him at:

International Outreach
Omega Ministries
P.O. Box 1788
Medford, OR 97501

Stuart also will come to individual churches to hold a four-day concentrated course on healing. Then the next couple of nights, he encourages the attendees to bring their friends and relatives, especially the sick ones, so that the people in the class can pray for them and see them healed.

At a minimum, I would encourage you to get Stuart's book, entitled *How To Heal The Sick*, and read it carefully (available from Omega Ministries at the preceding address). It has a wealth of information and actual illustrations of prayers in it that would be very beneficial to you. There is enough information in that book to instruct you step-by-step how to pray for yourself, loved ones and acquaintances. It also removes many of the former mysteries and misunderstandings of divine healing. For those wishing to go further, the book gives keys on how to present the gospel to strangers or larger groups, having your word confirmed with signs and wonders following.

I will give you one illustration here from the book. When Stuart was ministering in India one time, God gave him the story of Elijah and the contest with the prophets of Baal, and here is what happened:

"What a wonderful message you have given to me Lord," I thought excitedly. "The people in India love stories and I know this will really bring the point clearly to them."

"That's not all," the Lord said to me. "You are going to have a contest as well! You are going to challenge the local religious leaders to a competition! After you preach, you will call the lepers, the deaf and the dumb onto the platform. If their religious leaders can heal them through their idols' power, let them be God, but if I heal them, Jesus is Lord."

I was really taken aback! It was an exciting concept, but the thought of actually doing it horrified me.

I thought of all the wonderful men whom God had used in the healing ministry, and how great it would have been for them to have had this opportunity.

The apostle Paul would have revelled in it. Smith Wigglesworth would have done a great job. T.L. Osborn would have been a huge success. The trouble was . . . they weren't there . . . and I was! I had no choice. It was of little benefit continuing the way we had, leaving people worshipping both Jesus and idols.

Thousands poured into the grounds that night and I stood up and preached the message of Elijah versus Baal.

The people loved the story. They laughed at the failure of the false prophets. They applauded the miracle of Elijah, little realizing what was coming up next.

After I had finished, I said: "Your religious leaders tell you that YOUR gods forgive sin, but I'm telling you tonight that only Jesus can forgive sin.

"One of us tells the truth, the other lies.

"We are going to establish once and for all who is telling the truth. Tonight we are going to have a competition. We have the lepers, deaf, dumb and others here who need healing.

"Surely a God who has the almighty power to forgive our sins, can do something as simple as heal a person.

"I challenge the religious leaders to prove their gods' ability to forgive sin. Come up and heal the lepers; if they are healed we'll know your god is Lord. However, if my Jesus heals the leper, we'll know that He is Lord.

"Is that a fair competition?"

Everyone went completely silent.

"Is that a fair competition?" I repeated.

The people quietly nodded their heads. "Then come up here right now and represent your gods."

There was a stunned silence around the ground—nobody moved. I began to make a joke of them, just as Elijah did:

"What! Is there no one here to represent the local gods . . . nobody?

"At least the prophets of Baal made an attempt."

Still no one came.

I walked over to a leper, who had been in that condition for years, and said: "To show you that only One is able to forgive sin and that He is Lord . . . be healed in the Name of Jesus Christ."

That same power that flowed into Elijah's sacrifice flowed into the leper. He started to rub his hands together excitedly. Feeling and movement had been restored. He raised his hands to the crowd, waving excitedly and showing them how his leprosy had been healed.

"You have to make a decision tonight," I said to the crowd, "It is either your gods or Jesus!"

In one accord the people stood to give their lives to Jesus and renounce the other gods.

I can assure you that throughout the whole ordeal, I was a frightened man, hanging tightly onto God. I could totally identify with Paul when he was in Corinth: *"I was with you in weakness, in fear, and in much trembling, and my speech and my preaching were not with persuasive words of human wisdom, but in demonstration of the Spirit and of power, that your faith should not be in the wisdom of men but in the power of God." (1 Corinthians 2:3-5).*

I found through experience that God does want to demonstrate His power mightily, and will work through those who are willing to believe what he says . . . and do it!

—pp. 10-12

Not only does the admonition to be bold and "do it" apply to healing; it also applies to miracles and delivering people from demonic harassment.

God's supernatural power is for every Christian.

Chapter 12

POWER FOR MIRACLES AND DELIVERANCE

Today we need God's supernatural power for additional things other than taking the gospel to the world, although we certainly do need the power of God doing miraculous acts (usually healing) to validate the gospel and to draw the crowds. As we discussed in Chapter 10, manifestations of God's power will be one of the real keys to presenting the gospel during the end of this age.

We also need God's supernatural power in our lives and in the lives of our brothers and sisters in Christ for healing, as discussed in the last chapter. Only God can heal. All medicine can do primarily is to relieve the symptoms of a disease or illness while the body heals itself. The doctors of today do not heal; only God heals. There may be times of persecution ahead when we will not have doctors available to us. At that time, we will have to rely totally on the supernatural healing power of God Almighty.

Another area in which we need God's supernatural power is in dealing with demonic forces. Demons are just as real today as they were in the time of Jesus Christ. Jesus spent a great deal of time casting demons (evil spirits) out of people. Demons can harass Christians today to the extent that they are prevented from doing

God's will and God's work. Demons can still possess non-Christians. We must have God's supernatural power at work in us and through us to rid both believers and unbelievers of these demonic forces. We do not have any power within ourselves to achieve this. It must be by the miraculous supernatural power of God.

We also need the supernatural power of God just in our day-to-day spiritual lives and warfare. On occasion, we need it for a miracle that might even be life-saving to some precious soul. But without the supernatural power of God working through us, we could find ourselves in a time of desperate need with no power. How sad that would be, when that supernatural power is readily available to us through Jesus Christ our precious Lord and Savior.

SUPERNATURAL POWER FOR MIRACLES

The heading above is almost ridiculous in a way, because obviously any miracle is going to require supernatural power. When I speak of miracles here, I am referring to supernatural events other than healing and deliverance from evil spirits. These would be such things as multiplying food, calming a storm, cursing a fig tree which then withers and dies, and walking on water, to name a few of the miracles that occurred in Jesus' life.

One of these instances is recorded in Mark's gospel:

> **38 And He said to them, "How many loaves do you have? Go look!" And when they found out, they said, "Five and two fish."**
>
> **39 And He commanded them all to recline by groups on the green grass.**
>
> **40 And they reclined in companies of hundreds and of fifties.**

41 And He took the five loaves and the two fish, and looking up toward heaven, He blessed *the food* and broke the loaves and He kept giving *them* to the disciples to set before them; and He divided up the two fish among them all.

42 And they all ate and were satisfied.

43 And they picked up twelve full baskets of the broken pieces, and also of the fish.

44 And there were five thousand men who ate the loaves.

—Mark 6

It is wonderful that the supernatural power of God flowed through Jesus to perform the miracle of multiplying the food. You may think that this was great for those times, but that nothing of that nature would occur today. On the contrary, multiplying of food has happened many times in recent years. One such occurrence in the Indonesian revival is recorded in the book *Like a Mighty Wind* by Mel Tari. This event, and others from that book included in this chapter, occurred in the late 1960's:

> Another special miracle took place when the very first team went out to preach the Gospel. They came to a small village called Nikiniki about fifteen miles from our town of Soe. By this time, the Lord had used them to bring many people to the Lord Jesus.
>
> As is the custom, the team went to the pastor's house to stay with him. The pastor happened to be my uncle. That time my aunt, the pastor's wife, was embarrassed because so many people came and she had nothing to give them to eat. It was famine time in Timor. There were twenty on the team, but with the elders and all, there were more than fifty people at their home. She was supposed to feed them and there wasn't any food in the house. She went to her room and cried.

"Lord," she said, "I don't know what to do. Please show me."

At the same time, the Lord spoke to the leader of the team, and he went to my aunt and said, "Ma'm, the Lord told me that you had four tapioca roots in your cupboard and that you should take them and cook them. They will be sufficient for all of us."

"How do you know that I have four tapioca roots?" she asked.

"I didn't know; the Lord told me," he repeated.

She went to the kitchen and found exactly four roots as the Lord had revealed to the team member.

If the Lord told him about the roots, I had better obey the Lord and cook them, she thought.

After she had cooked the tapioca, the team leader said, "Please get water for tea."

My aunt had enough sugar and tea for only two or three cups, but she obeyed.

"Put the water, tea and sugar in the pitcher and mix it up for the people to drink as they eat the tapioca," the leader said. She did as he told her. Then she made a small flat loaf of bread out of the tapioca, put it on a plate, and prayed over it. The team leader also prayed. After they prayed, the Lord told them to give each of the guests a plate, which they did. They also handed out cups.

Then the Lord said to the team member, "Now tell the pastor's wife that she is to break the tapioca into pieces and give it to the people until their plates are full."

Even though she thought, "This is impossible to do, because there isn't even enough to fill one plate," she obeyed the Lord.

The first man who came for food was pretty glad. "If I am at the first of the line, I'll be sure to eat," he thought. But the man who was last in the line, who was a real good friend of mine, was quite upset because he liked to eat a lot. He was a big guy. I asked him later, "What did you feel that time?" He said, "I was really scared. I prayed real hard and said, 'Lord, I'm the last one in the line. There is only one tapioca loaf. Only three or four will have any. So, Lord Jesus, you had better perform a miracle, and please remember me, who's the last one in the line, because I'm really hungry.'"

My aunt then took the bread and broke it. Usually mathematics will tell you when you break one in half, you get two halves. That is not necessarily so in God's counting. My aunt broke one, and then the half in her right hand became whole again. The Lord told her to put the one that was in her left hand on the plate. She broke the one in her right hand again, and, as she did this, it made her cry because she realized that a miracle was taking place in her hand. So she just praised the Lord and cried and broke the bread and broke it.

The first man had a plateful and the second one, and the third one. Now everyone realized that a miracle was taking place. Even my friend who was the last one in line got a plateful. He too thanked the Lord and said, "Oh, Lord, You've done a miracle."

All of them, after they had eaten some tapioca bread, came for tea at the same time. When you eat tapioca it is so dry, if you don't get something to drink you feel terrible. My aunt wanted to put only a little bit in the cups, but the Lord said, "Just fill the cups up." She obeyed again, and the tea just kept coming until all of them had something to drink. Many of them had two or three glasses of tea. So all of the team ate until they were completely full.

As a matter of fact, there was food left over they couldn't eat. So even the dogs were satisfied; the Lord even took care of the animals.

—Creation House Publishers, pp. 41-43

As you can see, multiplying of food is still happening today. It will not happen when we can provide for ourselves, but if we get into a desperate situation, the Lord can well provide for us by His supernatural power.

Another basic type of miracle is that of control over nature. We see examples of this when Christ stilled the storm (Matthew 8:24-27) and when He cursed the fig tree (Matthew 21:19). There are many cases of supernatural control over weather in recent years. Earlier, I shared with you how the Lord led me on two occasions to take dominion over the rain and to command it to stop, in the name of Jesus Christ. When God tells you to do something like this, you can move ahead in faith because He will bring it to pass.

Another exciting display of God's miraculous power occurred with some Christian brothers and sisters who live in a town in southern Illinois. A tornado was coming right for their town, and all the people in the town had ducked into their storm cellars, except for these brothers and sisters who stood out on their front lawn. In the name of Jesus Christ, they took authority over this tornado, and commanded it to not hit their town. The tornado lifted on one edge of the town, jumped up completely over the town and hit the ground again, right on the other side of the town.

God's supernatural power is still working! There was a major hurricane that was headed for Norfolk, Virginia, where the CBN (Christian Broadcasting Network) headquarters stands. Pat Robertson, and many others joining with him, took authority over that hurricane, and it turned and missed their area completely.

During a severe drought in South Africa, Christians took authority over the weather. It rained just in their small area and not in anywhere else.

Perhaps you remember Elijah commanding it to not rain (1 Kings 17:1-7). Then, after he won the contest with the prophets of Baal at God's direction, he prophesied that it would rain again, and the rains returned (1 Kings 18:1, 2, 22-45).

There are other types of miracles, such as calling down fire from heaven and causing plagues to come upon the earth. As we mentioned earlier in this book, these awesome, miraculous gifts are going to be restored at the end of this age. We see this typified by the two witnesses that we read about earlier:

> **3 "And I will grant *authority* to my two witnesses, and they will prophesy for twelve hundred and sixty days, clothed in sackcloth."**
>
> **4 These are the two olive trees and the two lampstands that stand before the Lord of the earth.**
>
> **5 And if anyone desires to harm them, fire proceeds out of their mouth and devours their enemies; and if anyone would desire to harm them, in this manner he must be killed.**
>
> **6 These have the power to shut up the sky, in order that rain may not fall during the days of their prophesying; and they have power over the waters to turn them into blood, and to smite the earth with every plague, as often as they desire.**
>
> **—Revelation 11**

In review, we see that the two witnesses will have the power to call down fire from heaven, to take authority over the weather and cause it not to rain, and also to bring plagues on the earth. But remember, God can only entrust these awesome gifts to his bondslaves —to those He knows will be absolutely and totally obedient to Jesus Christ.

There are many other miracles that we could discuss. One of these would be raising someone from the dead. Jesus did this, but the Bible records that Elijah, Paul and Peter raised people from the dead as well. In

Like a Mighty Wind, Mel Tari shares one such modern incident:

> Not too long after that we were in another village called Amfoang where a man had died. He had been dead not only for a few minutes but for two days. The family invited us to the funeral because there were many people planning to come—as a matter of fact, hundreds—and they said, "Maybe you would have a word of comfort to give to the family." So we went.
>
> When we arrived there, there were more than a thousand people. That man had been dead for two days and was very stinky. In our tropical country, when you're dead six hours you start to decay. But after two days—oh, I tell you, you couldn't stand within 100 feet of him. You smelled that smell, and it was awful. In America you cannot understand that because in your funeral services they make everything very good. But it is because of your $2,000. In Indonesia, we don't have a way to make a dead person look so nice. The people there just look terrible in two days after they have died.
>
> When we were there and sitting with the mourners, suddenly the Lord said, "Now please go and stand around that dead person, sing songs and I will raise him back from the dead."
>
> When my brother-in-law told me that, I said, "Oh, my dear! The first time, the lady was dead only a few minutes. That was different. Now we will really get into trouble. This man has been dead two days. Oh no, this is too much!" I said to the others, "What do you think about this?" My computer was working again. Their computers were working, too. We began to wonder, shall we do it or not? All of a sudden we remembered how sad we had been when we failed to trust the Word of God. So I just prayed, "Oh Lord, give me a simple heart to believe your word."

I remembered the Scripture as Jesus came to the city of Jericho. Zacchaeus was waiting for Jesus, but he was waiting for Him in the wrong place. He was up in a tree. Jesus said, "Zacchaeus come down." The Lord visited with him in his house and Zacchaeus was so happy. He probably had to come down five or six feet out of the tree to find Jesus. But I believe we in this modern age don't need to come down three, four or six feet because we are not in trees. We only need to come down about a foot—from our minds to our hearts. We have all the words of God in our minds and we do all the figuring out there and we have lost the power of God. If we would only put the Word of God one foot down from our minds to our hearts, I am certain we could see the power of God move in a mighty way today.

Then I said to the Lord, "Oh Lord, please give me a simple heart, and move in our midst." So we decided in unison that we would obey the Lord because we had failed Him before. And we did.

We went and stood around this dead person. We began to sing. You know that time, the Devil said to me, "It is awful for you to sing by this stinky man. When you are 100 feet away it is bad enough. But now that you are standing near this dead person, when you open your mouth all that filth and stench comes into your mouth. It is foolish to do this."

This is true, but I must still obey the Lord, I thought. So we began to sing. But after the first song, nothing had taken place. So we started to wonder, *Lord if You're going to raise him up, please do it quickly because we can't stand to stay around this stinking man. We just can't sing any more songs by this terrible smell.*

Then we sang a second song, and nothing happened.

On the fifth song, nothing happened. But on the sixth song, that man began to move his toes—and the team began to get scared. We have a story in Indonesia,

> that sometimes when people die they wake up and hug a person by their coffin and then die again. However, we just went ahead and sang. When we sang the seventh and eight songs, that brother woke up, looked around and smiled.
>
> He didn't hug anybody. He just opened his mouth and said, "Jesus has brought me back to life! Brothers and sisters, I want to tell you something. First, life never ends when you die. I've been dead for two days and I've experienced it." The second thing he said was, "Hell and heaven are real. I have experienced it. The third thing I want to tell you is, if you don't find Jesus in this life you will never go to heaven. You will be condemned to hell for sure."
>
> After he had said these things, we opened our Bibles and confirmed his testimony by the Word of God. He not only found Jesus Christ as his Savior, but in that area more than 21,000 people came to know Jesus Christ as their Savior, because of the ministry of this man.
>
> —pp. 66-68

Isn't it fabulous that God used His supernatural power to bring this man back from the dead? As a result, the gospel went out in demonstration of the power of God and thousands came to know Jesus Christ as their Savior!

Turning to another exciting story from Mel Tari, I would like to share with you one additional incident of supernatural power bringing forth miracles that were not in the realm of healing or deliverance. He relates this amazing event in the same book:

> The Lord sent another team to an area in Timor where they had to cross a river. But there was no bridge. The Noemina river is about three hundred yards wide, and is the largest river we have in Timor. In flood time the river is about twenty to twenty-five feet deep. The

stream is very strong. Even the biggest trees get carried away out to the sea.

When the team came to the river they were scared. No one who had a good mind would want to cross the river during flood time. Even crazy people would never try that. So the team stopped at the edge of the river and prayed, "Lord, what must we do?"

One of the characteristics of the Indonesian revival is that before we go out to preach, the Lord gives us all the details of what we should do. We write it down on paper and follow it exactly as it is. If He tells us to stop at this place or minister in that place, we do just what the Lord tells us.

The Lord said to them, "You cross the river."

Usually when the teams go out in Indonesia it isn't during the rainy season. When it's the rainy season in Indonesia, it really rains, sometimes for forty days. It rains day and night without stopping. It's awfully hard to travel.

The most wonderful thing is that the Bible says, "God will supply all your needs."

Many times we go out and we do not have umbrellas or raincoats.

"Lord," we say, "You told us to go, but we don't have umbrellas or raincoats. Lord, protect us from the rain. Amen."

The Lord says, "Whatever you ask and believeth, you shall have it." We're not going to dance or fool around; we're going to preach the Gospel, so the Lord protects us from the rain.

We see the rain ten feet in front of us, ten feet behind us, ten feet to the right, and ten feet to the left. But not one single drop comes on our bodies.

When we come to the villages, the people say, "Where do you come from?"

"We have come from about fifty miles away," we answer.

"Did you walk in the rain?" they ask.

They see our feet are pretty muddy and wonder why our bodies didn't get wet. We tell them that the Lord protected us, and they just can't believe us. Many times they go out and try to find where we've hidden our umbrellas or raincoats, but they never find them, because God has protected us.

This was the way the Lord worked for the team that was supposed to cross the river. The people who saw them were amazed that they were still dry because it had rained all the time they were walking to that spot.

"Who are you?" asked many of the pagans who were gathered at the river.

"We're just a gospel team going to preach the Gospel," one of the team members answered.

"Where are you going?" they asked.

"We're going to the other side of the river, and the Lord has told us to cross the river now!" a team member replied.

"Don't do it. If you cross now you'll give your life to serve the Lord, because you'll surely drown," a pagan said.

Even some of the Christians who were watching the team said, "The Lord said you're to be as wise as the serpent. Now use your mind and stay here on the bank."

Sometimes Christians try to preach to you a nice sermon, but it isn't always from the Lord; sometimes the Devil preaches even better than we do, but he doesn't preach the Gospel.

"If you cross the river now and you die, then who will serve the Lord? It's better for you to wait two or three days. When the floods go down, we can help you across," the pagans continued.

"No, the Lord told us to cross now," the team members told the crowd. But even the team got to where they were wavering a little.

My brother-in-law and sister just stood there. They didn't really know what to do, because even their friends kept saying, "Don't do it now, don't do it now!"

Just then one of my cousins said, "The Lord is really moving in my heart. Team, if you want to hear the counsel of men, you just follow them. You can stay here for two or three days, but I want to follow the Lord and obey the Lord right now. The Lord said for us to cross now, and we're supposed to do it. Now! We're not supposed to do it another time. God said it to us like he did Joseph, when the angel told Joseph to take Mary and Jesus and get out of the country and go to Egypt now. How sad it would have been if Joseph hadn't obeyed God and would have waited for morning. Jesus would have been killed."

The others were still waiting because they were afraid and they didn't know what to do. But my cousin said, "You can stay here, but I'm going now."

He stepped into the water.

"Oh, no, don't do it. You'll die," the people screamed.

"But if I die, you can tell the people all over the world that I didn't die because I was stupid; I died because I obeyed the Lord," he said.

With the first step the water came between his ankle and knee. The second step, it was the same place. The third, fourth, fifth and with the sixth—the water never came above his knee.

When he came to the middle of the river, where it was supposed to be thirty feet deep, the water never came higher than his knee.

As my cousin was standing in the middle of the river, he called back to the team, "You had better come now; the water is not deep."

"Are you standing on the bottom or the top of the water?" they yelled back to him.

"I don't know," he said, "but I feel the bottom. The bottom is just under my feet." Yet everyone knew the water was twenty to thirty feet deep. As they watched him, it looked like he was standing on top of the water.

"You had better come, I'm telling you!" he said again.

The team talked it over and decided, "We'd better go, because God is in action now, and if we delay, afterwards we'll want to go and won't be able to. That will be terrible."

The entire team did what the first man had done, and stepped right in. They experienced the same feeling of touching the bottom of the river. When the rest of them saw this happen (pagans and Christians alike) they jumped in, thinking it wouldn't be deep. When they put their first foot in the water, they almost drowned. So the people all realized that a miracle had taken place. Then the Lord gave them the verse in Isaiah that says, "When you shall cross the river it shall not overflow you."

My people, that is the Word of God.

—pp. 37-41

What an exciting testimony of how God not only provided a divine umbrella by His supernatural power, but He also allowed this team to walk on water, just as Jesus had done. He blessed with His miracle power these Christians who were going out to present the gospel of Jesus Christ. The miracle happened because the first man was bold and "stepped into the water" in obedience to God. For miracles to occur in our lives, we must ***put action*** to our head faith. For miracles to occur, we must take a risk.

IF THERE IS NO RISK,
THERE IS NO FAITH.

Now let us move on to look at something that I think Christ wants every believer to be able to do—to deliver someone from an evil spirit, in the name of Jesus Christ and for His glory.

POWER FOR DELIVERANCE

When we talk about "deliverance," we are speaking of people being delivered from evil spirits (demons). In the last chapter, we read a few passages which showed that demons are sometimes the cause of some illnesses. Therefore, sometimes healing will involve casting out a demon. In this chapter, we will look further at the subject of deliverance in general.

Delivering people from unclean spirits was a major part of Christ's ministry. I love to teach through the book of Mark, especially to non-Christians or young Christians. Right in the very first chapter, we run into evil spirits:

> **21 And they went into Capernaum; and immediately on the Sabbath He entered the synagogue and *began* to teach.**
>
> **22 And they were amazed at His teaching; for He was teaching them as *one* having authority, and not as the scribes.**
>
> **23 And just then there was in their synagogue a man with an unclean spirit; and he cried out,**
>
> **24 saying, "What do we have to do with You, Jesus of Nazareth? Have You come to destroy us? I know who You are—the Holy One of God!"**
>
> **25 And Jesus rebuked him, saying, "Be quiet, and come out of him!"**
>
> **26 And throwing him into convulsions, the unclean spirit cried out with a loud voice, and came out of him.**
>
> **—Mark 1**

Here we see an example of Christ casting out an unclean spirit. Then, just four verses later in the same chapter, we read this:

> **32 And when evening had come, after the sun had set they *began* bringing to Him all who were ill and those who were demon-possessed.**
> **33 And the whole city had gathered at the door.**
> **34 And He healed many who were ill with various diseases, and cast out many demons; and He was not permitting the demons to speak, because they knew who He was.**
>
> **—Mark 1**

We can quickly see that one cannot teach through the Gospels about Jesus without teaching about casting out demons or "unclean spirits." This was an integral part of Jesus' life and ministry.

After the Lord's ascension into heaven, we learn that Peter and Paul were both in the "deliverance business." We read this about Peter:

> **14 And all the more believers in the Lord, multitudes of men and women, were constantly added to *their number;***
> **15 to such an extent that they even carried the sick out into the streets, and laid them on cots and pallets, so that when Peter came by, at least his shadow might fall on any one of them.**
> **16 And also the people from the cities in the vicinity of Jerusalem were coming together, bringing people who were sick or afflicted with unclean spirits; and they were all being healed.**
>
> **—Acts 5**

In verse 16, we see that people not only brought the sick but also those who were afflicted with unclean spirits, and they were being delivered or set free from those unclean spirits. The supernatural power of God so filled Peter that even his shadow passing over a person caused the power on him to flow to them in deliverances and healing. Peter did not do this in his own name; he did it only in the name of Jesus Christ of Nazareth.

Paul also commanded evil spirits to come out, in the name of Jesus Christ:

> **18 And she continued doing this for many days. But Paul was greatly annoyed, and turned and said to the spirit, "I command you in the name of Jesus Christ to come out of her!" And it came out at that very moment.**
>
> **—Acts 16**

Evidently, casting out evil spirits was a regular ministry of the power of God flowing through Paul. Just as people touched the garments of Christ and were healed, apparently a similar thing occurred with Paul:

> **11 And God was performing extraordinary miracles by the hands of Paul,**
>
> **12 so that handkerchiefs or aprons were even carried from his body to the sick, and the diseases left them and the evil spirits went out.**
>
> **—Acts 19**

Demons and evil spirits obviously existed in the time of Christ. Do they still exist today? The answer is a definite *"yes."* Do people still need delivering from evil spirits today? Again the answer is a resounding *"yes."* Another question that understandably arises—with which some people have a hard time dealing—is this: Can a Christian have a demon? Here, sadly, once again the answer is "yes." Let me hasten to add that a Christian cannot be demon possessed, but he can have a demon.

I could give many examples in support of this point. One is an outstanding traveling evangelist who moved in the power gifts, yet he had a secret habit of smoking. He came into a home meeting one time, and later in the evening one of the brothers there pointed to him and commanded the spirit of nicotine to come out of him in the name of Jesus Christ. All of the other people in the room thought that this man was mistaken; he must not know who he was dealing with, because this man was an outstanding evangelist. But then, the way this evangelist himself describes it, all of a sudden, something like an invisible golf ball came shooting out of his mouth. From that moment on, he never even had a desire for a cigarette. This evangelist is a friend of mine, and I have heard him tell this story personally.

An example from my own experience in casting out evil spirits involved a young lady in whom was manifested a spirit of mockery. As we began to cast it out, the most horrible mocking face came upon her sweet, beautiful, innocent countenance. I simply commanded it not to manifest itself and to come out immediately, which it did.

If an evil spirit hesitates to come out, we can remind ourselves of this situation with Christ and the demoniac:

> **26 And they sailed to the country of the Gerasenes, which is opposite Galilee.**
>
> **27 And when He had come out onto the land, He was met by a certain man from the city who was possessed with demons; and who had not put on any clothing for a long time, and was not living in a house, but in the tombs.**
>
> **28 And seeing Jesus, he cried out and fell before Him, and said in a loud voice, "What do I have to do with You, Jesus, Son of the Most High God? I beg You, do not torment me."**

29 For He had been commanding the unclean spirit to come out of the man. For it had seized him many times; and he was bound with chains and shackles and kept under guard; and *yet* he would burst his fetters and be driven by the demon into the desert.

30 And Jesus asked him, "What is your name?" And he said, "Legion"; for many demons had entered him.

31 And they were entreating Him not to command them to depart into the abyss.

32 Now there was a herd of many swine feeding there on the mountain; and *the demons* entreated Him to permit them to enter the swine. And He gave them permission.

33 And the demons came out from the man and entered the swine; and the herd rushed down the steep bank into the lake, and were drowned.

34 And when the herdsmen saw what had happened, they ran away and reported it in the city and *out* in the country.

35 And *the people* went out to see what had happened; and they came to Jesus, and found the man from whom the demons had gone out, sitting down at the feet of Jesus, clothed and in his right mind; and they became frightened.

36 And those who had seen it reported to them how the man who was demon-possessed had been made well.

37 And all the people of the country of the Gerasenes and the surrounding district asked Him to depart from them; for they were gripped with great fear; and He got into a boat, and returned.

38 But the man from whom the demons had gone out was begging Him that he might accompany Him; but He sent him away, saying,

39 "Return to your house and describe what great things God has done for you." And he went away,

proclaiming throughout the whole city what great things Jesus had done for him.

—Luke 8

As you can see in this passage, the spirits really did ***not*** want to be cast into the abyss. What the Lord has led me to do is to tell an evil spirit that, if he does not come out immediately, I have the authority through Jesus Christ to cast him into the abyss, and that is where I will cast him if he does not come out immediately. As a consequence, they come out and quickly. Jesus Christ cast those demons into hogs. He has led me to cast demons either into sharks in the ocean or out into "dry places." We have authority in the name of Jesus Christ not only to cast them out, but to tell them where to go.

What Christians must realize is that Jesus Christ has given us His power of attorney (His authority) over these evil spirits, and they must obey us, if we come against them in faith in the name of Jesus Christ. This authority and power was not given just to the disciples, but to all those who believe in Jesus Christ. Let's review a familiar passage, which contains the great commission in its totality:

15 And He said to them, "Go into all the world and preach the gospel to all creation.

16 "He who has believed and has been baptized shall be saved; but he who disbelieved shall be condemned.

17 "And these signs will accompany those who have believed: in My name they will cast out demons, they will speak with new tongues;

18 they will pick up serpents, and if they drink any deadly *poison*, it shall not hurt them; they will lay hands on the sick, and they will recover."

—Mark 16

We have quoted this passage before, but it is so very important. It tells us that "these signs" are going to accompany us because we have believed in Christ and that, among other things, in His name we ***"will cast out demons"!*** Clearly in this context, signs and wonders were meant to accompany the presentation of the gospel.

Do you believe what Jesus said? I certainly do. Then let's quit trying to explain it away or make it fit into some theological scheme. Let us simply believe fully what Jesus had to say and begin to utilize the power and the authority that He gave to us.

I would like to relate something that happened to me personally in connection with evil spirits. I went to Bozeman, Montana one year to minister, and the Lord tremendously used that time, not only with the church but also with the Christian leaders in the community. However, after I returned home, I seemed to be angry with everyone all the time. At times, I almost had the inclination to smash things, which really bewildered me because this was not like me. This went on for about two weeks. Then I was in prayer one morning, and the Lord told me to cast out a "bear spirit" from myself. In the name of Jesus Christ and with His authority, I bound and cast out the "bear spirit," and all of these inexplicable feelings of anger left me.

Later that day, I called a Christian brother in Montana where I had ministered and asked him if they had any trouble there with a "bear spirit"? He replied that they definitely did. In fact, he said that many of the Indians there worshiped the grizzly bear, and consequently they had a lot of difficulty in that regard. This was a validation and confirmation that what the Lord had shown me was really true. Somehow an evil bear spirit had attached itself to me when I was there. Whether it was inside or outside doesn't matter; it was necessary to cast it out in the name of Jesus Christ, before I could again have the peace that belongs to me as a gift from Jesus.

TERRITORIAL SPIRITS

There is another type of spirit that I would like to deal with before leaving this subject. First, we must realize that God is omnipresent; He is present everywhere. Satan does not have that power—he can only be in one place at a time. Consequently, he has set up a hierarchical structure. This is one like we see in the military, for example, where there are levels of authority and command. In the military, there are generals, and underneath them, colonels, then majors, lieutenants, sergeants, corporals and privates. There is a similar type of structure in many major corporations: there is a president, and underneath him, vice-presidents who are over supervisors, who in turn are over the clerical staff and other workers.

Evidently Satan has a hierarchical structure of this nature. Apparently it is based primarily on geography. It is likely that Satan has a "prince" over each country, then probably one over each state or province, possibly one over each county and maybe even over each town or city. We read about members of his hierarchy in a number of places. One example is this:

> **12 Then he said to me, "Do not be afraid, Daniel, for from the first that you set your heart on understanding *this* and on humbling yourself before your God, your words were heard, and I have come in response to your words.**
>
> **13 "But the prince of the kingdom of Persia was withstanding me for twenty-one days; then behold, Michael, one of the chief princes, came to help me, for I had been left there with the kings of Persia.**

14 "Now I have come to give you an understanding of what will happen to your people in the latter days, for the vision pertains to the days yet *future*."

—Daniel 10

According to this passage in Daniel, the "prince of Persia" was a demon prince of Satan's who warred with the messenger angel until the archangel Michael came to fight and free him up to go on to Daniel. This demon prince was evidently the one responsible for Persia. I call these "territorial spirits."

Paul summarizes this hierarchical structure of Satan's in this passage:

10 Finally, be strong in the Lord, and in the strength of His might.

11 Put on the full armor of God, that you may be able to stand firm against the schemes of the devil.

12 For our struggle is not against flesh and blood, but against the rulers, against the powers, against the world forces of this darkness, against the spiritual *forces* of wickedness in the heavenly *places*.

—Ephesians 6

In these verses from Ephesians, we also see that we are to be strong in the Lord and in the strength (power) of His might (power). The way that we are going to be able to stand against Satan and his hierarchical structure is by the supernatural power of God. In the July, 1989 *Evangelical Mission Quarterly*, Peter Wagner brings us up-to-date on these geographic or territorial spirits (Box 794, Wheaton, IL 60189):

> In a number of places at least some of these angelic governors are portrayed as hostile principalities and powers—the "world rulers of this darkness" of Eph. 6:12.

Bruce goes on to point out that what is implicit in Deuteronomy becomes explicit in Daniel 10, where three of these princes are named. Two of them are evil princes, the prince of Persia and the prince of Greece, and one is a good prince, Michael, called one of the chief princes.

As the story unfolds, a lesser unnamed angel who was sent by God to minister to Daniel battled the prince of Persia for 21 days and could not overcome him until Michael came to his rescue. If we take this account at face value, we see the awesome power that these world rulers of darkness can exercise (Dan. 10:10-21).

Territorial spirits and their dominance of geographical areas are taken for granted as the history of Israel unfolds. Joshua rebuked the Israelites for serving gods on the other side of the river and in Egypt (Josh. 24:14). Even in Canaan the Israelites did not cleanse the land as God commanded, but "forgot the Lord their God and served the Baals and Asherahs" (Judges 3:7).

Names of some of the specific principalities are mentioned, such as Succoth Benoth of Babylon, Nergral of Cuth, Ashima of Hamath, Nibhaz and Tartak of the Avites, and Adrammelech and Anammelech of the Sepharvites. (See 2 Kings 17:30-31.) The occult power of these principalities is reflected in previous references in the same chapter to witchcraft and soothsaying (2 Kings 17:17). Jeremiah refers to the fall of Babylon by such phrases as "Bel is shamed" and "Merodach is broken in pieces" (Jer. 50:2).

Perhaps a specific instance of the breaking of the power of a territorial spirit is seen in Paul's encounter with the sorcerer Elymas in eastern Cyprus. Elymas' close relationship with the political authority, the proconsul Sergius Paulus, suggests a spiritual dominance of the region. Although the principality is not named, when a power encounter broke the power of Elymas (called a "son of the devil"), the proconsul believed.

Satan's attempt to blind his mind failed. (See Acts 13:6-13)

Research on territorial spirits is so new that the same stories tend to get told over and over again. As time goes on, however, I do not doubt that credible stories of breaking the power of territorial spirits over areas large and small will multiply. Jamie Buckingham has told me of his sensing the presence of a specific power of evil over the city of Prague. He also reports that former Secretary of the Interior James Watt, through sensitivities acquired in his past occult dealings, perceived specific dark angels assigned to the White House.

In two of my books, *The Third Wave of the Holy Spirit* (Servant) and *How to Have a Healing Ministry* (Regal), I tell eight examples of dealing with territorial spirits. Let me summarize them here.

Thailand. A wave of conversions followed when the missionaries set aside one day a week for spiritual warfare.

Uruguay-Brazil border. People who were closed to the gospel on the Uruguay side of the town's main street became open when they crossed over to the Brazilian side.

Navajo Reservation. Herman Williams, a Navajo Alliance pastor, suffered serious physical symptoms which left him as he crossed the reservation boundary for treatment in the city, and recurred when he entered the reservation again. The spirits causing this were traced to a witch doctor whom they later killed.

Philippines. Lester Sumrall cast a spirit out of an inmate in Bilibid Prison, which was followed by a dramatic change in the receptivity of Filipinos to the gospel.

Argentina. Omar Cabrera by prayer and fasting exercises a ministry of identifying the spirits controlling certain cities, breaks their power, and finds little subsequent resistance to God's power for salvation and healing.

Korea. Paul Yonggi Cho attributes the contrast in receptivity to the gospel between Germany and Korea to the victories in spiritual warfare gained through the ministry of prayer of Korean Christians.

Argentina. Egardo Silvoso reports the accelerated multiplication of churches within a radius of 100 miles of the city of Rosario after a team broke the power of the spirit of Merigildo in 1985.

Although I cannot personally attest to the validity of these case studies, they have been reported by people of integrity with reputations as credible witnesses. We all need discernment as we evaluate them further.

Here are some other reports:

Greece. Loren Cunningham of Youth With a Mission tells an incident that happened in 1973. As 12 co-workers were praying and fasting for three days in Los Angeles, the Lord revealed to them that they should pray for the downfall of the prince of Greece. On the same day similar groups in New Zealand and Europe received the same word. All three groups obeyed and came against that principality. Within 24 hours a political coup changed the government of Greece and for the first time YWAM workers could preach the gospel in the streets.

Evanston, Illinois. While teaching a class for me in 1985, John Wimber gave a report from Vineyard pastor Steve Nicholson. After six years of ministry in Evanston, he had seen little fruit. They prayed for the sick and few got well. Then he started to pray and fast seriously.

At one point, a grotesque being appeared to him, saying, "Why are you bothering me?" It eventually identified itself as a demon of witchcraft who had supervision over that area. In the heat of the battle, Steve named the city streets and claimed them for God. The spirit said, "I don't want to give you that much."

Steve replied that through Jesus he was commanding him to give up the territory. The spirit argued some more and then left.

Immediately, the sick began to get well. In a little over three months, the church more than doubled from 70 to 150, most of them new converts from witchcraft. Almost all of them had to be delivered from demons as they were being saved.

Bermuda Triangle. Kenneth McAll spent many years as a missionary surgeon in China, then returned to England as a consulting psychiatrist. In China he began a deliverance ministry and did considerable research and writing on the subject. In 1972, he and his wife were sailing through the Bermuda Triangle. Many ships and airplanes had disappeared there without a trace, but they thought that such a thing could not happen to them. It did. They were overpowered by a fierce storm, but fortunately they were rescued. McAll discovered through his research that in the Bermuda Triangle the slave traders had thrown overboard some two million slaves who were either too sick or too weak to be sold and then collected insurance for them.

Sensing that God was leading him to do something, McAll recruited several Anglican bishops, priests, and others throughout England to celebrate a Jubilee Eucharist in 1977. Another was held shortly afterward in Bermuda itself. The stated purpose was to seek the "specific release of all those who had met their untimely deaths in the Bermuda Triangle." As a result, the curse was lifted. McAll reported in 1982, "From the time of Jubilee Eucharist until now—five years—no known inexplicable accidents have occurred in the Bermuda Triangle."

—pp. 281-284

You may want to prayerfully consider binding the territorial spirits over your city, county, state and nation.

When we bind Satan or an evil spirit, we do not know exactly for how long he is bound. Obviously, it is not forever. Possibly it is just for one day, because Jesus Himself said, "Sufficient unto the day *is* the evil thereof" (Matthew 6:34, *KJV*). We have seen that the Lord wants us to deliver individuals from evil spirits. (Those spirits will come back, if the vacuum is not filled with the Holy Spirit—Luke 11:24-26). We also have authority and power to cast out spirits from over geographic territories.

Coming back to casting out demons in general, I would like to give you two thoughts for your protection. First, as we have already mentioned, I think that it is best not to lay hands on a person with a demon. Second, ask God to cover you, all of your loved ones and anyone close to you with the blood of Jesus Christ. That way, the demon cannot get at you or any of them.

With this protection in place, we should have no fear of stepping out and boldly engaging the enemy. God gives us the supernatural power to win these spiritual battles.

SUMMARY AND CONCLUSION

As Christians, we want to follow Jesus' example and walk as He walked. We want to do the things that He Himself said we would do in Mark 16:17, 18 concerning the signs that would accompany those who have believed. In order to do so, we definitely need to have God's supernatural power flowing through us, just as it flowed through Jesus and the apostles.

We have seen that God's supernatural power has accomplished many glorious miracles, even in our current day and age.

By His supernatural power, God desires to use ***us*** to heal, to perform miracles and to deliver others from possession and harassment by evil spirits. He can also use us to liberate geographic regions from domination by evil spirits, in His name and by His power.

The skirmishes that we have today, I would have to put in the realm of spiritual battles. However, there is a major spiritual war coming that will far overshadow the battles that we are experiencing today. Let's learn about it, so we know how to be prepared.

God's supernatural power is for every Christian.

Chapter 13

POWER FOR THE COMING SPIRITUAL WAR

As we just discussed in the last chapter, we need supernatural power to fight day-to-day spiritual battles. These are not happening in the physical or fleshly realm but in the spiritual realm. Most Christians go through one spiritual battle after another, whether or not they are aware of it. We do need God's miraculous, spiritual power in order to come out victorious in those everyday skirmishes.

However, there is a very major spiritual war coming to planet earth in the not-too-distant future. This war will eclipse the spiritual battles that we have experienced to date.

The war I am speaking of is not a military war but a spiritual war. Spiritual battles have been fought upon the earth through the centuries, but there has never been a spiritual war like the one that looms ahead of us.

Before discussing this war specifically, we need to talk a little about the enemy, since there are so many misconceptions about who Satan is.

WHO IS SATAN?

If you were to ask most Christians who Satan is, they would likely respond that he is a fallen angel, in fact a fallen angel leader. If you were to ask them when he was kicked out of heaven, they might respond with anything from "during the Old Testament times" or "prior to the garden of Eden" to "he will be kicked out of heaven sometime in the future, right before the tribulation."

I have asked many Christians for their biblical basis for believing that Satan is who they think he is and for believing what they do about when he was, or will be, kicked out of heaven. I have found very few who have had a solid scriptural basis for what they believed. Take yourself as an example. You possibly believe that Satan is a fallen angel. On what Scripture do you base that?

It is likely that you are repeating what you have heard someone else say. We know from past experience that basing our beliefs on anything but the Scriptures can lead to all sorts of confusion and even error.

Why is there so much confusion concerning who Satan is and what his present status is? I believe the confusion comes because Satan is the great deceiver, the author of confusion, and the father of all lies. He tries to get Christians to believe false things about himself and to bring confusion anywhere he can. With the Lord as my guide and my protection, I would like to share with you some things that the Bible does say about Satan.

Let us first tackle the question of who Satan is. I cannot find a Scripture that says Satan is a fallen angel, although that is what I have been taught all my life. Let's look at some of the Scriptures that people might use to conclude that Satan is a fallen angel. The first of these is 2 Corinthians:

> **13 For such men are false apostles, deceitful workers, disguising themselves as apostles of Christ.**
>
> **14 And no wonder, for even Satan disguises himself as an angel of light.**

15 Therefore it is not surprising if his servants also disguise themselves as servants of righteousness; whose end shall be according to their deeds.

—2 Corinthians 11

We see that Satan is not called an angel in this passage; rather it says that he ***disguises*** himself as one. Another verse about him is found in Matthew:

41 "Then He will also say to those on His left, 'Depart from Me, accursed ones, into the eternal fire which has been prepared for the devil and his angels; . . .'"

—Matthew 25

Here we learn that eternal fire has been prepared for "the devil and his angels." Yet Christ also had angels who could protect Him if He jumped off the pinnacle of the temple (Luke 4:9-11), but that did not make him an angel. This passage no more makes Satan an angel than the fact that Christ had angels to serve Him made Christ an angel. Let's look further:

7 And there was war in heaven, Michael and his angels waging war with the dragon. And the dragon and his angels waged war,

8 and they were not strong enough and there was no longer a place found for them in heaven.

—Revelation 12

These verses depict a war in heaven between Michael and his angels and Satan and his angels. This could possibly imply that Satan and Michael were on equivalent levels, although it does not necessarily imply this. This is probably the strongest verse that could lead one to conclude that Satan was an angel, but it is far from conclusive.

Now let us examine some things that might lead us to believe that Satan might not be a fallen angel.

Is Satan a Fallen Cherub?

To examine the possibility that Satan might be a fallen cherub, we need to look at Ezekiel 28. In the first ten verses of this chapter of Ezekiel, the word of the Lord comes through Ezekiel to the "leader of Tyre." But then, beginning in verse 11, the word of the Lord comes to the "king of Tyre." It is possible that the first ten verses are talking about the human leader of Tyre, while the remaining verses of that chapter deal with Satan, the ruler or power behind that leader. Let's read those verses, and then we will see why they are possibly talking about Satan.

> **11 Again the word of the LORD came to me saying,**
> **12 "Son of man, take up a lamentation over the king of Tyre, and say to him, 'Thus says the Lord GOD,**
> **"You had the seal of perfection,**
> **Full of wisdom and perfect in beauty.**
> **13 "You were in Eden, the garden of God;**
> **Every precious stone was your covering:**
> **The ruby, the topaz, and the diamond;**
> **The beryl, the onyx, and the jasper;**
> **The lapis lazuli, the turquoise, and the emerald;**
> **And the gold, the workmanship of your settings and sockets,**
> **Was in you.**
> **On the day that you were created**
> **They were prepared.**
> **14 "You were the anointed cherub who covers,**
> **And I placed you *there*.**
> **You were on the holy mountain of God;**
> **You walked in the midst of the stones of fire.**
> **15 "You were blameless in your ways**

From the day you were created,
Until unrighteousness was found in you.
16 "By the abundance of your trade
You were internally filled with violence,
And you sinned;
Therefore I have cast you as profane
From the mountain of God.
And I have destroyed you, O covering cherub,
From the midst of the stones of fire.
17 "Your heart was lifted up because of your beauty;
You corrupted your wisdom by reason of your splendor.
I cast you to the ground;
I put you before kings,
That they may see you.

—Ezekiel 28

One thing that would lead us to think that this likely is talking about Satan is found is verse 13, where God says, "You were in Eden, the garden of God. " There is further evidence that this may be talking about Satan in verse 14, where God says, "You were the anointed cherub" and, "You were on the holy mountain of God; You walked in the midst of the stones of fire." To understand this part about walking in the midst of the stones of fire, let us first turn back to Chapter 10 of Ezekiel, where we get a description of the cherubim. (Cherubim is plural for cherub.)

8 And the cherubim appeared to have the form of a man's hand under their wings.

9 Then I looked, and behold, four wheels beside the cherubim, one wheel beside each cherub; and the appearance of the wheels was like the gleam of a Tarshish stone.

10 And as for their appearance, all four of them had the same likeness, as if one wheel were within another wheel.

11 When they moved, they went in *any of* their four directions without turning as they went; but they followed in the direction which they faced, without turning as they went.

12 And their whole body, their backs, their hands, their wings, and the wheels were full of eyes all around, the wheels belonging to all four of them.

13 The wheels were called in my hearing, the whirling wheels.

14 And each one had four faces. The first face *was* the face of a cherub, the second face *was* the face of a man, the third the face of a lion, and the fourth the face of an eagle.

15 Then the cherubim rose up. They are the living beings that I saw by the river Chebar.

16 Now when the cherubim moved, the wheels would go beside them; also when the cherubim lifted up their wings to rise from the ground, the wheels would not turn from beside them.

17 When the cherubim stood still, the wheels would stand still; and when they rose up, the wheels would rise with them; for the spirit of the living beings *was* in them.

18 Then the glory of the LORD departed from the threshold of the temple and stood over the cherubim.

19 When the cherubim departed, they lifted their wings and rose up from the earth in my sight with the wheels beside them; and they stood still at the entrance of the east gate of the LORD'S house. And the glory of the God of Israel hovered over them.

20 These are the living beings that I saw beneath the God of Israel by the river Chebar; so I knew that they *were* cherubim.

21 Each one had four faces and each one four wings, and beneath their wings *was* the form of human hands.

22 As for the likeness of their faces, they were the same faces whose appearance I had seen by the river Chebar. Each one went straight ahead.

—Ezekiel 10

From this description of cherubim, we see that they each had four faces, they had wings and underneath the wings were hands, like the hands of a man. In verse 22, Ezekiel says that these were the same beings that he had seen by the river Chebar. We find that vision back in the first chapter of Ezekiel:

2 (On the fifth of the month in the fifth year of King Jehoiachin's exile,

3 the word of the LORD came expressly to Ezekiel the priest, son of Buzi, in the land of the Chaldeans by the river Chebar; and there the hand of the LORD came upon him.)

4 And as I looked, behold, a storm wind was coming from the north, a great cloud with fire flashing forth continually and a bright light around it, and in its midst something like glowing metal in the midst of the fire.

5 And within it there were figures resembling four living beings. And this was their appearance: they had human form.

6 Each of them had four faces and four wings.

7 And their legs were straight and their feet were like a calf's hoof, and they gleamed like burnished bronze.

8 Under their wings on their four sides *were* human hands. As for the faces and wings of the four of them,

9 their wings touched one another; their *faces* did not turn when they moved, each went straight forward.

10 As for the form of their faces, *each* had the face of a man, all four had the face of a lion on the right and the face of a bull on the left, and all four had the face of an eagle.

11 Such were their faces. Their wings were spread out above; each had two touching another *being*, and two covering their bodies.

12 And each went straight forward; wherever the spirit was about to go, they would go, without turning as they went.

13 In the midst of the living beings there was something that looked like burning coals of fire, like torches darting back and forth among the living beings. The fire was bright, and lightning was flashing from the fire.

14 And the living beings ran to and fro like bolts of lightning.

—Ezekiel 1

In verse 13 of this passage, we see that these living beings had in their midst coals of burning fire. This ties back to "You walked in the midst of the stones of fire" that we read from Ezekiel 28:14. Verse 14 of Ezekiel 1 also says that the cherubim ran back and forth like bolts of lightning. At one point, Christ said that He saw Satan fall from heaven like lightning (Luke 10:18). This might be further evidence that the being talked about in the last half of Ezekiel 28 is indeed Satan.

One thing is clear: if the last half of Ezekiel 28 is talking about Satan, then Satan is no fallen angel. He is a fallen cherub. Cherubim are something totally different from angels, with a different function. We know from Revelation 4:4-8 that there are four of these cherubim. They are unique and are definitely not angels.

I do not believe that the Bible tells us explicitly and clearly who Satan is, but it seems to me that the best indications are that he is a fallen cherub, and not a fallen angel, nor a fallen created son of God (for a discussion of created sons of God, see pages 175-178 of my book *You Can Overcome*).

Whether Satan is a fallen cherub, a fallen created son of God, a fallen angel or something else, there are verses in Job which tell us that he had been roaming about the earth. Evidently, he had access both to the earth and to God's throne room, where he appeared among the sons of God and made his accusations against Job (Job 1:6-12; 2:2-7). This is still true today, as we will see. Satan has access to the earth, and yet he has access to the throne of God, because the Bible says that he accuses the brethren night and day before the throne of God:

> **9 And the great dragon was thrown down, the serpent of old who is called the devil and Satan, who deceives the whole world; he was thrown down to the earth, and his angels were thrown down with him.**
>
> **10 And I heard a loud voice in heaven, saying,**
>
> **"NOW the salvation, and the power, and the kingdom of our God and the authority of His Christ have come, for the accuser of our brethren has been thrown down, who accuses them before our God day and night. . . ."**
>
> **—Revelation 12**

This is part of one of John's visions of things yet to come. In verses such as the following, we also find that Satan is the ruler of this world:

> **30 "I will not speak much more with you, for the ruler of the world is coming, and he has nothing in Me; . . ."**
>
> **—John 14**

11 and concerning judgment, because the ruler of this world has been judged.

—John 16

Satan is also said to be the ruler of the "air," which is the space between sea level and the clouds. The fact that he is the prince (ruler) of the air is found in these passages:

1 And you were dead in your trespasses and sins,
2 in which you formerly walked according to the course of this world, according to the prince of the power of the air, of the spirit that is now working in the sons of disobedience.

—Ephesians 2

12 For our struggle is not against flesh and blood, but against the rulers, against the powers, against the world forces of this darkness, against the spiritual *forces* of wickedness in the heavenly *places*.

—Ephesians 6

We also know that Satan has power and authority, because he gives these to the first beast spoken of in Revelation:

1 And he stood on the sand of the seashore.
And I saw a beast coming up out of the sea, having ten horns and seven heads, and on the horns *were* ten diadems, and on his heads *were* blasphemous names.
2 And the beast which I saw was like a leopard, and his feet were *like those* of a bear, and his mouth like the mouth of a lion. And the dragon gave him his power and his throne and great authority.

—Revelation 13

In spite of his power and authority, Satan does not have many of the attributes of God that he would like to have. For example, as we discussed in the last chapter, he is not omnipresent; that is, he cannot be present everywhere at once. He can only be one place on the earth at a time.

SATAN'S WAR IN HEAVEN

We will need supernatural power, in the name of Jesus Christ, to fight and win the major spiritual war that Satan will bring to the earth. We know that Satan has access to the earth and to the air, that he has had this dual access at least since the garden of Eden, and that he still has it today. We also know that back in the time of Job, he also had access to God's throne room in heaven, and he still has that access today. One time I heard Pat Robertson say that "at this moment Satan is before the throne of God accusing the brethren." He is right. However, there will be a time when Satan will be kicked out of heaven, following a war with Michael and his angels, after which Satan will no longer have access to heaven, but will only have access to earth.

You may be thinking, "Wait a minute, James. I thought that the battle in heaven had already occurred and Satan had already been cast out of heaven." I would be very interested if someone could give me a passage of Scripture on which to base that, but you may have a bit of difficulty in finding one. I did.

This is one subject that always confused me. My "teachers" talked about Satan being kicked out of heaven in a passage back in Isaiah, yet I saw him being kicked out of heaven in Revelation and I could not reconcile the two. I could not figure out if this event had already occurred, if the expulsion from heaven was going to happen in the future, or if it was going to happen twice. Upon doing further research, I found that the passage many people refer to in Isaiah is probably not talking about Satan at all. To begin our search for truth on this subject, let's turn to Isaiah 14. We need to read a long passage from this chapter to get the context, so please be patient and read it all carefully:

3 And it will be in the day when the LORD gives you rest from your pain and turmoil and harsh service in which you have been enslaved,

4 that you will take up this taunt against the king of Babylon, and say,

"How the oppressor has ceased,
***And how* fury has ceased!**
5 "The LORD has broken the staff of the wicked,
The scepter of rulers
6 Which used to strike the peoples in fury with unceasing strokes,
Which subdued the nations in anger with unrestrained persecution.
7 "The whole earth is at rest *and* is quiet;
They break forth into shouts of joy.
8 "Even the cypress trees rejoice over you, *and* the cedars of Lebanon, *saying,*
'Since you were laid low, no *tree* cutter comes up against us.'
9 "Sheol from beneath is excited over you to meet you when you come;
It arouses for you the spirits of the dead, all the leaders of the earth;
10 It raises all the kings of the nations from their thrones.
"They will all respond and say to you,
'Even you have been made weak as we,
You have become like *us.*
11 'Your pomp *and* the music of your harps
Have been brought down to Sheol;
Maggots are spread out *as your bed* beneath you,

And worms are your covering.
12 "How you have fallen from heaven,
O star of the morning, son of the dawn!
You have been cut down to the earth,
You who have weakened the nations!
13 "But you said in your heart,
'I will ascend to heaven;
I will raise my throne above the stars of God,
And I will sit on the mount of assembly
In the recesses of the north.
14 'I will ascend above the heights of the clouds;
I will make myself like the Most High.'
15 "Nevertheless you will be thrust down to Sheol,
To the recesses of the pit.
16 "Those who see you will gaze at you,
They will ponder over you, *saying*,
'Is this the man who made the earth tremble,
Who shook kingdoms,
17 'Who made the world like a wilderness
And overthrew its cities,
Who did not allow his prisoners to *go* home?'
18 "All the kings of the nations lie in glory,
Each in his own tomb.
19 "But you have been cast out of your tomb
Like a rejected branch,
Clothed with the slain who are pierced with a sword,
Who go down to the stones of the pit,
Like a trampled corpse.
20 "You will not be united with them in burial,
Because you have ruined your country,
You have slain your people.
May the offspring of evildoers not be mentioned forever.
21 "Prepare for his sons a place of slaughter
Because of the iniquity of their fathers.

They must not arise and take possession of the earth
And fill the face of the world with cities."

22 "And I will rise up against them," declares the LORD of hosts, "and will cut off from Babylon name and survivors, offspring and posterity," declares the LORD. . . ."

—Isaiah 14

Who would you say this passage in Isaiah is talking about? Some people say that it is talking about Satan, because they read only verses 12-15. But if you read the whole passage in context, I believe you will see that it is clearly talking about a king of Babylon. This is a taunt that the children of Israel were to take up against the king of Babylon when he was defeated and they were set free. Verse 17 says that this king overthrew cities and would not let prisoners go home. Verses 19-20 say that he is going to go down into a pit like someone slain with a sword, and he will not have a nice tomb, because he ruined his country and slew his people. Verse 21 says this person (the king) had sons.

I am not sure how people justify applying a small segment out of the middle of this taunt to Satan, and using it to "prove" that he has already been cast out of heaven. Personally, I cannot find any justification for that. Let us now turn to another passage on the fall of Satan:

17 And the seventy returned with joy, saying, "Lord, even the demons are subject to us in Your name."

18 And He said to them, "I was watching Satan fall from heaven like lightning.

19 "Behold, I have given you authority to tread upon serpents and scorpions, and over all the power of the enemy, and nothing shall injure you.

20 "Nevertheless do not rejoice in this, that the spirits are subject to you, but rejoice that your names are recorded in heaven."

—Luke 10

Here Christ says that He was watching Satan fall from heaven like lightning. This could have a number of interpretations. One is that the battle in heaven occurred and Satan was kicked out at that point in time. Another is that Christ, in a visionary way, was looking back to a pre-Adamic event or forward to the battle and expulsion from heaven of Satan spoken of in Revelation. Probably a more plausible interpretation is that, as the seventy went out and conquered demons in the name of Christ, Satan fell from "heaven," which is another name for the "air," and did battle against them.

The Coming War in Heaven

Now let's look further at the passage that describes an event involving Satan that we are pretty sure still lies in the future:

7 And there was war in heaven, Michael and his angels waging war with the dragon. And the dragon and his angels waged war,

8 and they were not strong enough, and there was no longer a place found for them in heaven.

9 And the great dragon was thrown down, the serpent of old who is called the devil and Satan, who deceives the whole world; he was thrown down to the earth, and his angels were thrown down with him.

10 And I heard a loud voice in heaven, saying,

"NOW the salvation, and the power, and the kingdom of our God and the authority of His Christ have come, for the accuser of our brethren has been thrown down, who accuses them before our God day and night.

11 "And they overcame him because of the blood of the Lamb and because of the word of their testimony, and they did not love their life even to death.

12 "For this reason, rejoice, O heavens and you who dwell in them. Woe to the earth and the sea, because the devil has come down to you, having great wrath, knowing that he has *only* a short time."

—Revelation 12

Here in John's prophetic writings we see the first mention of a "war" in heaven, as a result of which Satan is "thrown down" to the earth and evidently no longer allowed access to God's throne. When this happens, Satan will realize that he has only a little while left, and so he will release his full wrath upon the earth (verse 12).

I therefore have to conclude that the actual war in heaven, when Satan is cast down to the earth and no longer allowed access to God's throne, is yet in the future. When that does occur, the persecution of Christians and spiritual warfare will get incredibly intense.

SATAN'S ARMY

Satan has a partial army in existence down here on the earth right now. It consists of demons and possibly some fallen angels. Demons are far different than fallen angels. There is never any evidence of an angel seeking to inhabit someone else's body, since angels have a body of their own. Demons are *"body-less"* evil spirits whose origin is not clearly specified in the Bible.

As far as I can tell, the Scriptures indicate that all non-Christians are also part of Satan's partial army.

44 "You are of *your* father the devil, and you want to do the desires of your father. He was a murderer from the beginning, and does not stand in the truth, because there is no truth in him. Whenever he speaks

a lie, he speaks from his own *nature*; for he is a liar, and the father of lies.

—John 8

7 Little children, let no one deceive you; the one who practices righteousness is righteous, just as He is righteous;

8 the one who practices sin is of the devil; for the devil has sinned from the beginning. The Son of God appeared for this purpose, that He might destroy the works of the devil.

9 No one who is born of God practices sin, because His seed abides in him; and he cannot sin, because he is born of God.

10 By this the children of God and the children of the devil are obvious: anyone who does not practice righteousness is not of God, nor the one who does not love his brother.

—1 John 3

In Revelation 12, we also read the following, speaking about the dragon (Satan) and his angels (the stars):

3 And another sign appeared in heaven: and behold, a great red dragon having seven heads and ten horns, and on his heads *were* seven diadems.

4 And his tail swept away a third of the stars of heaven, and threw them to the earth. . . .

—Revelation 12

As we have seen, joining this partial army here on planet earth at some point will be Satan and one third of the angels that are in heaven right now. These angels will join in the category of fallen angels. Let's reread a couple of verses:

9 And the great dragon was thrown down, the serpent of old who is called the devil and Satan, who deceives the whole world; he was thrown down to the earth and his angels were thrown down with him. . . .

12 "For this reason, rejoice, O heavens and you who dwell in them. Woe to the earth and the sea, because the devil has come down to you, having great wrath, knowing that he has *only* a short time."

—Revelation 12

The verbs in these verses are in past tense because John is describing a vision that he saw, but it is a prophetic vision of events yet to come, as is obvious if read in the context of the rest of the book of Revelation. We see here that not only will Satan be thrown out of heaven down to the earth, where he will no longer have access to the throne of God, but he will have a third of the angels with him. He will have only a short time here and he is going to be full of wrath. When that event occurs, the major coming "Spiritual War I" (SWI) will begin.

PREPARATION FOR THE SPIRITUAL WAR

Many Christians are going to be defeated in this coming spiritual war (SWI). They will be defeated first of all because they do not know that it is coming, and thus they are not making any preparations for it. You will likely not be prepared for something that you do not know is coming.

6 My people are destroyed for lack of knowledge. . . .

—Hosea 4

"Do not be weary of well doing my people. It is hard to prepare ahead of time and then wait, but your

patience will not be in vain. Keep waiting and watching, keep your eyes sharp, your mind keen and your heart open to Me," saith the Lord.

There are many things that you can do to prepare for spiritual battles that are going on today, and also for the major spiritual war (SWI) that is coming when Satan is kicked out of heaven. I go over these in the book *You Can Overcome* that I mentioned earlier. If you have never read a copy of this, I would encourage you to get one and read it. If you read it a number of years ago, you may wish to get out your copy and prayerfully read through it again.

In that book, I get into how to put on the armor of God and utilize it. Many people know that we should have on the armor of God but if you ask them, "When is the last time you put it on?" they give you a blank look. I believe we should put on the armor of God daily, because we are going out to do spiritual battles daily. Remember, what we are experiencing now is simply spiritual "battlefare"—the real spiritual warfare is yet ahead of us.

If I were to tell a person only one thing to do to get ready for the spiritual war and to have God's supernatural power, without hesitation I would say the very most important thing to do is to:

BECOME A BONDSLAVE OF GOD

What it means to be a bondslave of God was discussed in some length in Chapter 5. As I noted there, God's pattern through the centuries has always been to let His people go through a time of trouble and turmoil but to divinely protect them in it. He let Daniel go through the lion's den, but He divinely protected him in it. He allowed Shadrach, Meshach and Abed-nego to go through the fiery furnace, but He divinely protected them in the midst of it.

The children of Israel were in Egypt during the plagues but, by and large, the plagues did not touch them.

> **21 "For if you will not let My people go, behold, I will send swarms of insects on you and on your servants and on your people and into your houses; and the houses of the Egyptians shall be full of swarms of insects, and also the ground on which they *dwell.***
>
> **22 "But on that day I will set apart the land of Goshen, where My people are living, so that no swarms of insects will be there, in order that you may know that I, the LORD, am in the midst of the land.**
>
> **23 "And I will put a division between My people and your people. Tomorrow this sign shall occur."'"**
>
> **—Exodus 8**

> **4 "But the LORD will make a distinction between the livestock of Israel and the livestock of Egypt, so that nothing will die of all that belongs to the sons of Israel. . . ."'"**
>
> **6 So the LORD did this thing on the morrow, and all the livestock of Egypt died; but of the livestock of the sons of Israel, not one died.**
>
> **—Exodus 9**

In most of the plagues in Egypt, God divinely protected His people, as He did in these two instances. On all but the last plague, they had God's protection simply because they were there, but with the last plague a new dimension was added. With the last plague:

THEIR PROTECTION WAS DEPENDENT UPON THEIR OBEDIENCE

If they obeyed God and sacrificed the lamb, and sprinkled its blood over the doorpost, then they were protected from the death angel. If they did not obey God, they did not get His protection (Exodus 12:5-13).

Similarly, God wanted to protect Noah from the flood, but his protection was dependent upon his obedience. For one hundred and twenty-five years he preached righteousness and he built an ark which dramatically shows that it is not spiritual preparation *or* physical preparation that is important, but *both*. Noah's protection was dependent upon his obedience.

GOD'S BONDSLAVES

One exciting thing about God's pattern of protection is that He is going to do this one more time. He is going to let His people go through a time of trouble and turmoil, but He is going to divinely protect them in the midst of it. As we saw briefly in Chapter 5, God is going to seal His bondslaves on their foreheads:

> **2 And I saw another angel ascending from the rising of the sun, having the seal of the living God; and he cried out with a loud voice to the four angels to whom it was granted to harm the earth and the sea,**
>
> **3 saying, "Do not harm the earth or the sea or the trees, until we have sealed the bondservants of our God on their foreheads."**
>
> **—Revelation 7**

Why will they be sealed on their foreheads? It is for divine protection:

> **3 And out of the smoke came forth locusts upon the earth; and power was given them, as the scorpions of the earth have power.**

4 And they were told that they should not hurt the grass of the earth, nor any green thing, nor any tree, but only the men who do not have the seal of God on their foreheads.

5 And they were not permitted to kill anyone, but to torment for five months; and their torment was like the torment of a scorpion when it stings a man.

6 And in those days men will seek death and will not find it; and they will long to die and death flees from them.

—Revelation 9

In verse 4, we see that these locusts, which will be able to swarm all over men and sting them like scorpions sting, will not be able to touch the people who have the seal of God on their foreheads. Praise God!

Since I am an economist, frequently when I speak at Christian groups, people inquire if their MasterCard or VISA are part of the mark of the beast. They are also concerned about the black marks on the grocery store cans. I ask them to pause in all their worrying and fretting and I ask this question: "Do you think that Satan or the beast or anyone else could remove God's seal of protection from your forehead and replace it with the mark of the beast?"

The answer to this question has to be, "Absolutely not"; otherwise, that would be saying that Satan was more powerful than God. I advise such Christians to stop worrying about the mark of the beast and start being concerned about getting the seal of God on their foreheads. I believe that if one has the seal of God, it will be ***absolutely impossible*** to take on the mark of the beast.

But who is it that God said He was going to seal on their foreheads? He said that He was going to seal His bondslaves. In Chapter 5, we briefly examined what a bondslave of God really is, but it is of such significance that some of what we discussed there bears repeating with some elaboration at this point.

In thinking of "God's Bondslaves," an even better title would probably be "God's Volunteer Permanent Slaves." When we think of the word "slave," we may think of those people of Africa who were captured by force, taken to America and forced into slavery. We also might think of slaves in the ancient times, such as under the Roman Empire, when a country was captured and some or most of the people in the captured country were forced into slavery at the hands of the victors. Of course, children born to slave parents were born into slavery. Thus, our basic concept of slavery is that people are either forced into it or born into it.

It would be almost impossible for most people to conceive of a free person walking up to a slave master and volunteering to become a permanent slave. To us this would almost seem like an act of a psychotic, sadist, or a lunatic. Yet that is precisely what God asks us to do. To those who do not know God and Christ in an intimate way, to do so may indeed seem like lunacy or psychotic behavior, but those who know God can see that it is the only path to victory and an overcoming life.

Unfortunately, some of the newer translations of the Bible use the words *slave* and *servant* almost interchangeably. In many instances where the word would more accurately be translated "bondslave," it is unfortunately translated "bond-servant." The term *slave* and *servant* are far from interchangeable, as we saw in Chapter 5.

A servant gets paid a wage, however small it may be. That servant can then go out and buy with that wage anything he or she wants to buy. A servant also has days off, during which he can do anything that he desires. Thus, he has control over a good portion of his life. Servants may live in virtual poverty, or have a low standard of living, but they are still in control of their spending and a portion of their time.

On the other hand, a slave never receives any money of his own whatsoever. Anything that he wants he must ask of his master. If he wants some new clothes, he must ask his master for them. His master may say "yes" or "no" and, if the answer is "yes," he might also specify what kind and what color. If the slave wants to take a wife, he goes and asks his master if he may have one. His master answers "yes" or "no." If the answer is "yes," the master can also decide who the slave must marry. The slave has no "rights" to marry whomever he pleases. He does his master's bidding. If the slave wants to live in a different house, have a piece of furniture or anything else, he cannot make the decision himself, for he has no money to purchase these items. He must go to the master and ask him, and then do whatever the master says or receive whatever the master gives.

Similarly, there is never any "time off" from being a slave. He does not have any days off. His time is 100 percent under the control of his master. He may be dead tired and need a vacation, but if his master says, "Work," he works. He may be sick, but if his master tells him to do something, the slave must do it, in spite of his sickness. *His time is not his own.*

In the time of the feudal lords where there were feudal slaves, the slaves were used as part of the army of the feudal lord in the event of any attack. Thus, if a master told a slave to go out into battle and charge up a particular hill, the slave had to do it, even if it meant his death. For a person to voluntarily become a slave, he was voluntarily making a commitment to die for his master, if his master wanted him to die, to have no possessions except what the master gave him, to have no discretionary spending money of his own, to have no time of his own and no rights at all. As you can see, being a slave is far, far different from being a servant.

If one is a servant, one can quit whenever one wants to. If one is a slave, one can never quit.

Now let's take a look at bondslaves in the Old Testament and examine what implications this has for you and me.

A BONDSLAVE IN THE OLD TESTAMENT

The concept of a bondslave (a voluntary slave) in the Old Testament is found in many places. One of the best descriptions of it is in Deuteronomy:

> **12 "If your kinsman, a Hebrew man or woman, is sold to you, then he shall serve you six years, but in the seventh year you shall set him free.**
>
> **13 "And when you set him free, you shall not send him away empty-handed.**
>
> **14 "You shall furnish him liberally from your flock and from your threshing floor and from your wine vat; you shall give to him as the LORD your God has blessed you.**
>
> **15 "And you shall remember that you were a slave in the land of Egypt, and the LORD your God redeemed you; therefore I command you this today.**
>
> **16 "And it shall come about if he says to you, 'I will not go out from you,' because he loves you and your household, since he fares well with you;**
>
> **17 then you shall take an awl and pierce it through his ear into the door, and he shall be your servant forever. And also you shall do likewise to your maidservant.**
>
> **18 "It shall not seem hard to you when you set him free, for he has given you six years *with* double the service of a hired man; so the LORD your God will bless you whatever you do. . . ."**
>
> **—Deuteronomy 15**

As you can see in this passage, if a person has come to be your temporary slave, for whatever reason—whether because he owed you money or because he sold himself to you to raise money—at the end of the seventh year, you were to set him free. When you set him free, you were to give him some of your material possessions so that he did not go away empty-handed.

On the other hand, he could say to you that he did not want to go away and be free again, but instead he wanted to voluntarily become your permanent slave (bondslave). If he told you that, you would stand him against the doorpost and pierce his ear with an awl. The pierced ear was the mark of a permanent slave. Since he was not born into slavery, but he voluntarily became a permanent slave, he was called a bondslave.

Remember, this required a two-sided commitment, the master and the slave each committing themselves to the other and each assuming certain responsibilities.

It is true that the master had gotten a slave for life who would have to do his bidding, work for him, fight for him and even die for him. But, the master was also taking on the obligation and responsibility to care for that slave for the rest of his life, to protect him and to provide for him.

What would cause an individual to voluntarily become a permanent slave? One certainly would not want to do so if the master were cruel, harsh or unjust. However, if the master were loving, kind, considerate and just, and if serving him were a joy, one might well consider being a voluntary permanent slave. Even though a slave might live in material luxury, he still had no freedoms of his own.

The concept of voluntarily becoming a permanent slave, because of love for the master, is also recorded in a passage we read earlier from Exodus:

2 "If you buy a Hebrew slave, he shall serve for six years; but on the seventh he shall go out as a free man without payment.

3 "If he comes alone, he shall go out alone; if he is the husband of a wife, then his wife shall go out with him.

4 "If his master gives him a wife, and she bears him sons or daughters, the wife and her children shall belong to her master, and he shall go out alone.

5 "But if the slave plainly says, 'I love my master, my wife and my children; I will not go out as a free man,'

6 then his master shall bring him to God, then he shall bring him to the door or the doorpost. And his master shall pierce his ear with an awl; and he shall serve him permanently. . . ."

—Exodus 21

I think this is a very beautiful passage because it outlines what happened if a temporary slave plainly said that he was staying because he loved his master.

This also clearly affirms that even a temporary slave had no rights at all. If the master had given the slave a wife and they had children, the wife and the children still belonged to the master. If the slave decided to leave, he had to leave his wife and children with the master. As you can see, when one is a slave, everything that a person has, including his wife (or her husband) and children, belong to the master and not to the slave. Yet that is a temporary condition of one who is a temporary slave. But if one volunteers to become a permanent slave, that becomes a permanent condition.

So we see that a bondslave has no money nor possessions of his own, no rights nor time of his own, and he is obligated to do anything that the master tells him to do. The question that arises is this: Are all Christians bondslaves of God? Unfortunately, I and most of the Christians with whom I speak, including Christian leaders, would readily admit that all Christians are not bondslaves of God. Many of them have possessions of their own and money of their own which they use as they please.

But who is going to get sealed with the seal of the living God on their foreheads? ***Only*** the bondslaves of God will be sealed. The rest of the Christians will not be sealed. God wants every Christian to become a bondslave, and I certainly encourage every Christian to be a bondslave of God, but unfortunately they all are not.

The cost of becoming a bondslave is not high—it is total. Once you buy that, you will never be able to buy anything else again in your life. Once you make a commitment to God to be His bondslave, God will hold you to it.

As I mentioned in Chapter 5, if you would like to make a commitment to become a bondslave of God, for your convenience there is a form on the next to last page of this book that might be of help to you. It has a prayer of commitment to God on it and a place to sign and date it. It would be wonderful if you sent it, or a copy of it to the address given, so that we could have a record of it and include you when we correspond with others who have made this bondslave commitment. However, since this is a commitment between you and *God*, you may just want to sign it and keep it for yourself. If God is speaking to your heart, you might want to pause right now and do that. (If you do make this commitment to God, I would strongly encourage you to get the book *You Can Overcome* which I believe will be a tremendous help to you.)

SUMMARY AND CONCLUSION

We have seen that there is a spiritual war coming, the likes of which we have never seen and—once it is over—we will never see again. The spiritual war down here on the earth will immediately follow the spiritual war in heaven, wherein Satan will be defeated and thrown out of heaven and will no longer have access to the throne of God.

We know that this war is yet ahead of us (it will occur as part of the fulfillment of Revelation 12) and it certainly did not occur during or prior to the time of Job, when Satan had access to both the throne of God and the earth. Once the war happens and Satan is defeated, he will no longer have access to the throne of God.

God is raising up an end-time, bondslave army, so that once Satan hits planet earth, he is going to be defeated down here as well. He will lose in heaven and then he will lose again on earth. Let's review a couple of verses that we read earlier:

> **9 And the great dragon was thrown down, the serpent of old who is called the devil and Satan, who deceives the whole world; he was thrown down to the earth, and his angels were thrown down with him.**
>
> **10 And I heard a loud voice in heaven, saying,**
>
> **"NOW the salvation, and the power, and the kingdom of our God and the authority of His Christ have come, for the accuser of our brethren has been thrown down, who accuses them before our God day and night.**
>
> **11 "And they overcame him because of the blood of the Lamb and because of the word of their testimony, and they did not love their life even to death. . . ."**
>
> **—Revelation 12**

Verse 11 is speaking of Satan being overcome by the overcomers, the bondslaves, those who have the divine seal of protection of God on their foreheads. This will be Spiritual War I (SWI), and we need the supernatural power of God to fight it and win it.

God is going to bring back the awesome power gifts, such as calling down fire from heaven and causing it to rain or not to rain. As we have discussed, these gifts are exemplified by the two witnesses spoken of in the book of Revelation (Revelation 11:3-6). However, God can only give those power gifts to people whom He can trust to be totally obedient to Him. As bondslaves, we become accustomed to walking moment-by-moment in obedience to the Lord under the direction of the Holy Spirit.

The next major move of God is not going to be a renewed, revived charismatic movement. I believe the next move of God is going to come to and through the bondslaves. Please hear me—we are not talking about an elite group in any way; there is no such thing as a ***proud slave***. This is a humble, servant group of those who are totally surrendered to God. Our Lord Jesus Christ was a bondslave, and He was a humble servant:

> **5 Have this attitude in yourselves which was also in Christ Jesus,**
>
> **6 who, although He existed in the form of God, did not regard equality with God a thing to be grasped,**
>
> **7 but emptied Himself, taking the form of a bond-servant, *and* being made in the likeness of men.**
>
> **8 And being found in appearance as a man, He humbled Himself by becoming obedient to the point of death, even death on a cross.**
>
> **—Philippians 2**

Jesus was a bondslave of God and He had an attitude of humility and obedience to the Father. Verse

5 tells us that we are to have that same attitude in ourselves.

Jesus said, "Learn of Me for I am meek and lowly" (Matthew 11:29, *KJV*). How many Christian leaders today that you see on television and at major conventions would you consider to be "meek and lowly"? It appears that many of them have a lot to learn about being a bondslave, becoming like Jesus Christ and learning from Him about meekness and lowliness. If they will do this, God will mightily use them in the next move of God. If they will not become bondslaves of God, they will be left behind in the next move of God.

In summary, Satan coming down to planet earth with a third of the angels is yet in the future. When that occurs, we must have God's supernatural power to combat him and win.

As part of this gigantic spiritual war, and probably for a period of time before it, there will be persecution of Christians. Believers in Jesus Christ have been persecuted through the centuries, but there is massive persecution ahead of us, according to Jesus. Supernatural power is essential to go through persecution with victory. Let us take a look at how the power of God pertains to the subject of going through persecution.

God's supernatural power is for every Christian.

Chapter 14

POWER TO WITHSTAND PERSECUTION

We are going to need supernatural power for a number of things, particularly as this age comes to a close and Jesus Christ returns in power and glory to rule and reign here on the earth for a thousand years.

Some people might acknowledge that persecution is coming in a general way, yet question whether persecution is coming to America. If persecution is coming to America, we certainly are going to need God's divine power to withstand it and go through it, proclaiming the truth of Jesus Christ. God never brings anything upon His people without first warning them. I believe God is warning Christians in America today.

I believe that persecution is indeed coming to Christians in America. Billy Graham warns of this in his book *Till Armageddon*; Dave Wilkerson warns of it in his book *The Vision*, and many other outstanding Christian leaders have warned that persecution is coming to Christians in America.

The Bible also warns that persecution is coming. In answering the disciples' question of what things would be like at the end of this age and right before He came back, Jesus Christ said the following:

6 "And you will be hearing of wars and rumors of wars; see that you are not frightened, for *those things* must take place, but *that* is not yet the end.

7 "For nation will rise against nation, and kingdom against kingdom, and in various places there will be famines and earthquakes.

8 "But all these things are *merely* the beginning of birth pangs.

9 "Then they will deliver you to tribulation, and will kill you, and you will be hated by all nations on account of My name.

10 "And at that time many will fall away and will deliver up one another and hate one another. . . ."

—Matthew 24

The fact that persecution is an integral part of the time of birth pangs that precedes the great tribulation is confirmed in Luke 21, which also amplifies on what the persecution will be like:

10 Then He continued by saying to them, "Nation will rise against nation, and kingdom against kingdom,

11 and there will be great earthquakes, and in various places plagues and famines; and there will be terrors and great signs from heaven.

12 "But before all these things, they will lay their hands on you and will persecute you, delivering you to the synagogues and prisons, bringing you before kings and governors for My name's sake.

13 "It will lead to an opportunity for your testimony.

14 "So make up your minds not to prepare beforehand to defend yourselves;

15 for I will give you utterance and wisdom which none of your opponents will be able to resist or refute.

16 "But you will be delivered up even by parents and brothers and relatives and friends, and they will put *some* of you to death,

17 and you will be hated by all on account of My name.

18 "Yet not a hair of your head will perish.

19 "By your endurance you will gain your lives. . . ."

—Luke 21

In verse 12 of the preceding passage, Christ says that ***before*** all of the rest of the things in the time of birth pangs, we will be persecuted. Then He gives some details about who is going to betray us.

It may seem strange to you that I am writing about preparing for persecution, since most of the readers of this book will live in America where there is so much religious freedom and where being "born again" is still somewhat popular, even among governmental leaders and celebrities. However, there is a great deal of persecution of Christians going on around the world. It is even increasing here in America, and I believe it will become very intense in the not-too-distant future.

You might be thinking, "Wait a minute—God loves me and He wouldn't allow me to be tortured or physically harmed or killed. He wouldn't allow me to be imprisoned or to live in constant danger."

Let me ask you a question. Did God love Paul? Let's see what the Bible says happened to him:

23 Are they servants of Christ? (I speak as if insane) I more so; in far more labors, in far more imprisonments, beaten times without number, often in danger of death.

24 Five times I received from the Jews thirty-nine *lashes.*

25 Three times I was beaten with rods, once I was stoned, three times I was shipwrecked, a night and a day I have spent in the deep.

26 *I have been* on frequent journeys, in dangers from rivers, dangers from robbers, dangers from *my*

countrymen, dangers from the Gentiles, dangers in the city, dangers in the wilderness, dangers on the sea, dangers among false brethren;

27 *I have been* in labor and hardship, through many sleepless nights, in hunger and thirst, often without food, in cold and exposure.

28 Apart from *such* external things, there is the daily pressure upon me *of* concern for all the churches.

—2 Corinthians 11

God loved Paul and he was persecuted. Concerning the assumption that "if God loves me He wouldn't allow me to suffer persecution," consider this: we know that God loved Jesus Christ, yet He allowed His very own Son to be persecuted. Likewise, one could ask, did God love the Christians who died in the Colosseum in Rome by horrible deaths? Did He love the millions of Christians who have died under communism? The mere fact that we might suffer and die for Jesus does not mean that He does not love us.

PERSECUTION IS COMING

Do you believe what Christ said? Of course you do. Let's see what He had to say about persecution:

20 "Remember the word that I said to you, 'A slave is not greater than his master.' If they persecuted Me, they will also persecute you; if they kept My word, they will keep yours also. . . ."

—John 15

Here we read that Jesus said, "If they persecuted Me, they *will* also persecute you." Jesus Himself said that you were going to be persecuted. This is borne out other places in Scripture. Let's just turn to one of them:

12 And indeed, all who desire to live godly in Christ Jesus will be persecuted.

—2 Timothy 3

In the preceding verse, Paul says that those who desire to live godly in Jesus Christ ***will*** be persecuted. Are you being persecuted? If not, guess what! The more godly (in God's will) you live, the more the persecution increases. This persecution may or may not be physical in nature.

Almost everywhere Jeani and I go, we experience varying forms of persecution. In most every city, there are some pastors and Christian leaders warning their flock not to hear me. When I was ministering in Hattiesburg, Mississippi one year, there was one lady who was warned not to come to the meetings where I was speaking; the reason she was given was that I would instill in her a spirit of fear. She came anyhow, and the opposite happened. God brought her closer to Himself and there was a real sense of peace and joy in her soul, as she later reported to me. She went back to tell those who had warned her how wrong they had been.

We could read of many other incidents in the Scriptures—such Stephen being stoned to death in Acts 7—which let us know that, even though God loved the precious first-century Christians, He allowed them to suffer persecution. Jesus told them that they should expect it, because it ***was*** coming to them.

Christians around the world are beginning to feel more and more that the end of this age is at hand. If this is true, it means that Christians living today will experience the time of birth pangs that precedes the great tribulation. One of the major things that occurs during the time of birth pangs is persecution of Christians. This means that, in all likelihood, Christians living today will experience significant persecution.

This persecution could come from many sources. It could come from our own government, from Communists, from deprogrammers, from religious leaders (that is where it came from for Christ), from Muslims and even from the "organized" Catholic church, to name a few potential sources. What the Lord has laid on my heart is that from whatever source the persecution does come, many Christians will not be prepared, and some might even deny Christ. They need the power of God.

When Corrie ten Boom was traveling in China, one of the Chinese bishops told her that their people had not been prepared for persecution. He encouraged her to go back and alert and help prepare Christians in America for persecution. Of course the main preparation is walking surrounded by the supernatural power of God.

SUPERNATURAL POWER FOR PROTECTION

One of the reasons we need divine power in connection with persecution is for protection from harm. I am sure that you can think of many cases in the Bible in which God's divine power provided protection for His people. One of these was the incident that took place in Babylon when Nebuchadnezzar threw the three Hebrew men into the fiery furnace. We read about this in the book of Daniel:

> **17 "If it be *so*, our God whom we serve is able to deliver us from the furnace of blazing fire; and He will deliver us out of your hand, O king.**
>
> **18 "But *even* if *He does* not, let it be known to you, O king, that we are not going to serve your gods or worship the golden image that you have set up."**
>
> **19 Then Nebuchadnezzar was filled with wrath, and his facial expression was altered toward Shadrach, Meshach and Abed-nego. He answered by giving orders**

to heat the furnace seven times more than it was usually heated.

20 And he commanded certain valiant warriors who *were* in his army to tie up Shadrach, Meshach and Abed-nego, in order to cast *them* into the furnace of blazing fire.

21 Then these men were tied up in their trousers, their coats, their caps and their *other* clothes, and were cast into the midst of the furnace of blazing fire.

22 For this reason, because the king's command *was* urgent and the furnace had been made extremely hot, the flame of the fire slew those men who carried up Shadrach, Meshach and Abed-nego.

23 But these three men, Shadrach, Meshach and Abed-nego, fell into the midst of the furnace of blazing fire *still* tied up.

24 Then Nebuchadnezzar the king was astounded and stood up in haste; he responded and said to his high officials, "Was it not three men we cast bound into the midst of the fire?" They answered and said to the king, "Certainly, O king."

25 He answered and said, "Look! I see four men loosed *and* walking *about* in the midst of the fire without harm, and the appearance of the fourth is like a son of *the* gods!"

26 Then Nebuchadnezzar came near to the door of the furnace of blazing fire; he responded and said, "Shadrach, Meshach and Abed-nego, come out, you servants of the Most High God, and come here!" Then Shadrach, Meshach and Abed-nego came out of the midst of the fire.

27 And the satraps, the prefects, the governors and the king's high officials gathered around *and* saw in regard to these men that the fire had no effect on the bodies of these men nor was the hair of their head singed, nor were their trousers damaged, nor had the smell of fire *even* come upon them.

28 Nebuchadnezzar responded and said, "Blessed be the God of Shadrach, Meshach and Abed-nego, who has sent His angel and delivered His servants who put their trust in Him, violating the king's command, and yielded up their bodies so as not to serve or worship any god except their own God.

29 "Therefore, I make a decree that any people, nation or tongue that speaks anything offensive against the God of Shadrach, Meshach and Abed-nego shall be torn limb from limb and their houses reduced to a rubbish heap, inasmuch as there is no other god who is able to deliver in this way."

—Daniel 3

Here we see Shadrach, Meshach and Abed-nego bound by ropes and thrown into a furnace so hot that the men who threw them in were killed. Yet in the midst of the fire, there was one like the son of God (Jesus). When they came out of the blazing furnace, their hair and clothes did not even smell like smoke, yet the ropes that had bound them had been burnt off! The fire that is coming upon the earth is going to destroy many, but set free those who are the true bondslaves of God, and they will have His divine protection, as well as His divine power.

Also in the book of Daniel, we find the story of Daniel being cast into a pit full of hungry lions:

16 Then the king gave orders, and Daniel was brought in and cast into the lions' den. The king spoke and said to Daniel, "Your God whom you constantly serve will Himself deliver you."

17 And a stone was brought and laid over the mouth of the den; and the king sealed it with his own signet ring and with the signet rings of his nobles, so that nothing might be changed in regard to Daniel.

18 Then the king went off to his palace and spent the night fasting, and no entertainment was brought before him; and his sleep fled from him.

19 Then the king arose with the dawn, at the break of day, and went in haste to the lions' den.

20 And when he had come near the den to Daniel, he cried out with a troubled voice. The king spoke and said to Daniel, "Daniel, servant of the living God, has your God, whom you constantly serve, been able to deliver you from the lions?"

21 Then Daniel spoke to the king, "O king, live forever!

22 "My God sent His angel and shut the lions' mouths, and they have not harmed me, inasmuch as I was found innocent before Him; and also toward you, O king, I have committed no crime."

23 Then the king was very pleased and gave orders for Daniel to be taken up out of the den. So Daniel was taken up out of the den, and no injury whatever was found on him, because he had trusted in his God.

24 The king then gave orders, and they brought those men who had maliciously accused Daniel, and they cast them, their children, and their wives into the lions' den; and they had not reached the bottom of the den before the lions overpowered them and crushed all their bones.

25 Then Darius the king wrote to all the peoples, nations, and *men of every* language who were living in all the land: "May your peace abound!

26 "I make a decree that in all the dominion of my kingdom men are to fear and tremble before the God of Daniel;

> **For He is the living God and enduring forever,**
> **And His kingdom is one which will not be destroyed.**
> **And His dominion *will be* forever.**

27 "He delivers and rescues and performs signs and wonders
In heaven and on earth,
Who has *also* delivered Daniel from the power of the lions."

—Daniel 6

Here we see the supernatural power of God protecting Daniel from the lions. Again, the result was that God got the glory.

As we saw in an earlier chapter, the book of Revelation tells us that God is going to seal His bond-slaves on their foreheads:

2 And I saw another angel ascending from the rising of the sun, having the seal of the living God; and he cried out with a loud voice to the four angels to whom it was granted to harm the earth and the sea,

3 saying, "Do not harm the earth or the sea or the trees, until we have sealed the bond-servants of our God on their foreheads."

—Revelation 7

The reason that God will have the angel seal His bondslaves on their forehead with the seal of the living God is for their protection, as we see two chapters later:

2 And he opened the bottomless pit; and smoke went up out of the pit, like the smoke of a great furnace; and the sun and the air were darkened by the smoke of the pit.

3 And out of the smoke came forth locusts upon the earth; and power was given them, as the scorpions of the earth have power.

4 And they were told that they should not hurt the grass of the earth, nor any green thing, nor any tree, but only the men who do not have the seal of God on their foreheads.

5 And they were not permitted to kill anyone, but to torment for five months; and their torment was like the torment of a scorpion when it stings a man.

6 And in those days men will seek death and will not find it; and they will long to die and death flees from them.

—Revelation 9

The locusts described in this passage will be able to swarm all over a man and sting him like scorpions sting. They will be able to torment for five months and men will be in such agony that they will want to die. However, we are told in verse 4 that the bondslaves of God, who have the seal of God on their foreheads, cannot be touched by this plague. Isn't that exciting? Once more God is going to provide protection by His supernatural power.

Of course, we are not protected by anything other than the power of God:

5 who are protected by the power of God through faith for a salvation ready to be revealed in the last time.

—1 Peter 1

There are many other examples in the Scriptures of God's divine protection, as well as innumerable ones from history. For example, back in the days of the Inquisition, a young man who firmly stood up for Jesus Christ was tied to a stake, and fire was set under his feet. The flames rose up, then separated and went around him and formed an archway over his head. This kept going on, and it looked as if he was ***not*** going to be burned to death. Finally, one of the inquisitors took a spear and rammed it through him to kill him.

Many have read books concerning the persecution of Christians in the Soviet Union. The following is one incident that stands out in my mind. A Christian man, Ivan Moiseyev, was later imprisoned for his faith, where he came under severe persecution by the prison officials. Prior to that, while he was still in the army, he was required to stand outside all night, in a summer uniform at 25 degrees below zero Centigrade (equivalent to minus 13 degrees Fahrenheit). This was intended by his superiors as a severe punishment to persuade him to stop talking about God. However, the power of God flowed around him, clothed him and kept him warm all night long! Isn't it great that God's power can protect us in every way? This story is recorded in the book entitled *Vanya* by Myrna Grant:

> When Gidenko spoke, it was wearily. "I am sorry, Moiseyev, that you persist in your irregular behavior. It will achieve nothing for you except discomfort. However, I feel you will come to your senses with a little discipline and be cured of your delusions of angels and talking gods. I am going to order you to stand in the street tonight after taps are played until you are willing to come to me and apologize for the nonsense you have been circulating around the base about yourself and your so-called experiences with God. Since the temperature is likely to be some twenty-five degrees below zero, for your sake, I hope you quickly agree to behave sensibly. Tomorrow we shall make a plan together for your political reeducation. You are dismissed."
>
> Gidenko was unaccountably irritated by the courage with which Moiseyev seemed to take the order. He had expected a hesitation, a reconsidering, but Moiseyev's face was quiet and his shoulders squared as he walked the correct pace to the door.
>
> "Comrade private!"
>
> Ivan turned. Gidenko observed he was a trifle pale. He *had* understood the order, then.

"You will obey my instructions in summer uniform. That is all."

The aging corporal in the quartermaster corps was incredulous at Ivan's requisition for the issue of a summer uniform. Was not the snow already two feet in the fields? . . .

A brusque telephone verification from the Polit-Ruk sped the light trousers, shirt, jacket, and side cap into Ivan's hands. The corporal was silent, handing the articles to Ivan with a grave shaking of his white head. Ivan could almost hear the labored thoughts behind the sympathetic eyes. It was to be a bitter night.

A wind came up as the moon rose, lifting powdery snow from the corners of the buildings and swirling it across the well-swept streets. It was already cold in the barracks as the soldiers undressed for the night, huddling in their bunks under the heavy blankets for warmth. . . .

Ivan was getting tired of telling his story. The news of this new punishment had spread like wildfire through the mess hall at supper. The private assigned to ladeling the soup at his table had heard the account from the quartermaster corporal, and he distributed the news with every bowl of borscht. Ivan had been questioned or admonished at least a dozen times as he made his way out of the hall after supper.

And his answer sounded absurd. "At taps I am to report to the duty officer and stand outside in the street." He didn't blame the men for smiling. If the Polit-Ruk wanted to make a public example of Ivan, they were succeeding. Now, the men listening to Ivan and Igor jumped into the conversation. "How long are you going to stay out in the cold?" "You will have to give in. You will die of the cold." "Why do you refuse to be quiet about religion?" "Why can you not believe and be silent?" "You will be inside after five minutes."

Igor raised his voice above the others, quieting them. "Ivan! Why? What is it that you believe, that you would do this?"

"I believe God wants men to know that He exists, and loves man, and came in the form of Jesus Christ, as a real man, to this earth. It is almost Christmas. At this time we believers celebrate the coming of Christ to Bethlehem as a baby. All over the world, believers observe this great thing that God did and give glory to God. I believe He came to die for the sin of every man who wants forgiveness. For me. For you too, Igor." . . .

. . . In the distance the soft notes of a bugle could be heard. The light was immediately switched off. Hurrying, Ivan made his way to the door. From the window the brilliant moon lit the aisle between the bunks as he passed. There was silence behind him as he made his way down the stairs and to the street outside.

At first the cold was a shock slamming into his face with an impact that left his head aching and his eyes full of water. He recoiled from the icy wind that burned at his ears. He knew faces at the darkened barracks windows would be peering into the street. The moon lit the road and the snowbanks against the buildings. He stiffened against the freezing blast, glancing at his watch. It was one minute after ten o'clock.

He would have a long time to pray. He began haltingly, a slow fear rising in him that he tried to push away. How long *could* he stand out here? What if he became so cold he gave in? What if he froze to death? Would they let him freeze to death? He tried to concentrate on praying, but a panic constricted his chest. How long would it take to freeze to death? Would it be quick? What if he were *almost* frozen by morning but revived? He had heard the pain of frozen limbs was terrible. What if they had to amputate? He had to get his mind off it. He began to sing. "The joy of the Lord is your strength. The joy of the Lord is your strength."

Suddenly the glory of the morning revisited him. He looked at the park in the central square, distant in the moonlight but visible. An angelic light seemed to linger upon it. "Do not be afraid. I am with you!" The angel's words! They had been for tonight! Even the warmth of those moments seemed to resettle upon him. Fervently Ivan opened his mouth and softly began to pray.

It was twelve-thirty when his attention was distracted by the crunching of steps in the snow. Bundled in their greatcoats, three officers slowly were making their way toward him from the barrack.

Their voices were gruff and almost blown away by the wind.

"Well, Moiseyev, have you reconsidered? Are you ready to come in? Have you had enough of standing out here?"

Even in the moonlight Ivan could see that they were looking at him with a measure of apprehension. Was it possible that he was warm?

"Thank you, comrade officers. I would like very much to come in and go to bed. But I cannot agree to remain silent about God."

"Then you're going to stand out here all night long?" Each of their faces was twinged with fear.

"I'd rather not. But I don't see how anything else is possible, and God is helping me." Ivan was rubbing his hands with his fingertips as he stood at attention. Excitement shook his voice. His hands were cold, but no colder than they had been while dressing in the barracks. He tentatively wiggled his toes. They moved easily, without discomfort. A feeling of astonishment grew in him. He looked at the officers in excitement. He could see that even in their coats they were cold. They were stamping their feet and slapping their hands, shifting their weight, impatient to return to their heater in the barracks. He would feel differently in another hour, the senior officer mumbled as they wheeled away. Ivan couldn't resist a wondering laugh.

Soon the surge of relief subsided and a feeling of brokenness took its place. He was not better than any of the young people in his congregation at home. His parents had suffered in difficult situations for years. He knew of pastors who had been questioned, arrested, even sent to prison camps. Yet he was touched again and again by God's direct power and deliverance. Something in him pulled away from such magnificent singling out. He didn't want to be special, he didn't deserve miracles and mysteries. He *ought* to be freezing. He wasn't good enough. Hot tears rimmed his eyes.

By three o'clock in the morning he was dozing on his feet. His prayers of repentance were long over. His intercessions for all the believers he knew he had made over and over. He had sung Christmas carols. He had prayed for every officer he knew and knew of. He had cried out to God on behalf of the men in his unit. But gradually his mind seemed to be floating somewhere outside of his head. As much as he tried to command prayer, it eluded him.

Suddenly a voice in his ear startled him fully awake. The senior officer on duty was speaking gently.

"All right, Moiseyev, you are to come inside." The moon had set and the wind died down, and in the pitch-black, Ivan strained to see his face. The officer hesitated, standing still beside Ivan, the yellow light from the barracks caught in the gold oak-leaf insignia of his hat. His voice was intense. "What kind of person are you?"

"Sir?"

"What kind of person are you that the cold does not bother you?"

Ivan also spoke softly. "Oh, comrade, I am a person just like you. But I prayed to God and was warm."

> The officer turned and began walking very slowly back to the barracks, touching Ivan's arm as a signal to accompany him. "Tell me about this God," he said.
>
> —Creation House, pp. 54-59

Is that not a marvelous testimony of how God's power took care of Ivan? Another example of God's miraculous intervention is Nora Lam, a beautiful Chinese lady who was also protected by the divine power of God welling up within her. As a Christian dedicated to Jesus Christ, she stood before a firing squad in a Chinese prison. They fired, and because of God's power, *every single bullet missed her.*

We will all need God's supernatural power to protect us during times of persecution.

POWER FOR STRENGTH

Because of God's providence, not all Christians will be spared; some indeed will be martyred. God's power can give us the strength to sing as we "go to the lions," just as the first century Christians did. Rather than screaming with fear, by His power, we can face such a trial praising Jesus Christ.

I would like to share with you a few of the many stories wherein God gave strength to Christians to praise Him during persecution and even death. I could paraphrase these, but I think it would be better to let you read them from the source. These were taken from *Foxe's Book of Martyrs,* published in 1968. In a portion wherein the author is describing the eighth persecution under the Roman Empire, we read this touching account:

> Laurentius, generally called St. Laurence, the principal of the deacons, who taught and preached under Sextus, Bishop of Rome, followed him to the place of

execution; when Sextus predicted that he should meet him in heaven three days after. Laurentius considered this as a certain indication of his own approaching martyrdom, at his return collected all the Christian poor, and distributed amongst them the treasures of the Church which had been committed to his care. His conduct alarmed the persecutors, who seized on him, and commanded him to give an immediate account to the emperor of the Church treasures.

Laurentius promised to satisfy them. Then with great diligence he collected together a great number of aged, helpless, and impotent poor, and repaired to the magistrate, presenting them to him saying, "These are the true treasures of the Church."

Fancying the matter meant in ridicule, the governor ordered him to be immediately scourged. He was beaten with iron rods, set upon a wooden horse, and had his limbs dislocated. He endured these tortures with such fortitude and perseverance, that he was ordered to be fastened to a large gridiron, with a slow fire under it, that his death might be more tedious. But his astonishing constancy during these trials, and his serenity of countenance under such excruciating torments, gave the spectators so exalted an idea of the dignity and truth of the Christian religion, that many immediately became converts.

Having lain for some time upon the gridiron, the martyr cheerfully lifted up his eyes to heaven, and with calmness yielded his spirit to the Almighty. This happened August 10, A.D. 258.

—Fleming H. Revell Company, p. 23

What a joy to be able to die in the peace of Jesus, even in such circumstances! There is the story of a father and son who died with this peace which I feel I should share with you. This happened in 1556, and it is also recorded in *Foxe's Book of Martyrs*:

While they were thus examined, each of them made an open confession of their faith, and, not long after, were put to the torture, to make them reveal who frequented their house. Four or five days after they were convened again before their judges, and after many words passed, they asked them whether they would submit themselves to the will of the magistrates. Robert Oguier and Baudicon his son, with some deliberation, said, "Yea, we will."

Then demanding the same of Martin, the younger brother, he answered that he would not submit himself thereto, but would accompany his mother; so he was sent back again to prison, whilst the father and the son were sentenced to be burnt to ashes. One of the judges, in pronouncing sentence, spoke as if he were transported with fury in beholding the great patience of these two servants of Christ. Having received the sentence of death, they returned to the prison joyful that the Lord conferred on them the honour of enrolling them in the number of his martyrs. They no sooner entered the prison than a band of friars came; one amongst the rest told them the hour was come when they must die. Robert Oguier and his son answered, "We know it well; but blessed be the Lord our God, and now, delivering our bodies out of this vile prison, will receive our souls into His glorious and heavenly kingdom."

One of the friars endeavoured to turn them from their faith, saying,"Father Robert, thou art an old man; let me entreat thee in this thy last hour, to think of saving thine own soul; and if thou wilt give ear unto me, I warrant thee thou shalt do well."

The old man answered, "Poor man! how darest thou attribute that to thyself which belongs to the eternal God, and so rob him of his honour? For it seems by thy speech, that if I will hearken to thee, thou wilt become my saviour. No, no; I have only one Saviour, Jesus Christ, who by-and-by will deliver me from this miserable world. I have one teacher whom the heavenly Father hath commanded me to hear, and I purpose to hearken to none other."

Another exhorting him to take pity on his soul, "Thou willest me (said Robert) to pity mine own soul; dost thou not see what pity I have on it, when, for the name of Christ, I willingly abandon this body of mine to the fire, hoping today to be with him in paradise? I have put all my confidence in God, and my hope is wholly fixed upon the merits of Christ, his death and passion; he will direct me the right way to his kingdom. I believe what the holy prophets and apostles have written, and in that faith will I live and die." The friar, hearing this, said, "Out, dog! thou are not worthy the name of a Christian; thou, and thy son with thee, are both resolved to perish."

As they were about to separate Baudicon from his father, he said, "Let my father alone, and trouble him not thus: he is an old man, and hath an infirm body; hinder him not, I pray you, from receiving the crown of martyrdom."

When at the place of execution, the son pulled a cross of wood out of his father's hands, saying, "What cause hath the people to be offended at us for not receiving a Jesus Christ of wood? We bear upon our hearts the cross of Christ, the Son of the ever-living God, feeling his holy word written therein in letters of gold."

A band of soldiers attended them to execution, just as if it had been a prince who was being conducted into his kingdom. Baudicon was then dragged to the stake, where he began to sing the 16th Psalm. The friar cried out, "Do you not hear, my masters, what wicked errors these heretics sing to beguile the people with?" Baudicon, hearing him, replied, "How, simple idiot, callest thou the psalms of the prophet David errors?" Then, turning his eyes towards his father, who was about to be chained to the stake, he said, "Be of good courage,

> father; the worst will be past by-and-by." Then he often reiterated these short breathings: "O God, Father everlasting, accept the sacrifice of our bodies, for thy well-beloved Son Jesus Christ's sake." And thus, during these conflicts, Baudicon bent his eyes to heaven, and, speaking to his father, said, "Behold, I see the heavens open, and millions of bright angels ready to receive us, rejoicing to see us thus witnessing the truth in the view of the world. Father, let us be glad and rejoice, for the joys of heaven are opened unto us." Fire was forthwith put to the straw and wood. In the end, the fire growing hot, the last words they were heard to pronounce were, "Jesus Christ, thou Son of God, into they hands we commend our spirits." And thus they fell asleep in the Lord.
>
> —pp. 88-89

Another story in this same book tells of how the power of God gave John Huss strength. He was an author and a dedicated Christian, who was labeled a heretic and was burned at the stake. This is what happened in the year 1380:

> Shortly after the petition was presented, four bishops and two lords were sent by the emperor to the prison, in order to prevail on Huss to recant. But he called God to witness, with tears in his eyes, that he was not conscious of having preached or written anything against the truth of God, or the faith of his orthodox Church.
>
> On the 4th of July he was, for the last time, brought before the council. After a long examination he was commanded to abjure, which, without hesitation, he refused to do. The council censured him for being obstinate and incorrigible, and ordained that he should be degraded from the priesthood, his books publicly burnt, and himself delivered to the secular power.

He received the sentence without the least emotion; and at the close of it kneeled down, and lifting his eyes towards heaven, exclaimed, with the magnanimity of a primitive martyr, "May thy infinite mercy, O my God! pardon this injustice of mine enemies. Thou knowest the injustice of my accusations: how deformed with crimes I have been represented; how I have been oppressed with worthless witnesses, and a false condemnation; yet, O my God! let that mercy of thine, which no tongue can express, prevail with thee not to avenge my wrongs."

A serenity appeared in his looks, which indicated that his soul was approaching the realms of everlasting happiness; and when the bishop urged him to recant, he turned to the people and addressed them thus:—

"These lords and bishops do counsel me that I should confess before you all that I have erred; which thing, if it might be done with the infamy and reproach of man only, they might, peradventure, easily persuade me to do; but now I am in the sight of the Lord my God, without whose great displeasure I could not do that which they require. For I well know that I never taught any of those things which they have falsely alleged against me, but I have always preached, taught, written, and thought contrary thereunto."

The bishops then delivered him to the emperor, who handed him over to the Duke of Bavaria. His books were burnt at the gates of the church; and on the 6th of July he was led to the suburbs of Constance to be burnt alive.

Having reached the place of execution, he fell on his knees, sung several portions of the Psalms, and looked steadfastly towards heaven, saying, "Into thy hands, O Lord! do I commit my spirit: thou has redeemed me, O most good and faithful God."

As soon as the faggots were lighted, the martyr sung a hymn, with so cheerful a voice, that he was heard above the cracklings of the fire and the noise of the multitude. At length his voice was interrupted by the flames, which soon put an end to his existence.

—pp 101-102

What a glorious way to die—praising God!

Reading *Foxe's Book of Martyrs* in its entirety will give you courage as you see how Christians endured persecution through the years. Even if they were to be martyred, God gave them the strength to face death with a song in their hearts. It is the supernatural power of God that enables you to do this to God's glory.

POWER TO REMAIN SILENT

If as a Christian, you are imprisoned and forced to endure interrogation, one of the things the Lord can do is to give you the power to remain silent. Whether it is interrogation like in the Inquisition, or by Communists, deprogrammers, or any other type of authority, God can certainly empower you in this manner. This was a primary thing that the power of God enabled Jesus to do when He was facing persecution to the point of death on a cross:

> **32 Now the passage of Scripture which he was reading was this:**
> **"HE WAS LED AS A SHEEP TO SLAUGHTER;**
> **AND AS A LAMB BEFORE ITS SHEARER IS SILENT,**
> **SO HE DOES NOT OPEN HIS MOUTH.**
> **33 "IN HUMILIATION HIS JUDGMENT WAS TAKEN AWAY;**
> **WHO SHALL RELATE HIS GENERATION?**
> **FOR HIS LIFE IS REMOVED FROM THE EARTH."**

34 And the eunuch answered Philip and said, "Please *tell me,* of whom does the prophet say this? Of himself, or of someone else?"
35 And Philip opened his mouth, and beginning from this Scripture he preached Jesus to him.

—Acts 8

We see this Spirit-directed silence a number of times in the Scriptures. For example, when Christ was before Herod, here is what happened:

8 Now Herod was very glad when he saw Jesus; for he had wanted to see Him for a long time, because he had been hearing about Him and was hoping to see some sign performed by Him.
9 And he questioned Him at some length; but He answered him nothing.
10 And the chief priests and the scribes were standing there, accusing Him vehemently.
11 And Herod with his soldiers, after treating Him with contempt and mocking Him, dressed Him in a gorgeous robe and sent Him back to Pilate.

—Luke 23

As we can see in the preceding verses, in spite of vehement accusations, mocking and being treated with contempt, Jesus answered nothing. He did not even attempt to defend Himself. The same thing was true when Christ was before Pilate. Here is what happened:

1 And early in the morning the chief priests with the elders and scribes, and the whole Council, immediately held a consultation; and binding Jesus, they led Him away, and delivered Him up to Pilate.
2 And Pilate questioned Him, "Are You the King of the Jews?" And answering He said to him, "*It is as* you say."

3 And the chief priests *began* to accuse Him harshly.

4 And Pilate was questioning Him again, saying, "Do You make no answer? See how many charges they bring against You!"

5 But Jesus made no further answer; so that Pilate was amazed.

—Mark 15

Jesus did the same when He went before the high priest:

59 Now the chief priests and the whole Council kept trying to obtain false testimony against Jesus, in order that they might put Him to death;

60 and they did not find *any*, even though many false witnesses came forward. But later on two came forward,

61 and said, "This man stated, 'I am able to destroy the temple of God and to rebuild it in three days.'"

62 And the high priest stood up and said to Him, "Do You make no answer? What is it that these men are testifying against You?"

63 But Jesus kept silent. And the high priest said to Him, "I adjure You by the living God, that You tell us whether You are the Christ, the Son of God."

—Matthew 26

There may be times when the Holy Spirit wants you to be silent or to give minimal information, like Jesus did. It will take the supernatural power of God to enable you to do this. It may be that if you were interrogated by the Communists, some governmental authority or deprogrammers, the Lord would lead you to be silent or to give a minimal amount of information.

Most Christians are not aware of the many cases of real persecution that are going on here in America.

There have been many Christian young people kidnapped from Christian farms and communes in order to be deprogrammed. There is a book written about a Jewish young man who had become a Christian. His orthodox Jewish parents tried everything they could do to get him to renounce Jesus Christ and Christianity. He would not. Just before his wedding rehearsal, they had him kidnapped by deprogrammers who attempted to get him to renounce Jesus Christ. The name of this book is *Kidnapped For My Faith,* by Ken Levitt with Ceil Rosen. These deprogrammers try to cause these young people to renounce Christ, they attempt to discredit the elders of the church or group to which they belong, and their goal is to return them to their "normal family." Their tactics are exactly the same techniques that the Communist brainwashers use. I spoke at a conference once at which the following situation ensued: A father was threatening all sorts of things to have his daughter returned home. He was not a Christian and was afraid that she might have been entrapped by a "cult." This conference was held in a Christian community and was with a very solid and good Christian organization. I wrote a letter to the girl's father on her behalf and it took care of the situation. However, in a different situation, he too could have had her kidnapped by deprogrammers and attempted to break her faith.

A question that I have for all of you with a position of responsibility in a church or a Christian body is this: *Are your young people prepared to cope with the brainwashing techniques of deprogrammers? It could happen to them. You have a spiritual responsibility to be sure that they know what to do in the event that something like that did happen to one of them.*

If you were to become a "Prisoner Of the Spiritual War" (POSW), in many ways you might need to behave like military personnel are trained to do in the event that one of them becomes a POW.

A POW is instructed to give only his name, rank and serial number. Anything else that he gives to his captors helps them; they can use his own words to break him. The same thing is true for a POSW, except in this case, if the Lord so leads, you would give only your name, when you became a Christian, and that you love Jesus with all your heart. If I were in such a situation, they might ask me a question such as this: "Do you believe the Bible has any inconsistencies?" I would say, "My name is James McKeever, I received Christ as my Savior on May 22, 1952, and I love Him with all my heart." ***PERIOD***. They might then ask me if I believed Christ was the only way to heaven. My answer would be, "My name is James McKeever, I received Christ as my Savior on May 22nd, 1952, and I love Him with all my heart."

Do not give the deprogrammers any additional information. It will be used against you to help break you. In general, Christians today are so naive and so used to casting their pearls before swine. In most cases, they really do not have the spiritual discernment necessary for a situation like this. These deprogrammers might say this: "Tell me what you believe about Jesus." Most Christians would think that this was a wonderful chance to witness and would dump the whole load on them. Deprogrammers have been trained to use such beliefs to question, probe and tear apart a person's faith. Witnessing in such an instance would be casting your pearls before swine.

Deprogrammers also frequently use the "good guy and bad guy" approach. One of the interrogators is a harsh, tough, rough individual. After he gets through with you, they take you to another room where a "good guy" offers you tea or coffee and a sympathetic ear, and talks about how mean and bad Mr. X was. Frequently a POW or a POSW will then gush out all the information to the "good guy" that he stubbornly refused to give to the "bad guy." This is especially true if they want to know about your relatives or family. *Do not tell them anything about anyone you love.*

There are many examples, such as when the Chinese Communists took over mainland China and they captured Christians, wherein information found out about families has been used against those being interrogated. One man was told that his wife had been killed by the personnel at the American Embassy. This just about destroyed this particular Christian man. He almost had heart failure. Much later, when he was released, he found his wife alive and well. Interrogators will lie, they will twist, they will play on your emotions. They want to know about your family, so that they know where to stick in the emotional knife. Only give them your name, when you become a Christian and that you love Jesus Christ with all your heart—***nothing else!***

INTERROGATIONS

One of the favorite tactics of both the Communists and the deprogrammers is long, long interrogations, while depriving the "captive" of sleep, food and sometimes even bathroom facilities. There are frequently at least three interrogators who work on 8-hour shifts. Thus, they come in fresh and you are tired. They can keep you up 24 hours a day. They have patience; they are in no hurry. They know that the average person will crack sooner or later.

In looking at all of this questioning, there are three very significant things to remember. The first one is to never, ***never***—under any circumstances—deny Jesus Christ as your Savior and the Son of God. One Chinese Christian bishop, in undergoing such interrogation, finally thought to himself, "If I just deny Christ in front of this interrogator and they let me go, then I can live rather than being killed and I could do much productive work for Christ." He did deny Christ and was released. However, about twenty years later as he was dying, he cried out encouraging people never to deny Christ, because he lived in total spiritual blackness ever since his release from prison. The Spirit of God in no way allowed him to be used of God. He felt that it would have been far better to have died in prison than to have agonized for twenty years in this horrible spiritual vacuum.

The second thing to remember is never to tell a lie; always tell the truth. Remember that all lies are generated from Satan. In John, we read this:

> **44 "You are of *your* father the devil, and you want to do the desires of your father. He was a murderer from the beginning, and does not stand in the truth, because there is no truth in him. Whenever he speaks a lie, he speaks from his own *nature*; for he is a liar, and the father of lies. . . ."**
>
> **—John 8**

Particularly if people are arrested for distributing Bibles, such as in the U.S.S.R., the captors will normally separate these individuals into different rooms and leave them alone, frequently in the cold and dark, for hours and hours. Then they will bring them out one by one and interrogate them. If some or all of them lie about part of their trip or activities, then the Communists have a case against the whole group. Frequently, their hotel rooms have been searched and they may have been under surveillance, so the Communists may well know what the activities have been anyhow. Lying does not ever bring glory to the Lord.

However, I must hasten to add that there is a vast difference between ***honesty*** and ***openness.*** Christ was always honest (He told the truth), yet He did not always say everything that was on His heart and mind. He was not always "open," as is pointed out in the following verses:

> **24 But Jesus, on His part, was not entrusting Himself to them, for He knew all men,**
> **25 and because He did not need any one to bear witness concerning man for He Himself knew what was in man.**
>
> **—John 2**

The difference between honesty and openness was a difficult lesson for my wife, Jeani, to learn. She has a tendency to be completely honest and open when asked any question. (This can be another form of casting our pearls before swine.) We must have discernment as to ***when*** to be open, and to what degree.

To answer a question in this manner: "I decline to answer that," "That is something I choose not to reveal" or "That is my private affair" is giving a truthful answer, but not an open answer. It is possible that this is a type of response that the Lord would have you to give if you are ever in an interrogation situation. You should not lie, but you can choose either to remain silent or to give one of the above-type of answers that is honest, though not open. Christians who feel they must "tell all" in answer to interrogation questions could well endanger the lives of their fellow Christians and family.

If the Communists were to come into control of America, an intelligent interrogator could point out to a Christian that there were now new "laws of the land" and that a Christian was commanded to obey the laws of the land; since the law of the land says that they must give this information, they would be going against God if they did not disclose all. This type of logic would possibly trip up some Christians, again because of a lack of proper teaching.

Most Christians do not realize that it is frequently impossible to obey all of the commands in the Bible. One must, under the guidance of the Holy Spirit, give priorities to the various commands. For example, in the early days of Christianity, the Roman law—which was then "the law of the land"—was that you should worship only Caesar, and renounce all other gods. Christians were also admonished strongly never to renounce Jesus Christ. To obey both would be impossible. Therefore, the early Christians, many of whom were martyred in the Roman Colosseum, faced a priority decision of whether or not to keep the command of obeying the law of the land.

Another example of this priority decision is that a wife is told to be submissive to her husband. The Christian woman is also commanded in the Bible not to steal. What if a non-Christian husband told his Christian wife to steal? She could not keep the commandment to be submissive to her husband *and* the commandment not to steal. She would have to make a priority choice of which one was the most important to obey. Most non-Christians would not tell their Christian wives to steal, but they could well tell them to not go to church. Since the Bible tells us not to forsake the assembling of ourselves together, again the wife would have to make a choice as to what the priority sequence should be between being submissive to her husband and obeying the command not to forsake the assembling of ourselves together.

We could continue with many such examples. I wish there were more teaching that would give Christians guidance in making these priority judgments. The bottom line is that one must seek the Holy Spirit's guidance as to which is the highest priority command any time there is a conflict. Do not feel guilty about breaking those that the Holy Spirit tells you are of a lower priority. Guilt is a form of self-accusation and, remember, Satan is the great *accuser of Christians.*

Back to our interrogation situation: If the interrogator uses this "obey the new laws of the land" tactic on a Christian, the Christian should be aware of what is happening. In many cases, it will be necessary to make a priority decision, as did the Christians of the first two centuries, to stand true to Christ and to brothers in Christ, and to let obeying the law of the land be a lower priority. We do not want to tell a lie, but we do not have to be open in answering questions of an interrogator.

If we feel that the Lord is leading us not to answer questions, we may have to suffer the consequences. This may mean prison, removal of privileges, or even death. If it does mean these things, the power of God can come upon us and give us the strength to endure them. The Holy Spirit can give us guidance and comfort. All that we need is found in God through the Lord Jesus Christ.

POWER TO SPEAK THE WORDS THAT GOD WOULD HAVE YOU TO SPEAK

In a time of persecution, the Holy Spirit may lead you to be silent or He may lead you to speak out boldly for Jesus Christ. If you speak out boldly, you will need the power of God behind your message. God promises that on such an occasion, He will give you the words:

> **12 "But before all these things, they will lay their hands on you and will persecute you, delivering you to the synagogues and prisons, bringing you before kings and governors for My name's sake.**
>
> **13 "It will lead to an opportunity for your testimony.**

> **14 "So make up your minds not to prepare beforehand to defend yourselves;**
>
> **15 for I will give you utterance and wisdom which none of your opponents will be able to resist or refute. . . ."**
>
> **—Luke 21**

POWER FOR PRAISE DURING PERSECUTION

You are likely familiar with the instance when Paul was in a prison in Philippi. We read this passage once in an earlier chapter, but it bears repeating here. After having been arrested and beaten, Paul was in what was probably a smelly cell, possibly with rats crawling over his feet. There with his feet and hands in stocks, he and Silas were praising God at midnight:

> **23 And when they had inflicted many blows upon them, they threw them into prison, commanding the jailer to guard them securely;**
>
> **24 and he, having received such a command, threw them into the inner prison, and fastened their feet in the stocks.**
>
> **25 But about midnight Paul and Silas were praying and singing hymns of praise to God, and the prisoners were listening to them;**
>
> **26 and suddenly there came a great earthquake, so that the foundations of the prison house were shaken; and immediately all the doors were opened, and everyone's chains were unfastened.**
>
> **27 And when the jailer had been roused out of sleep and had seen the prison doors opened, he drew his sword and was about to kill himself, supposing that the prisoners had escaped.**
>
> **28 But Paul cried out with a loud voice, saying, "Do yourself no harm, for we are all here!"**

29 And he called for lights and rushed in and, trembling with fear, he fell down before Paul and Silas,
30 and after he brought them out, he said, "Sirs, what must I do to be saved?"
31 And they said, "Believe in the Lord Jesus, and you shall be saved, you and your household."

—Acts 16

In verse 25, we see that Paul and Silas were singing hymns of praise to God at midnight. After having been beaten and cast into horrible confinement in a torturous prison, do you think that it took supernatural power for Paul and Silas to be singing and praising God? I believe that it did indeed. The jailer was so impressed when he saw them free that he fell on his knees and asked what he needed to do to be saved. This is evangelism with the power of God in demonstration. God's miraculous power provided the strength to praise in the midst of a time of persecution. Without His supernatural power, Christians will be unable to praise during a very dark hour, such as that which Paul and Silas experienced.

A similar thing occurred with the early Christians in the Colosseum at Rome. They were led out to a very terrible death at the mouths of lions, tigers or gladiators, yet the supernatural power of God allowed them to sing praises to Jesus as they were being led out to slaughter. One cannot do that in one's own strength. It requires the miraculous power of God working in you to be able to sing His praise during a time like that.

I have heard many Christians say, "I don't know if I have the strength to go through persecution and torture in prison." It's true; you ***don't*** have the strength or power to endure it. However, if you have the supernatural power of God working in you, then you indeed will have all the power necessary for such a trial, with power left over, because God's supernatural power is without limit.

We will need the supernatural power of God working in us to enable us to praise Him in times of extreme distress or persecution. However, I think that other times, praise is itself a powerful offensive weapon or tool that we can engage to our advantage. As we choose to praise God, as an act of faith out of obedience and trust, even though we may not ***feel*** like it, that praise can help usher in a release of the power of God to see us through our difficulty in victory. God inhabits the praises of His people (Psalm 22:3, *KJV*)!

SUPERNATURAL POWER TO LOVE YOUR ENEMIES

Christians today are so oriented towards "peace" that they can easily fall into the trap of thinking that one should not have any enemies. This is certainly not the case, if you look at the Bible.

IT IS OKAY TO HAVE ENEMIES.

David certainly had enemies, in the Philistines and many others. Joshua had enemies, as he conquered the promised land. He fought and killed his enemies. Elijah had enemies; he killed 850 false prophets of Baal and Asherah. Even Jesus Christ had enemies. As you well know, His enemies ultimately killed Him.

It is okay to have enemies. When persecution comes, you will indeed have many enemies. But the Lord tells us that we are to love our enemies and to pray for those who despitefully use us:

> **44 "But I say to you, love your enemies, and pray for those who persecute you**
> **45 in order that you may be sons of your Father who is in heaven; for He causes His sun to rise on *the***

evil and *the* good, and sends rain on *the* righteous and *the* unrighteous.

46 "For if you love those who love you, what reward have you? Do not even the tax-gatherers do the same?

47 "And if you greet your brothers only, what do you do more *than others*? Do not even the Gentiles do the same?

48 "Therefore you are to be perfect, as your heavenly Father is perfect. . . ."

—Matthew 5

These are not my words; these are the words of Jesus Christ. No matter how badly those persecuting you may be treating you or your loved ones, you are to love them—not hate them—and you are to pray for them. If the Lord so leads you, you could let them know that you love them and care for them. Let them know that you are praying that they might know the joy and peace that comes from having Christ as one's Savior. Let them know of your love by words and actions. This will bring glory to the Lord.

In his book *Tortured For Christ* (published by Diane Books, Glendale, CA), Richard Wurmbrand said that after a rough time of physical or emotional persecution or torture, when he was placed back in his cell he would spend time praying and asking the Lord for real love for his persecutors. This seemed to make his ordeal less painful. If the Holy Spirit leads and compels you to witness, then you can witness freely and openly to an interrogator. However, do not do this unless you feel a direct compulsion from the Holy Spirit. If you cast your pearls before swine, the swine will turn upon you and devour you.

I believe that blessing your enemies goes a step beyond just loving your enemies. When you bless them, you are wishing them well, you are wishing them prosperity, you are wishing them good health. A command to bless your enemies is found in Romans:

> **14 Bless those who persecute you; bless and curse not.**
>
> **—Romans 12**

We see the act of blessing one's enemies beautifully portrayed in the death of Stephen:

> **57 But they cried out with a loud voice, and covered their ears, and they rushed upon him with one impulse.**
> **58 And when they had driven him out of the city, they *began* stoning *him*, and the witnesses laid aside their robes at the feet of a young man named Saul.**
> **59 And they went on stoning Stephen as he called upon *the Lord* and said, "Lord Jesus, receive my spirit!"**
> **60 And falling on his knees, he cried out with a loud voice, "Lord, do not hold this sin against them!" And having said this, he fell asleep.**
>
> **—Acts 7**

If some foreign soldier or enemy of yours were to kill your children and your spouse, what would your reaction be? Most of us would want to go for his throat. If they had a gun, many men would probably waste that individual on the spot. However, the Lord tells us that we are to love our enemies and bless them, no matter how badly they persecute and hurt us. Not only does it take the filling of the Holy Spirit, but overflowing with the supernatural power of God in order to love our enemies in cases of severe persecution and possibly even torture.

POWER TO DESTROY YOUR ENEMIES

We have seen that there are times when the Holy Spirit would have you be silent by the power of God, and there are other times when He would guide you to speak boldly by the power of God. Likewise, there are times when the Lord would have you be very non-aggressive towards your enemies, and there are other times when the Holy Spirit might lead you to kill your enemies.

Let us reread a passage we read in Chapter 5, wherein God led Elijah to call down fire from heaven:

> **9 Then *the king* sent to him a captain of fifty with his fifty. And he went up to him, and behold, he was sitting on the top of the hill. And he said to him, "O man of God, the king says, 'Come down.'"**
>
> **10 And Elijah answered and said to the captain of fifty, "If I am a man of God, let fire come down from heaven and consume you and your fifty." Then fire came down from heaven and consumed him and his fifty.**
>
> **11 So he again sent to him another captain of fifty with his fifty. And he answered and said to him, "O man of God, thus says the king, 'Come down quickly.'"**
>
> **12 And Elijah answered and said to them, "If I am a man of God, let fire come down from heaven and consume you and your fifty." Then the fire of God came down from heaven and consumed him and his fifty.**
>
> **13 So he again sent the captain of a third fifty with his fifty. When the third captain of fifty went up, he came and bowed down on his knees before Elijah, and begged him and said to him, "O man of God, please let my life and the lives of these fifty servants of yours be precious in your sight.**
>
> **14 "Behold fire came down from heaven, and consumed the first two captains of fifty with their fifties; but now let my life be precious in your sight."**

15 And the angel of the LORD said to Elijah, "Go down with him; do not be afraid of him." So he arose and went down with him to the king.

—2 Kings 1

As we discussed in Chapter 5, God did not lead Elijah to do the same thing in all three instances. However, he did twice call down fire from heaven to destroy his enemies. We also saw that the same type of thing is going to occur again, in the future:

3 "And I will grant *authority* to my two witnesses, and they will prophesy for twelve hundred and sixty days, clothed in sackcloth."

4 These are the two olive trees and the two lampstands that stand before the Lord of the earth.

5 And if anyone desires to harm them, fire proceeds out of their mouth and devours their enemies; and if anyone would desire to harm them, in this manner he must be killed.

—Revelation 11

As you see, this passage says that the enemies of the two witnesses ***"must"*** be killed in the manner described.

Certainly, most people are familiar with the story of Joshua killing all of the people of Jericho. In addition, he and the Israelites killed many other people in the land of Palestine while they were conquering the promised land. David killed Goliath and tens of thousands of Philistines. There are times when God calls His people to destroy their enemies.

We must be extremely careful always to be in the will of God and under the guidance of the Holy Spirit. However, it is a great comfort to know that, if necessary, the supernatural power of God can indeed destroy our enemies during a time of persecution by bringing fire down from heaven or by some other means.

PROVISION DURING PERSECUTION

Another one of the reasons that we will need the supernatural power of God during persecution is for God's supernatural provision. During persecution, it can be difficult to come by even the fundamental things necessary for life, such as food. In Romania, where there was severe persecution of Christians, there were times when there was no food in the home and the table was set with empty plates. The Christians thanked God by faith for the food that they were going to get, and through supernatural provision (God using various means) food was provided.

There are many instances that we could give of God supernaturally multiplying food. We shared one of the contemporary ones in Chapter 12. If you are ever in a situation like the widow of Elijah's time, who had only a little meal and a little oil, during times of persecution be encouraged to know that God can keep multiplying that food for many months. Let's read of the way God provided for this widowed lady:

> **8 Then the word of the LORD came to him, saying,**
>
> **9 "Arise, go to Zarephath, which belongs to Sidon, and stay there; behold, I have commanded a widow there to provide for you."**
>
> **10 So he arose and went to Zarephath, and when he came to the gate of the city, behold, a widow was there gathering sticks; and he called to her and said, "Please get me a little water in a jar, that I may drink."**
>
> **11 And as she was going to get *it*, he called to her and said, "Please being me a piece of bread in your hand."**

12 But she said, "As the LORD your God lives, I have no bread, only a handful of flour in the bowl and a little oil in the jar; and behold, I am gathering a few sticks that I may go in and prepare for me and my son, that we may eat it and die."

13 Then Elijah said to her, "Do not fear; go, do as you have said, but make me a little bread cake from it first, and bring *it* out to me, and afterward you may make *one* for yourself and for your son.

14 "For thus says the LORD God of Israel, 'The bowl of flour shall not be exhausted, nor shall the jar of oil be empty, until the day that the LORD sends rain on the face of the earth.'"

15 So she went and did according to the word of Elijah, and she and he and her household ate for *many* days.

16 The bowl of flour was not exhausted nor did the jar of oil become empty, according to the word of the LORD which He spoke through Elijah.

—1 Kings 17

Isn't it exciting to know that God can and does multiply food? He can also miraculously provide food, just as He did for the children of Israel during the time that they were in the wilderness. He told them to bring some food with them out of Egypt—He told them to make some preparation. However, when all of the preparation that they had made ran out, God miraculously took over and, by His supernatural power, provided food for the next forty years. However, as soon as they entered the promised land and could eat of the fruit of the land, God's miraculous provision stopped:

12 And the manna ceased on the day after they had eaten some of the produce of the land, so that the sons of Israel no longer had manna, but they ate some of the yield of the land of Canaan during that year.

—Joshua 5

It is wonderful to know that if we have no food to multiply, God's power can take care of that too. In his book *The Gentle Breeze of Jesus,* Mel Tari shares something that happened to one of the gospel teams that went out in the Indonesian revival of this century:

> After a long walk the team finally reached the village, hungry and tired. But they found bad news waiting for them. The village was in the middle of a famine. The pastor with whom the Lord had told them to stay didn't have a bit of food in his whole house.
>
> Of course the pastor wanted them to go someplace else where they could find some food. The most embarrassing thing he could think of was to have his guests stay in his house the three days the meetings lasted without giving them a single bite to eat the whole time. But my brother-in-law stood firm. He was going to obey the Lord by staying with the pastor even if it meant the whole team would have to suffer.
>
> But I believe that my Jesus was watching them from His palace in heaven. It just blessed and thrilled His heart to pieces to see how His children wanted to honor Him and follow His leading no matter what it cost them. They had proved their love for Him. And like someone has said, "The Lord is no man's debtor." So the Lord Jesus decided that He was going to abundantly shower His love and mercy on the team by doing something for them that they had never before experienced in their whole life.
>
> That night after the first meeting was over, the team came home terribly, terribly hungry. Then the Lord Jesus told my brother-in-law to gather the team, the pastor, and his family together for a prayer meeting. As my brother-in-law led out in prayer, a wonderful thing happened. The Lord gave every one of them there the same vision.

Some beautiful angels came down from heaven carrying a table. They spread it with a snowy white tablecloth—the Timorese people had never seen anything so pretty! And then do you know what those angels did? After setting the plates and spoons, they put a beautiful red rose beside each one's place. Jesus even wanted the table to look pretty for them.

And then came the food, bowl after bowl of it: rice, pork, chicken, vegetables, and some tea. When everything was ready, those having the vision saw themselves seated around the table, and they began to eat. Oh, I tell you, it was really a feast! The chefs in heaven had really prepared a masterpiece that time. It was so delicious that some of the people sitting in the room having the vision were actually smacking their lips out loud.

Finally when everyone had enough to eat and was full, my brother-in-law finished his prayer and said amen. (He'd been praying out loud the whole time.) Then everybody looked around at each other with a surprised look on their faces. They weren't hungry anymore. In fact, they were so full they could hardly move.

The Lord gave them this same vision every mealtime until the meetings were over. The food in the vision must have had a lot of vitamins and protein in it, because somehow it gave them enough energy to serve Him happily.

Now why would Jesus do a sweet thing like that? I believe He wanted to draw them all even closer to Himself so that He could just bathe them in His love. He knows that only by living close to His side, right next to His heart, will we ever find contentment and satisfaction in life. Only then will we know the joy and happiness God created us to experience.

—New Leaf Press, pp. 41-43

Like Joseph, Noah or the children of Israel we too need to make whatever preparations God tells us to make for the coming famines and persecutions. However, if we are obedient to Him, I am absolutely convinced that once those preparations run out, God will miraculously multiply the food or even provide food until we can once again provide for ourselves. It is exciting to contemplate that the supernatural power of God will be our sustenance through whatever might come. We Christians are going to need His miraculous power working through us to be able to go through those days.

THE LOVE OF CHRIST

The love of the Lord is even more important than supernatural power. We must love Him with all of our heart, soul, mind and strength, and be conscious of how much He loves us. As you read the following passage, ask yourself this question: Is there any kind of persecution that can separate us from the love of the Lord?

> **35 Who shall separate us from the love of Christ? Shall tribulation, or distress, or persecution, or famine, or nakedness, or peril, or sword?**
>
> **36 Just as it is written,**
>
> **"FOR THY SAKE WE ARE BEING PUT TO DEATH ALL DAY LONG;**
> **WE WERE CONSIDERED AS SHEEP TO BE SLAUGHTERED."**
>
> **37 But in all these things we overwhelmingly conquer through Him who loved us.**
>
> **38 For I am convinced that neither death, nor life, nor angels, nor principalities, nor things present, nor things to come, nor powers,**

39 nor height, nor depth, nor any other created thing, shall be able to separate us from the love of God, which is in Christ Jesus our Lord.

—Romans 8

Isn't that fantastic? In the first century and in the Old Testament times, there were people dying for the Lord, but they were dying wrapped in His love and, in most cases, in His supernatural power.

There are other aspects of persecution that we could consider, such as the power to withstand brainwashing or to flee to the mountains (or wilderness). The main thing to realize, however, is that whatever may happen during a time of persecution, the supernatural power surrounding you and flowing out of you, under the guidance of the Holy Spirit and in the sovereignty of God for the glory of Jesus Christ, will be sufficient for all of your needs.

God's supernatural power is for every Christian.

Chapter 15

HOW YOU CAN HAVE SUPERNATURAL POWER

Actually the title of this chapter is not a very good one, because if you have been filled with the Holy Spirit, you have the power of God. Jesus Christ promised that:

> **8 but you shall receive power when the Holy Spirit has come upon you; and you shall be My witnesses both in Jerusalem, and in all Judea and Samaria, and even to the remotest part of the earth."**
>
> **—Acts 1**

This is not physical power to lift weights or to do pushups. It is not mental power to figure out complicated equations and situations. The power Jesus is talking about here is supernatural power. If you have been filled with the Holy Spirit, you have all of the power that you will ever need. There is no need to ask for more power. The secret is to let the power that is there flow through you to achieve the miracles that God wants to achieve.

I certainly do not claim to have an equation, a "quick fix" or an instant way for you and me to have supernatural power. Most likely the way for each Christian is going to be different. But I do know that

God desires that each believer have this power to use, in the name of Jesus Christ and for His glory, to expand His kingdom.

I must also confess that I am certainly not walking in this perfectly myself. With many of the books that I have written, I felt that I was well on the way to walking out the subject matter that was of a personally challenging nature. However, with this book I feel that I am just in the beginning stages of really utilizing the supernatural power of God that He has given to me.

After writing the first part of this book, I had to fall on my face before God and cry out, *"Oh God, help me to share Your heart and Your mind with the precious people who read this book. Help me to help them, in the best way possible, to come into the place where the full, supernatural, miracle power of God can be theirs, to use for Your glory and the glory of Your Son, Jesus Christ."*

In answer to that prayer, I believe He gave me a few general things that would apply to all of us, and also some specific things. Let's look at the general things first.

IF YOU WANT TO PROCEED

Following is an enumeration of some of the general things you should be doing if you want the supernatural power of God to flow from you out to others:

1. Be filled with the Holy Spirit (a prerequisite)
2. Make a bondslave commitment to God
3. Acknowledge that you are weak
4. Humble yourself (James 4:10)
5. Clean up your power filter
   (get rid of defilements)
6. Turn your time over to God
   (don't be too busy)
7. Let genuine love be your motivation
8. Press toward becoming like Jesus Christ

We will discuss some of these; others we have covered in previous chapters. But first we need to remind ourselves of a couple of things. One is that ***love and compassion are more important than power.*** The emphasis of this book has been on acquiring and utilizing God's supernatural power, for His glory. We have not attempted to balance this teaching with the fruit of the Spirit (gentleness, faithfulness, longsuffering and so on—Galatians 5:22, 23). There are good books available that go into that subject in depth. Nor have we tried to balance this message about power with detailed discussion of the sovereignty of God, yet this too is a very vital element in the life of a Spirit-filled Christian seeking to be a channel for God's power.

Alan Langstaff, formerly a Charismatic leader in Australia who is now pastoring a church in Minneapolis, has stated that a prophet's message is not a balanced message, but a message to ***bring balance.*** In the Bible, if a prophet saw something that was way out of balance, he would hit it hard from just one side in order to bring the situation back into balance. He gave the example that if you had gone to the "First Church of John the Baptist" and all you heard Sunday after Sunday was "Repent, Repent," it may have seemed a little harsh and unbalanced. It was not a balanced message; it was a message to bring balance.

I humbly look at this book in this way. It is not intended to present a balanced message. Rather, it is a message to "bring balance"—to restore supernatural power to its rightful place in our lives, in our presentation of the gospel, and to enable us to victoriously go through the troubled end-time days that lie ahead.

Christianity started out as a supernatural religion and it has never stopped being one. God wants all of His people, every single Christian, to be partakers of supernatural power. Let's now examine some steps that we might need to take in order to have this power filling us and overflowing to others.

MAKE A BONDSLAVE COMMITMENT TO GOD

In Chapters 5 and 13 I have already discussed what it means to make a bondslave commitment to God. As we discussed earlier, Jesus Himself was a bondslave:

> **5 Have this attitude in yourselves which was also in Christ Jesus,**
> **6 who, although He existed in the form of God, did not regard equality with God a thing to be grasped,**
> **7 but emptied Himself, taking the form of a bond-servant, *and* being made in the likeness of men.**
> **—Philippians 2**

Because His desire was to do the Father's will, God was able to pour out supernatural power through Jesus like the world had never seen before. Likewise, as His disciples followed His example and laid down their lives for the Lord, God was able to work mighty miracles through them as well. In like manner, it is as we choose to voluntarily become bondslaves of God that He will begin to be able to entrust us with His supernatural power, knowing that it will be used to His glory.

ACKNOWLEDGE THAT YOU ARE WEAK—HUMBLE YOURSELF

If we want God's power, we must stop trusting in our own strength and power. We must stop leaning on our intellect and understanding (Proverbs 3:5, 6). Jesus said that we were to learn from Him for He was meek and lowly (Matthew 11:29, *KJV*). We know that Paul gloried in his infirmities and weaknesses so that the power of Christ could rest upon him:

> **9 And he said unto me, My grace is sufficient for thee: for my strength is made perfect in weakness. Most gladly therefore will I rather glory in my infirmities, that the power of Christ may rest upon me.**
>
> **10 Therefore I take pleasure in infirmities, in reproaches, in necessities, in persecutions, in distresses for Christ's sake: for when I am weak, then I am strong.**
>
> **—2 Corinthians 12, *KJV***

Here Paul said that he was going to glory ("boast") in his infirmities ("weaknesses" in the *NAS*) and, by doing so, the power of Christ could rest upon him. Paul boasted about being weak, so that God would get the glory for all that was done, rather than people honoring Paul for what he had achieved.

How many Christians have you recently heard boast about their weaknesses? How many Christian leaders have you recently heard boast about their weaknesses? Often, if you ask the average Christian how things are going for him, everything is usually "fine" or "wonderful"; "things are growing" or "we are getting stronger and bigger everyday." Very often there is no mention at all that it is God's power accomplishing all of these marvelous things. It seems that this type of attitude is the opposite of boasting in our weakness in order that God may be glorified. Perhaps it is the opposite of being humble, meek and lowly, as Jesus was (Matthew 11:29, *KJV*).

There are people who have a heart attitude of being strong and self-sufficient, who give no evidence of having any problems or weaknesses. God cannot readily use such Christians as a funnel of His tremendous supernatural power as He would like to, because they are the ones who would get the glory, in the eyes of other people.

If you would like to see the power of God flow through you, let people know about your weaknesses, your hurts and your "clay feet." In other words, learn of Christ, for He was meek and lowly.

Let's take a closer look at the word "glory" *(KJV)* in 2 Corinthians 12:9 that we just read (translated "boast" in the *NAS*). The Greek word used is *"kauchaomai."* According to *Vine's Expository Dictionary,* one of the major uses of this Greek word, "kauchaomai" is *"rejoice."* That is the sense in which Paul was using it in the passage we read, when he said that he would "boast" or "rejoice" in his weaknesses. As a result, God's power could be shown strong in him.

CLEAN UP YOUR POWER FILTER

In Chapters 6 through 9, we looked at things that could hinder God's power resting upon you and flowing out from you to other people to achieve God's purposes and missions. Toward the end of Chapter 9, we gave a number of Scriptures that listed various items that could keep one from inheriting the kingdom of God or that would defile one or bring on God's wrath. Most Christians are involved in some or all of these, and yet they may not realize it.

We need to clean up our spiritual "power filter" (air filter), so the supernatural power of God can flow freely through us.

Periodically, you may wish to prayerfully review the passages of Scripture quoted in Chapter 9, asking God to reveal to you any areas of defilement in your life. As He does so, be diligent to repent of those things that are clogging up your "power filter," that He may cleanse you from all unrighteousness (1 John 1:9). Remember, the less "debris" you have clogging up your power filter, the more freely God can use you as an ambassador of His power and grace.

TURN YOUR TIME OVER TO GOD

As we mentioned earlier in this book, when you make a decision to be a bondslave of God, you really also commit your time to the Lord. It is no longer your own. I mention it specifically here, because the way in which you choose to spend your time can make a tremendous difference in how much God can use you as a channel of His supernatural power.

More than anything else you can offer Him, God desires to have an intimate relationship with you. Relationships require ***time***. They are not "instant."

> **6 For I delight in loyalty rather than sacrifice,**
> **And in the knowledge of God rather than burnt offerings.**
>
> **—Hosea 6**

Matthew 17:14-21 describes an incident in which the disciples were unable to cast a demon out of a boy. When Jesus rebuked the demon, it came out at once. As part of His reply to the disciples, when they asked Him why they were unable to cast it out, Jesus said this:

> **21 "But this kind does not go out except by prayer and fasting."**
>
> **—Matthew 17**

Evidently Jesus Himself felt a need to spend much time alone with the Father in prayer:

> **16 But He Himself would *often* slip away to the wilderness and pray.**
>
> **—Luke 5**

35 And in the early morning, while it was still dark, He arose and went out and departed to a lonely place, and was praying there.

—Mark 1

12 And it was at this time that He went off to the mountain to pray, and He spent the whole night in prayer to God.

—Luke 6

If Jesus needed that kind of quality time communicating with God the Father, we certainly do too! It was out of that lifestyle of continual communion with God that God's power was able to flow through Him to perform many miracles.

Paul knew how crucial it was to devote time to prayer and getting to know God better. He encouraged the Thessalonians to "pray without ceasing" (1 Thessalonians 5:17). He prayed that the Colossians would "be filled with the knowledge of His will" and would increase "in the knowledge of God" (Colossians 1:9-12). Getting to know Him requires spending some time with Him and learning to hear His voice.

As a side note here, I believe it is also important that you become a worshiper. We are told that God inhabits the praises of His people (Psalm 22:3, *KJV*). We are exhorted repeatedly in the Scriptures to offer the Lord the praise and glory that is due His name:

4 Enter His gates with thanksgiving
***And* His courts with praise.**
Give thanks to Him; bless His name.

—Psalm 100

Power is released in worship. Many times people have been healed in the midst of a worship service. As they get their eyes off of themselves and begin to worship God and receive from Him, He sovereignly meets them at their point of need and heals them.

As you spend time getting to know God better, you will naturally want to worship Him for who He is and all that He has done for you. When you have a heart to worship and honor Him, it will be your desire to give Him the glory for any works that He accomplishes through your hands. He will then better be able to use you as a vessel to reach out in supernatural power to those who are in need.

LET YOUR MOTIVATION BE *LOVE*

Anything that we do in the power of God should be done in ***love.*** In fact, if you consider the life of Jesus, who is our Example of how to walk in the supernatural power of God, love preceded manifestations of the power of God. He was willing to come to earth and to die for us, because of ***love.*** Many times, the Scriptures reveal to us that Jesus was moved with compassion because of His genuine, selfless love for people, and ***then*** the power of God flowed out from Him to perform healing and other miracles in a response to the needs:

> **14 And when He went ashore, He saw a great multitude, and felt compassion for them, and healed their sick.**
>
> **—Matthew 14**

> **34 And moved with compassion, Jesus touched their eyes; and immediately they regained their sight and followed Him.**
>
> **—Matthew 20**

41 And moved with compassion, He stretched out His hand, and touched him, and said to him, "I am willing; be cleansed."

42 And immediately the leprosy left him and he was cleansed.

—Mark 1

13 And when the Lord saw her, He felt compassion for her, and said to her, "Do not weep."

14 And He came up and touched the coffin; and the bearers came to a halt. And He said, "Young man, I say to you, arise!"

15 And the dead man sat up, and began to speak. And *Jesus* gave him back to his mother.

—Luke 7

As we can see in these examples, it was the caring that came first. Jesus truly cared for people. Love ***precedes*** power, and it is a very important ingredient in our daily walk with the Lord.

Exhibiting the supernatural power of God requires that we put aside selfishness. It is a selfless act to risk being made to look foolish in order to obey God and allow His power to flow through you to meet the needs of others. Remember, God can use anything—even a donkey (Numbers 22:21-34). You are simply a tool for His great love to flow out to others. Check your heart and motivation, and ask God to give you a heart of compassion like Jesus had.

BECOME LIKE JESUS

The real bottom line is that if you want to have God's power resting upon you as it rested upon Jesus, then you need to *become like Jesus.*

THE MORE YOU BECOME LIKE JESUS, THE MORE GOD'S POWER WILL WORK THROUGH YOU.

All believers in Jesus Christ have Christ dwelling within them. The fact that Christ lives inside of us is our hope of glory. As Paul was writing to the Christians at Galatia, He knew that Christ dwelt in them, but He yearned for something much more wonderful for them:

> **19 My children, with whom I am again in labor until Christ is formed in you . . .**
>
> **—Galatians 4**

Paul yearned that Christ would not just dwell in them, but that *Christ would be formed in them.* If Christ were formed within them, they would have every thought captive to the obedience of Jesus (2 Corinthians 10:5). They would be living holy, pure lives, obedient to the will of God. The more Christ was formed within them, the more God's power would rest upon them and be able to flow out from them.

As a young Methodist boy, I read a book entitled *In His Steps* by Charles M. Shelton. This was a novel about a group of people who tried to walk daily in the steps of Jesus and to follow Him as their Example. I tried to do that and it was a dismal failure. It was a failure because I did not know Christ personally at that time, nor did I have any supernatural power in my life. However, in recent years, I find that this concept of walking in His steps is very biblical:

> **21 For you have been called for this purpose, since Christ also suffered for you, leaving you an example for you to follow in His steps, . . .**
>
> **—1 Peter 2**

This verse clearly says that Christ left us an example to follow and that we should daily follow this example and walk in His steps. What kind of example did He leave for us? Jesus gave us an example of how we are to live!

The apostle Paul spent his life trying to imitate (become like) Jesus:

> **1 Be imitators of me, just as I also am of Christ.**
> **—1 Corinthians 11**

Have you ever seen a child striving to imitate an adult? Have you seen little girls playing "dress up?" The imitation isn't perfect, but they are trying with all their little hearts to imitate the people they are representing or the people they admire. You might ask yourself, are you trying with all your heart to imitate Jesus? If not, why not? Paul was doing so. Shouldn't you and I also try to imitate Jesus?

If we use a cookie cutter on dough, the dough conforms to the image of the cookie cutter. If we pour plaster of Paris into a mold, out comes a casting that is perfectly conformed to the image of the mold. God desires that you and I be conformed to the image of His Son, Jesus:

> **29 For whom He foreknew, He also predestined *to become* conformed to the image of His Son, that He might be the first-born of many brethren; . . .**
> **—Romans 8**

This verse says that we are to be poured into the mold of Jesus and come out "looking like" Him. You might be thinking, "If that were true, I would essentially be perfect." The answer is, "Yes, you would be, and that is exactly what God wants you to be."

Jesus Commanded Us to Be Perfect

Would Jesus ever command you to do anything that was impossible? If so, He is an intolerant, unreasonable task master. However, I believe that He would never ask you or me to do anything that was impossible. Let's look at one of Christ's commands to us:

> **48 "Therefore you are to be perfect, as your heavenly Father is perfect. . . ."**
>
> **—Matthew 5**

This is not a suggestion from Jesus, nor something that He would like for you to do halfheartedly. It is a direct command from Jesus Christ, just as much as any of His other commands.

Satan will say to you: "You could never be perfect. Don't bother trying." Yet Jesus says to you: "You can become perfect; you can become like me. Go for it." Who are you going to believe? If you believe Jesus and really press on toward becoming an imitator of Him and becoming conformed to His image, yet only get 98 or 99 percent there, how much better off you will be than if you believe Satan's lie and don't even bother trying.

Many ministries and churches emphasize the five-fold ministries. Yet we need to examine why these ministries are given. Let's first look at what the Bible has to say:

> **11 And he gave some, apostles; and some, prophets; and some, evangelists; and some, pastors and teachers;**
>
> **12 For the perfecting of the saints, for the work of the ministry, for the edifying of the body of Christ:**
>
> **13 Till we all come in the unity of the faith, and of the knowledge of the Son of God, unto a perfect man, unto the measure of the stature of the fulness of Christ: . . .**
>
> **—Ephesians 4, *KJV***

As we can see, the fivefold ministries are given for "the perfecting of the saints." That means that these ministries are given so that they can help the saints become perfect, so they can help believers become like Jesus Christ.

Did you notice how verse 13 ends? Another reason that these ministries are given is to help each Christian become "a perfect man, unto the measure of the stature of the fulness of Christ." These ministries are to help Christians become perfect in the full likeness of Jesus Christ.

In evaluating the ministry of an apostle, prophet, pastor, teacher or evangelist, you might ask yourself if that individual is really fulfilling the biblical purpose of that ministry. Is he or she helping Christians to become perfect, to become like Jesus Christ?

If you are a man or woman called into these ministries, you may want to reevaluate your ministry to see if the main thrust of it really fulfills this purpose of helping Christians become perfect (become like Jesus Christ).

In our churches and ministries, we frequently set goals. If you were to ask many television ministers what their goal was, it might be to have their television programs broadcast in every country in the world, for example. If you were to ask the head of a campus ministry what his goal was, it might be to double his staff so that they could reach more campuses. If you were to ask some pastors what their goal was, it might be to conduct an evangelistic campaign in their neighborhood that would reach every home.

Similarly, before June, 1982, I had a goal for Omega Ministries to grow and expand in order to get the vital end-times message out to the body of Christ. I also had goals for my financial newsletter and I had personal goals. I spent much of the month of June, 1982, in prayer and fasting. During that month, the Lord completely changed my goal. My goal from that time forward has simply been "to become like Jesus Christ." The Lord told me, during that month, that at the end of the trail, when I stand before the judgment seat of Christ, it will not matter how big or small my ministry became or how "successful" I became. The key question as I stand before Him is going to be: ***How much like Jesus did I become***?

Pressing Towards the Goal

It is not enough simply to have a goal. For a goal to have any meaning, we need to press toward it. To help you understand this, I would like to share with you something that happened when I was in high school.

I was on the track team and I ran the sprints—the 100-yard dash and the 220 dash. After school, we sprinters would take a few sprints and then lie around on the grass and make fun of the distance runners, who ran round and round the oval track to build up their wind and endurance.

One day we were in a significant track meet and our quarter miler was sick. The coach asked me to run the quarter-mile race and told me that we really needed to win it in order to win the track meet. I was in no shape to run a quarter mile. My wind and endurance were not up to it. But since I had to run it, I figured that the only way I could win that race was not to let anybody pass me.

The starting gun sounded and I shot out like a sprinter and got way ahead of the pack. Then I slacked off on my running pace. When I heard the sound of someone coming up behind me, I began to sprint again until I was able to put some distance between him and myself, and then I eased off again. When I heard someone come up behind me again, I would floor it and put some distance between me and whomever was behind me. This happened time after time. As we were rounding the final curve into the finish line, my legs were burning like fire and I was gasping for breath, but I was so determined to hit that tape before anyone else that it would have taken the front line of a professional football team to have stopped me. My eyes were probably white-hot with determination to hit that tape first, and I did.

That is the same sort of determination and concentration that we need to have in pressing toward the goal of becoming like Jesus Christ. We need to press toward it with every fiber of our being. I think this is what Paul must have had in mind when he was writing to the Philippians:

> **7 But whatever things were gain to me, those things I have counted as loss for the sake of Christ.**
>
> **8 More than that, I count all things to be loss in view of the surpassing value of knowing Christ Jesus my Lord, for whom I have suffered the loss of all things, and count them but rubbish in order that I may gain Christ,**
>
> **9 and may be found in Him, not having a righteousness of my own derived from *the* Law, but that which is through faith in Christ, the righteousness which *comes* from God on the basis of faith,**
>
> **10 that I may know Him, and the power of His resurrection and the fellowship of His sufferings, being conformed to His death;**
>
> **11 in order that I may attain to the resurrection from the dead.**
>
> **12 Not that I have already obtained *it*, or have already become perfect, but I press on in order that I may lay hold of that for which I also was laid hold of by Christ Jesus.**

13 Brethren, I do not regard myself as having laid hold of *it* yet; but one thing *I do*: forgetting what *lies* behind and reaching forward to what *lies* ahead,

14 I press on toward the goal for the prize of the upward call of God in Christ Jesus.

—Philippians 3

Here Paul encourages us to forget what is behind us—what happened yesterday, last month or last year—and to press on towards the goal of becoming like Christ Jesus. I urge you with every fiber of your being to press toward the "finish line" of being conformed to His image.

SPECIFIC THINGS FOR GOD'S POWER

What we have just covered are some general things that you might need to do in order to let God's power flow through you freely. Let us now look at some specific things that relate to this area of supernatural power. If you are serious about desiring God's power, here are some things you can do:

1. Continuously ask God for His power to clothe you.
2. Each day ask God to bring someone across your path who needs a miraculous touch from Him.
3. Believe Jesus when He said that if you believe in Him, the works that He did, you will do also (John 14:12).
4. Ask Him to increase your faith and to get rid of your fear. (Fear is from Satan; faith is from God.)
5. Be willing to take a risk. (If there is no risk, there is no faith.)

6. Be bold and take the initiative. (Ask someone who is sick if he would like to be well and if he would like to have you pray for him.)
7. Put faith to work. (Step out of the boat. Lay hands on the sick and pray with authority, for Jesus promised that if you laid hands on the sick, they would recover.)

The bottom line is this. You have the power. You have the promise of Jesus. What you need to do is to put your faith into action and start ***doing it!***

You need to be sensitive to what the Father is saying and to what His will is. He will lead you to the right ones to pray for.

Ask the Lord for the gift of discernment to see if an illness is caused by evil spirits or is from a physical source. If He shows you, pray accordingly. If He does not, then first pray binding the evil spirit and casting it out in the powerful name of Jesus Christ. Then pray as though the cause is physical in nature.

In praying for the sick particularly, lay hands on them. Think of your hands like the high-voltage power lines that carry power from the generating plant (God) to the person in need, just as electrical wires carry electricity. Your hands are the conductive wires for the power of God to flow into these people. Jesus was so clothed with the power of God, that even when people touched His clothing, they were healed.

Use the authority that Jesus Christ gave you, and speak in an authoritative voice. In most cases where a miracle, a healing or a deliverance is needed, a quiet prayer won't do. Jesus stood up and "commanded" the sea to be calm; He didn't whisper to it. Certainly when you are casting out a demon, taking authority over nature, or things of this nature, you should speak in a commanding voice. Other times, when you are laying hands on someone to release the healing power of God to flow into him, you need not necessarily be loud in your prayer, but still remember to pray with the authority that is yours in the name of Jesus Christ.

We must command *using the name of Jesus Christ*. It is important to say "Jesus Christ" or "Jesus Christ of Nazareth." There are thousands of young men all over Latin American who are named "Jesus." There are also many false prophets claiming to be Christ. It is important that we use both His name, Jesus, and His title, Christ, to uniquely identify whose name it is that we are using. Then the forces of illness and evil will know that we are speaking with His authority.

In modern terms, you could say that we have His "power of attorney." If I gave you power of attorney over my checking account, then you could write a check, sign your name and cash any amount that you wanted. The same thing is true here. Jesus Christ has given us His full power of attorney over the area of sickness, disease and evil spirits. We need to step out in faith and with boldness begin to use that authority, in His name and for His glory.

Realize that sometimes healing takes time. All healings do not take place instantly, even as the case was with Jesus and the blind man. But if you lay hands on someone and pray for him, the power of God has gone from you into that individual and the healing process has begun. In speaking of the signs that will accompany those who have believed, Mark 16:17-18 says that we will lay hands on the sick in Jesus' name and they *"will recover."* Sometimes "recovery" is a process.

Also, realize that everyone that you pray for is not going to be healed. An average rate of healings among even those with the gift of healing is about 80 to 90 percent. When you begin to learn to exercise your authority in the name of Jesus Christ, your percentage may even be a little lower than that, at first. Even Christ could not heal many in His hometown of Nazareth, because of their lack of faith. Don't be discouraged by that. Say that you pray for ten people and eight get healed, and two do not. That does not mean that you should not pray for the eight, just because of the two who don't get healed. We do not understand everything there is to know about healing. Remember, God is sovereign. But don't allow a "fear of failure" to keep you from stepping out in faith to pray and see God's healing power released through you.

Many of these things we have discussed earlier in this book. We are simply reviewing them here so that the Lord can refresh them to your mind. One area that needs to be addressed in a little more detail is the following.

CONTINUOUSLY ASK FOR GOD'S POWER TO CLOTHE YOU

The reason God wants us to ask for things, when He already knows that we need them, is that we need to express our dependence upon Him (living independent of God is the essence of sin). God wants us to ask for His guidance in our everyday affairs, as well as in the major decisions in life.

Certainly where the power of God is concerned, one reason we may not be experiencing it is because we have not been asking for it and expecting it. James, the brother of Jesus, emphasizes this point:

> **2 . . . You do not have because you do not ask.**
> **3 You ask and do not receive, because you ask with wrong motives, so that you may spend *it* on your pleasures.**
>
> **—James 4**

Even though Jesus Christ has given us His power and authority, we need to ask God to use us, as humble meek children. James continues in the next verse to tell us that even when we do ask, we must not ask with wrong motives. Why do you want to have the supernatural power of God to rest upon you? Is it because you want everyone to see what a super Christian you are? Is it so that your church or your ministry might grow? Perhaps you have had questionable motives.

On the other hand, if your motive is compassion for sick people and people with twisted limbs such that you yearn to see them get well and be whole again, that would be a very good motive. If you are angry about seeing people bound up under demonic harassment and you yearn to see them set free, that would be a good motive. Our motives need to be unselfish and pure.

I believe that Jesus wanted God's supernatural power working through Him so that He might "work the works of the Father who sent Him" (John 9:4). He needed God's supernatural power to do God's mission. Evidently the mission came first, and then the power.

It is not enough to simply just ask once for the power of God. It is something that we must ask for continuously. Every time Jesus spoke on prayer, or gave a parable about prayer, He referred to praying in the continuous tense. Most English translations do not give us that progressive present tense in the correct way that it should be translated from the original language. Let's take a familiar verse for example:

> **7 "Ask, and it shall be given to you; seek, and you shall find; knock, and it shall be opened to you.**
>
> **8 "For everyone who asks receives, and he who seeks finds, and to him who knocks it shall be opened. . . ."**
>
> **—Matthew 7**

In the Greek, this actually says to "keep on asking," "keep on seeking," and "keep on knocking." The *Wil-*

liams translation is one English version that translates this so very beautifully:

> **7 "Keep on asking, and the gift will be given you; keep on seeking, and you will find; keep on knocking, and the door will open to you.**
>
> **8 "For everyone who keeps on asking, receives, and everyone who keeps on seeking, finds, and to the one who keeps on knocking, the door will open. . . ."**
>
> **—Matthew 7, *Williams***

If you are seeking for supernatural power to flow through you, you must keep on asking. When the disciples asked Jesus to teach them to pray, here is what He said:

> **1 And it came about that while He was praying in a certain place, after He had finished, one of His disciples said to Him, "Lord, teach us to pray just as John also taught his disciples."**
>
> **2 And He said to them, "When you pray, say:**
> **'Father, hallowed be Thy name.**
> **Thy kingdom come.**
>
> **3 'Give us each day our daily bread.**
>
> **4 'And forgive us our sins,**
> **For we ourselves also forgive everyone who is indebted to us.**
> **And lead us not into temptation.'"**
>
> **5 And He said to them, "Suppose one of you shall have a friend, and shall go to him at midnight, and say to him, 'Friend, lend me three loaves;**
>
> **6 for a friend of mine has come to me from a journey, and I have nothing to set before him';**
>
> **7 and from inside he shall answer and say, 'Do not bother me; the door has already been shut and my children and I are in bed; I cannot get up and give you *anything.*'**

8 "I tell you, even though he will not get up and give him *anything* because he is his friend, yet because of his persistence he will get up and give him as much as he needs. . . ."

—Luke 11

As part of His teaching concerning prayer, Jesus gave the example in verses 5-8. In essence, He said that if one of the disciples were continuously knocking on this man's door, he finally would get what he wanted because of *persistence.*

We will take just one other example in which Christ taught on prayer to show you that He expects prayer to be continuous:

1 Now He was telling them a parable to show that at all times they ought to pray and not to lose heart,

2 saying, "There was in a certain city a judge who did not fear God, and did not respect man.

3 "And there was a widow in that city, and she kept coming to him, saying, 'Give me legal protection from my opponent.'

4 "And for a while he was unwilling; but afterward he said to himself, 'Even though I do not fear God nor respect man,

5 yet because this widow bothers me, I will give her legal protection, lest by continually coming she wear me out.'"

—Luke 18

Here Jesus again tells us to keep praying, "not to lose heart" and to pray at all times. He gave the example of a widow who finally got what she wanted because she kept asking the judge.

I believe the first thing that you should do, if you want the supernatural power of God, is to begin to ask God (with good motives) and to keep on asking, day after day, month after month, and, if necessary, year after year. Do not lose heart; ***keep on asking.***

SUMMARY AND CONCLUSION

In this chapter, we have seen that God wants His supernatural power to flow through every Christian. That power is available to all of us, young and old, black and white, male and female. If we want the power of God to flow through us, we need to:

1. Be filled with the Holy Spirit (prerequisite)
2. Be a bondslave of God the Father
3. Rejoice in our weaknesses and infirmities
4. Humble ourself before God
5. Clean up our "power filter" (turn from wicked ways)
6. Turn our time over to God
7. *BECOME LIKE JESUS* (the more we become like Jesus Christ, the more the power of God can rest upon us)

To help you in this process, I would recommend three books, all of which I have mentioned before in this book. The first, *You Can Overcome*, deals with the three stages of the Christian life, including the bondslave relationship with Father God:

1. The salvation stage (Jesus Christ)
2. The filling of the Spirit stage (Holy Spirit)
3. The bondslave stage (Father God)

That book will help you make a bondslave commitment to Father God, which is the entryway into the third stage of Christian life. As we read earlier, Philippians 2 says that Jesus Christ was a bondslave of God. That is the place that we too must begin, if we want to become like Him and have the power of God rest upon us, as it rested upon Jesus. Becoming a bondslave of God is the entryway into what someday may well be called the "Victory Movement" or the "Power Movement" of God.

Then the second book that I believe would be a tremendous help to you in your spiritual life is *Become Like Jesus.* It tells us what God is going to do with us, through us and for us, after we move into the third stage of the Christian life. This book has literally transformed the lives of so many who have read it. One minister said that if he could only have two books in his library, they would be the Bible and *Become Like Jesus.*

The third book that I would recommend is *How to Heal the Sick* by Stuart Gramenz. This book can help you "get out of the boat" in the area of healing. It is very practical and it is filled with actual examples, situations and suggestions.

All three books may be obtained through the ministry of which I am president:

Omega Ministries
P.O. Box 1788
Medford, OR 97501, USA

Also, if you are interested in going on a "JESUS HEALS" campaign with Stuart Gramenz, wherein you will get hands-on experience, you can write to him at the preceding address.

To glorify Jesus Christ and Father God, we must desire to be a channel of God's power, even if we are unknown and remain unknown. We must simply want to be His obedient bondslaves because of our love for Him. As we come into this glorious relationship with Father God, wonderful love and power will flow through us, which in turn we will want to funnel to others to honor and glorify His Son, Jesus Christ.

I hate to close this book because I feel that I have only scratched the surface of the subject at hand. But I am excited to see the things we have discussed here walked out and lived out in the lives of Christians around the world. At first, there will be tens and hundreds, then thousands and perhaps millions of Christians who will begin to move in the full supernatural power of God. Then and only then will we see the mighty revival for which we all yearn. Then and only then will God be able to bless us in the way that He wants us to be blessed. Then we will see souls converted into the kingdom of God by the numbers that we would love to see, for the glory of Jesus.

Do pause and pray about the things that you have read in this book. Don't just set it aside and rush off for "business as usual." It is critical to make that bondslave ***commitment*** to Father God and a ***commitment*** to press toward becoming like Jesus. While it is on your heart and mind, decide now to make the goal of your life to become like Jesus Christ. Make the ***commitment*** to God to clean up your act and remove anything from your life that would hinder His power from resting upon you and flowing through you. Make a ***commitment*** to take a risk, to "step out of the boat," to be bold, to put your faith into action and to start doing the works of Jesus that He said you could do. I encourage you to pause, review what we have discussed here and make those commitments now.

As you begin to pray with authority and to command in the name of Jesus Christ, you ***will*** begin to see people healed, people set free, people converted and perhaps other miracles.

POWER IN THE END TIMES

Most churches in America, as well as churches in many other countries, are essentially powerless. For the body of Christ to go through the end times of this age in a way that will glorify the Lord, a return to the regular use of supernatural power is essential. As non-Christians see signs and wonders, they will know that Christianity is not just another religion; they will know that we truly speak from God and represent Him and His Son, Jesus Christ.

It is very likely that the body of Christ as a whole will basically ignore this call to supernatural power, along with the companion call to live holy, pure and clean lives. However, there will be pockets of believers, a local assembly here and there, as well as individuals in various churches who will listen to this call, whom God will mightily use in the end times of this age as a powerful end-time army.

God will not send out an army without giving them the power to win the victories. God will give His army supernatural power along with supernatural protection. Let's remember the words of the old (but true) hymn (by George Duffield):

STAND UP, STAND UP FOR JESUS

Stand up, stand up for Jesus,
ye soldiers of the cross
Lift high His royal banners,
it must not suffer loss
From victory unto victory,
His army shall He lead
'Til every foe is conquered
and Christ is Lord indeed

Another well-known hymn that speaks of our victory is this one (by Sabine Baring-Gould):

ONWARD, CHRISTIAN SOLDIERS

Onward Christian Soldiers, marching as to war
With the cross of Jesus, going on before
Christ the royal Master, leads against the foe
Forward into battle, see His banners go . . .

Crowns and thrones may perish, kingdoms rise and wane
But the church of Jesus, constant will remain
Gates of hell can never 'gainst that church prevail
We have Christ's own promise, and that cannot fail

We have Christ's promise that we will lay hands on the sick and they will recover. We have the promise of Jesus Christ Himself that in His name we will cast out demons. The victory will be ours through God's supernatural power resting upon us to the glory and honor of Jesus Christ, God's only begotten Son and our precious Savior.

God's supernatural power is for every Christian.

Appendix A

HOW TO BECOME A CHRISTIAN

If you are reading this, I am assuming that you are not sure that you have received Jesus Christ as your personal Savior. Not only is it possible to know this for sure, but God wants you to know.

> **11 And the witness is this, that God has given us eternal life, and this life is in His Son.**
>
> **12 He who has the Son has the life; he who does not have the Son of God does not have the life.**
>
> **13 These things I have written to you who believe in the name of the Son of God, in order that you may know that you have eternal life.**
>
> **—1 John 5**

These things are written to us who believe in the name of the Son of God, so that we can know that we have eternal life. It is not a "guess so," or "hope so" or "maybe so" situation. It is so that we can know for certain that we have eternal life. If you do not have this confidence, please read on.

In order to get the point of knowing that we have eternal life, we first need to review some basic principles. It is important to note that all things that God created (the stars, trees, animals, and so on) are doing exactly what they were created to do, except man. Isaiah 43 indicates why God created us:

> **7 ". . . Everyone who is called by My name,**
> **And whom I have created for My glory,**
> **Whom I have formed, even whom I have made."**
> **—Isaiah 43**

This says that humans were created to glorify God. I am sure that neither you nor I have glorified God all of our lives in everything that we have done. This gives us our first clue as to what "sin" is. We find more about it in Romans:

> **23 for all have sinned and fall short of the glory of God, . . .**
> **—Romans 3**

This says that we all have sinned and we all fall short of the purpose for which we were created—to glorify God. I have an even simpler definition of sin. I believe that sin is "living independent of God." A young person out of high school can choose which college to attend. If he makes this decision apart from God, it is "sin." This was the basic problem in the garden of Eden. Satan tempted Eve to eat the fruit of the tree of "the knowledge of good and evil." He said that if she would do this, she would know good from evil and would be wise like God. This would mean that she could make her own decisions and would not have to rely on God's wisdom and guidance. Since you and I fit in the category of living independent of God and not glorifying Him in everything we do, we need to look at what the results of this sin are.

First let me ask you what "wages" are. After thinking about it, because you probably receive wages from your job, you will probably come up with a definition something like "wages are what you get paid for what you do." That is a good answer. Now let's see what the Bible has to say concerning this:

23 For the wages of sin is death, but the free gift of God is eternal life in Christ Jesus our Lord.
—Romans 6

Here we see that the wages of sin is death—spiritual, eternal death. Death is what we get paid for the sin that we do. Yet this passage also gives us the other side of the coin: that is, that through Jesus Christ we can freely have eternal life, instead of eternal death. Isn't that wonderful!

But let's return for a moment to this death penalty that the people without Christ have hanging over their heads, because of the sin that they live in. In the Old Testament, God made a rule: "The soul who sins will die" (Ezekiel 18:4). If we were able to live a perfect, sinless life, we could make it to heaven on our own. If we live anything less than a perfect life, according to God's rule, we will not make it to heaven, but instead will be sentenced to death. All through the Bible, we find no one living a good enough life to make it to heaven.

This brings us to the place where Jesus Christ fits into this whole picture. His place was beautifully illustrated to me when I was considering receiving Christ as my Savior, by a story about a judge in a small town.

In this small town, the newspapermen were against the judge and wanted to get him out of office. A case was coming up before the judge concerning a vagrant—a drunken bum—who happened to have been a fraternity brother of the judge when they were at college. The newspapermen thought that this was their chance. If the judge let the vagrant off easy, the headlines would read, "Judge Shows Favoritism to Old Fraternity Brother." If the judge gave the vagrant the maximum penalty, the headlines would read, "Hard-hearted Judge Shows No Mercy to Old Fraternity Brother." Either way they had him. The judge heard the case and gave the vagrant the maximum penalty of thirty days or $300 fine.

The judge then stood up, took off his robe, laid it down on his chair, walked down in front of the bench and put his arm around the shoulders of his old fraternity brother. He told him that as judge, in order to uphold the law, he had to give him the maximum penalty, because he was guilty. But because he cared about him, he wanted to pay the fine for him. So the judge took out his wallet and handed his old fraternity brother $300.

For God to be "just," He has to uphold the law that says "the soul who sins will die." On the other hand, because He loves us, He wants to pay that death penalty for us. I cannot pay the death penalty for you, because I have a death penalty of my own that I have to worry about, since I, too, have sinned. If I were sinless, I could die in your place. I guess God could have sent down millions of sinless beings to die for us. But what God chose to do was to send down one Person, who was equal in value, in God's eyes, to all of the people who will ever live, and yet who would remain sinless. Jesus Christ died in order to pay the death penalty for you and me. The blood of Christ washes away all of our sins, and with it the death penalty that resulted from our sin.

The judge's old fraternity brother could have taken the $300 and said, "Thank you," or he could have told the judge to keep his money and that he would do it on his own. Similarly, each person can thank God for allowing Christ to die in his place and receive Christ as his own Savior, or he can tell God to keep His payment and that he will make it on his own. What you do with that question determines where you will spend eternity.

Referring to Christ, the book of John says this:

12 But as many as received Him, to them He gave the right to become children of God, *even* to those who believe in His name, . . .

—John 1

16 "For God so loved the world, that He gave His only begotten Son, that whoever believes in Him should not perish but have eternal life. . . ."

—John 3

Here we see that if we believe in Christ we won't perish, but we will have everlasting life and the right to become children of God. Right now you can tell God that you believe in Christ as the Son of God, that you are sorry for your sins and that you want to turn from them. You can tell Him that you want to accept Christ's payment for your sins, and yield your life to be controlled by Christ and the Holy Spirit. (You must accept Christ as your Savior *and your Master.*)

If you pray such a prayer, Christ will come and dwell within your heart and you will know for sure that you have eternal life.

If you have any questions about what you have just read, I would encourage you to go to someone that you know, who really knows Jesus Christ as his Savior, and ask him for help and guidance. After you receive Christ, I would encourage you to become a part of a group of believers in Christ who study the Scriptures together, worship God together and have a real love relationship with each other. This group (body of believers) can help nurture you and build you up in your new faith in Jesus Christ.

If you have received Christ as a result of reading these pages, I would love to hear from you. My address is at the end of this book.

Welcome to the family of God.

James McKeever

Appendix B

SUPERNATURAL POWER OF SATAN

In this book we have talked primarily about supernatural power from God. We also must realize that Satan has supernatural power that he can give to his followers.

For example, in talking about the end of this age, Christ says this:

> **24 "For false Christs and false prophets will arise and will show great signs and wonders, so as to mislead, if possible, even the elect.**
> **25 "Behold, I have told you in advance. . . ."**
> **—Matthew 24**

As Jesus Himself tells us here, at the end of the age false prophets are going to arise who are going to be able to do great signs and wonders. The Greek says, *"attesting miracles."* This is going to mislead many Christians ("the elect"). And Christ told us earlier in that same chapter that many Christians would be misled:

> **11 "And many false prophets will arise, and will mislead many. . . ."**
> **—Matthew 24**

If some of the teachers and prophets who are giving forth false information and not the truth of God were to begin to do miracles, Christendom at large would flock to them. However, we need to use the spirit of discernment, because miracles alone do not mean that a man is from God or is walking with God.

In fact, the book of Revelation tells us that there is a "beast" coming (a dictator beast, not "the Antichrist") to whom Satan will give his full power:

> **4 and they worshiped the dragon, because he gave his authority to the beast; and they worshiped the beast, saying, "Who is like the beast, and who is able to wage war with him?"**
>
> **5 And there was given to him a mouth speaking arrogant words and blasphemies; and authority to act for forty-two months was given to him.**
>
> **6 And he opened his mouth in blasphemies against God, to blaspheme His name and His tabernacle, *that is*, those who dwell in heaven.**
>
> **—Revelation 13**

In addition to the dictator beast, there will be the prophet beast, who will cause people to worship the dictator beast. This is what we are told about him:

> **11 And I saw another beast coming up out of the earth; and he had two horns like a lamb, and he spoke as a dragon.**
>
> **12 And he exercises all the authority of the first beast in his presence. And he makes the earth and those who dwell in it to worship the first beast, whose fatal wound was healed.**
>
> **13 And he performs great signs, so that he even makes fire come down out of heaven to the earth in the presence of men.**
>
> **—Revelation 13**

Verse 13 says that this prophet beast, who will cause people to worship the dictator beast, will perform great signs. He will even be able to bring fire down from heaven. So you see that the mere fact that someone can bring fire down from heaven does not necessarily mean that he is of God or working with God.

As we read in Chapter 13, Satan disguises himself as an angel of light and his followers disguise themselves as servants of righteousness:

> **13 For such men are false apostles, deceitful workers, disguising themselves as apostles of Christ.**
>
> **14 And no wonder, for even Satan disguises himself as an angel of light.**
>
> **15 Therefore it is not surprising if his servants also disguise themselves as servants of righteousness; whose end shall be according to their deeds.**
>
> **—2 Corinthians 11**

Satan is a great counterfeiter, imitating the works of God at times, in an attempt to deceive the undiscerning. It is essential that we exercise the spirit of discernment in regard to signs and wonders to determine if the source is God or the evil one. However, it is a grave and unfortunate mistake to disregard the supernatural out of fear of the deceiver and to allow him to rob you of the supernatural power that God wants to flow through you. Greater is He who is in us, than he who is in the world (1 John 4:4)! The victory is ours in Christ Jesus our Lord!

Appendix C

SUPERNATURAL POWER OF THE GODHEAD

Each person of the Godhead has power. The Scriptures refer to the power of the Holy Spirit:

> **13 Now may the God of hope fill you with all joy and peace in believing, that you may abound in hope by the power of the Holy Spirit.**
>
> **—Romans 15**

The verse above points out clearly that the Holy Spirit has power to fill us with joy and peace.

We also know that Jesus Christ has power that can rest upon us:

> **9 And he said unto me, My grace is sufficient for thee: for my strength is made perfect in weakness. Most gladly therefore will I rather glory in my infirmities, that the power of Christ may rest upon me.**
>
> **10 Therefore I take pleasure in infirmities, in reproaches, in necessities, in persecutions, in distresses for Christ's sake: for when I am weak, then am I strong.**
>
> **—2 Corinthians 12, *KJV***

The power of Christ gives us strength when we are weak. We also find this in other places in the Scriptures:

> **13 I can do all things through Him who strengthens me.**
>
> **—Philippians 4**

We have seen that the Holy Spirit has power and that Jesus Christ has power, but God the Father also has power:

> **8 And the temple was filled with smoke from the glory of God and from His power; and no one was able to enter the temple until the seven plagues of the seven angels were finished.**
>
> **—Revelation 15**

The Old Testament is full of statements about the power of Father God. For example:

> **16 "But, indeed, for this cause I have allowed you to remain, in order to show you My power, and in order to proclaim My name through all the earth. . . ."**
>
> **—Exodus 9**

> **6 "Thy right hand, O LORD, is majestic in power,**
> **Thy right hand, O LORD, shatters the enemy. . . ."**
>
> **—Exodus 15**

It was this power of God the Father that would come down into the holy of holies in the tabernacle. It was this power of God that so filled the house of the Lord, when King Solomon dedicated the temple, that the priests could not even stand to minister.

When Jesus was on the earth, He laid aside His privileges, emptied Himself, and took the form of a bondslave, being made in the likeness of men (Philippians 2:5-7). In other words, He did not have access to any power at that time that He has not also made available to us. The Bible seems to imply that it was the power of Father God that was present for Jesus to perform healings:

> **17 And it came about one day that He was teaching; and there were *some* Pharisees and teachers of the law sitting *there*, who had come from every village of Galilee and Judea and *from* Jerusalem; and the power of the Lord was *present* for Him to perform healing.**
>
> **—Luke 5**

As we have talked about the "power of God" in this book, we have not tried to delineate if it was the power of Christ, the power of the Holy Spirit or the power of God the Father. In fact, I deliberately left it ambiguous, so that you could think of it more as the "power of the Godhead." In my heart and spirit, I feel that it is the power of God the Father that we are talking about, although I certainly could not quibble with anyone who felt differently.

In the Evangelical movement, Jesus Christ was the person of the Trinity who was emphasized. In the Charismatic movement, the Holy Spirit began to be emphasized, along with Christ. However, I feel that Father God is the neglected one of the Trinity, and that the next major movement of God is going to emphasize God the Father.

GOD THE FATHER

In circles of born-again Christians, as I said, the neglected person of the Trinity tends to be Father God. There is a great deal of preaching and teaching that presents Jesus Christ as our Savior. Praise God, we ***should*** do that. It is at the name of Jesus that every knee will bow and every tongue will confess that He is the Son of God and the Savior of the world (Philippians

2:10, 11). We never ever want to take anything away from Jesus, our Lord.

The Holy Spirit's job is to glorify Jesus. There are some meetings that emphasize the Holy Spirit and the gifts of the Spirit so much that it is the Holy Spirit who gets glorified. If the Holy Spirit gets glorified, then that meeting is not *of* the Spirit, because if the Holy Spirit were in control, Jesus would be the one glorified. Yet there indeed needs to be some emphasis placed on the Holy Spirit; the fruits of the Spirit, which grow out of our lives; the gifts of the Spirit, which He gives as He decides and when He decides; and the filling or the baptism of the Holy Spirit, which is a prerequisite for receiving the power of God the Father.

Many Christians talk a lot about Jesus and the Holy Spirit, but if they were to evaluate themselves realistically, they spend very little time talking about God the Father. All Christians should have a good relationship with Jesus Christ, and many of them have a good relationship with the Holy Spirit as well, but very few Christians have a good relationship with Father God.

You may be thinking, "Wait a minute. I have a good relationship with Father God." It is possible that you might, but let's look at a modern-day parable to see if you truly do.

Let's say that you had a son about ten years old and he tried to build a bookcase, which was the first time he did anything with carpentry. His saw marks did not exactly follow the pencil lines, many of the nails that he drove in either were broken off or bent, and when he set it down on the floor, it was not level and it wobbled. What would you do? Would you tell him that it was terrible and that he should never try carpentry again? Of course not! You would tell him that for the first time that was pretty good and the next time, with your help, he would do even better.

Or let's say that you have a daughter about eight or nine who tried to make a doll's dress for the very first time. When she hemmed the bottom of it, the hem did not come out even. In fact, when she got all the way around, it did not match by about half-an-inch, and the buttonholes were giant gaping holes too big for the buttons. Would you tell her that it was the worst piece of sewing that you had ever seen, and that she should never try to sew again? No! You would tell her that for the first time, it was good. Next time you would help her and she would do even better, and eventually she would be making beautiful doll clothes and later on even some of her own clothes. You love her, so you would encourage her.

Let's consider one more modern-day parable. Then we will discuss how these relate to our relationship with God the Father. Suppose you had a son who was about twelve and he was playing football for the first time. He got the ball and started around right-end and a big giant from the other team hit him and knocked the ball up in the air. The other team grabbed it and ran for a touchdown. Would you go out onto the field, kick him off, and say, "You clumsy little oaf—you should never play football again." No, of course not! You would pick him up, dust him off, and tell him to get back in there and go for it.

You encourage your children and overlook their failures or poor performance because you love them. Let me ask you this: *Does God love you as much as you love your children?* Of course He does! In fact, He loves you infinitely more than you love your children. If we encourage our children, say nice things to them, and are proud of them when they do well, does our heavenly Father do less for us?

When was the last time you heard Father God say to you, "You did a nice job?" When is the last time you heard Father God say, "I like the way you handled that?" When was the last time you heard Father God say, "I'm proud of you?" Sadly, many Christians have never heard Father God say those things to them. We love our children and we say those kinds of encouraging things to them, don't we? God loves us and He is going to express this love. Sending His Son, Jesus Christ to die for us was the ultimate, incredible expression of His abounding love, but He also expresses His love on a day-to-day basis.

God *is* saying those kinds of things to you. He *does* love you. He wants to encourage you. If you are not hearing them, what is the problem? The problem is that you do not have the good close relationship with God the Father that you likely have with Jesus and the Holy Spirit.

The next major movement of God on planet earth is going to be centered around God the Father. We had the Evangelical movement in which Christ was the person of the Trinity who was truly exalted. Then we had the Pentecostal and Charismatic movements in which the Holy Spirit played a significant role (and unfortunately got exalted at times). The next movement of God may be called something like the *"Victory movement"* or the *"Power movement,"* and God the Father is going to be the person of the Trinity who receives the majority of the emphasis.

Jesus Christ said that He came to bring us into the right relationship with the Father. He said, "I am the way, and the truth and the life; no one comes to the ***Father*** but through me" (John 14:6). He said, "whatever you ask of the ***Father*** in My name, He may give to you" (John 15:16). It was *the Father, the Father, the Father.*

Jesus Christ came to bring you into right relationship with Father God. If you do not have a wonderful, glorious relationship with Father God, then you have stopped short of what Jesus Christ came to do.

It is from God the Father and our relationship to Him that we are going to get supernatural power. In Acts 1:8, Jesus told us that God was going to give us His supernatural power when we were baptized in the Holy Spirit. I do not totally understand the relationship between the two, but supernatural power is a gift from the Father at the time when we are filled with the Holy Spirit.

Do you want the supernatural power of God to fill you, just as it rested upon Jesus, Peter, Paul, the disciples and the believers of the first century? It will flow out of your relationship with Father God, which is so essential. Jesus Christ came to bring you into a right relationship with Father God. Your loving, heavenly Father wants to give you the power to use for His glory and for the glory of His Son Jesus Christ. Yet He asks you to be in total surrender to Him—to be a bondslave of His. You could call it "being an overcomer." You could say that it is the Christians who are walking in holiness, righteousness and purity before God. It does not matter what label you place on it. It is this group of totally-dedicated people to whom God is going to give His supernatural power and He will use them in a mighty way during the end times of this age.

Appendix D

MEET THE AUTHOR

Dr. James McKeever

Dr. James McKeever is an international consulting economist, lecturer, author, world traveler, and Bible teacher. His financial consultations are utilized by scores of individuals from all over the world who seek his advice on investment strategy and international affairs.

Dr. McKeever is the editor and major contributing writer of the *Money Strategy Letter*, an economic and investment letter with worldwide circulation and recognition. The *Hulbert Financial Digest*, an independent newsletter-rating service, rated this newsletter the *Number One* most profitable newsletter in the nation three out of four years (1985, 1986 and 1988)! It showed an average profit of 66.25 percent per year for the eleven full years that it included a Model Portfolio (1978-1988).

Dr. McKeever has been a featured speaker at monetary, investment and tax haven conferences in London, Zurich, Bermuda, Amsterdam, South Africa, Australia, Singapore and Hong Kong, as well as all over the North American continent and Latin America.

As an economist and futurist, Dr. McKeever has shared the platform with such men as Ronald Reagan, Gerald Ford, William Simon, William Buckley, Alan Greenspan, heads of foreign governments, and many other outstanding leaders.

For five years after completing his academic work, Dr. McKeever was with a consulting firm which specialized in financial investments in petroleum. Those who were following his counsel back in 1954 invested heavily in oil.

For more than ten years Dr. McKeever was with IBM, where he held several key management positions. During those years, when IBM was just moving into transistorized computers, he helped that company become what it is today. With IBM, he consulted with top executives of many major corporations in America, helping them solve financial, control and information problems. He has received many awards from IBM, including the "Key Man Award" and the "Outstanding Contribution Award." He is widely known in the computer field for his books and articles on management, management control and information sciences.

In addition to this outstanding business background, Dr. McKeever is an ordained minister. He has been a Baptist evangelist, pastor of Catalina Bible Church for three and a half years (while still with IBM) and a frequent speaker at Christian conferences. He has the gift of teaching, an in-depth knowledge of the Bible, and has authored twelve best-selling Christian books, seven of which have won the prestigious "Angel Award" given for excellence in media.

Dr. McKeever is president of Omega Ministries, which is a nonprofit organization established under the leading of the Holy Spirit to minister to the body of Christ by the traveling ministry of anointed men of God, through books, cassettes, seminars, conferences, and video tapes. He is the editor of the widely-read newsletter, *End-Times News Digest* (published by Omega Ministries), which relates the significance of current events to biblical prophecy and to the body of Christ today. The worldwide outreach of Omega Ministries is supported by the gifts of those who are interested.

DETAILED OUTLINE

COMMITMENT TO BE A BONDSLAVE AND AN OVERCOMER TO THE GLORY OF GOD THE FATHER, AND HIS SON, JESUS CHRIST

TO THE GOD OF ETERNITY,

I am voluntarily becoming a bondslave of Yours. I have no property nor possessions of my own. I have no time nor rights of my own. I am willing to permanently be Your slave.

I am willing to put on Your armor and to fight against Your enemies. I am willing to do absolutely anything You tell me to do, even if it goes against my knowledge of what is good. I am willing to die for You. Nothing is more important than doing Your will—not my family, my (former) possessions, my job, nor even my own life.

Through Your power I will be an overcomer, not to my glory, but only to Your glory and the glory of Your Son and my Savior, Jesus Christ.

I make this lifetime commitment, not because I have to, nor because of rewards. I make it because of my love for You, because I desire to please You, and because I want to be as close to You as possible throughout eternity.

Signed ______________________________ Date ___________

Witness _____________________________ Date ___________

JOIN WITH US

If you would like to join with other committed bondslaves to keep in touch and to possibly help each other, send us a copy of this page. We feel that the Lord is raising up an army and we want to be part of His special troops. Perhaps this part of God's army will become known as "The Omega Force." At some point, we may have a conference just for bondslaves that will not be announced to anyone else.

We are going to need each other when persecution starts. Let's help one another to be good soldiers for Jesus Christ.

To: James McKeever, P.O. Box 1788, Medford, Oregon 97501

☐ Yes, I would like to keep in touch with others who have also made a commitment to be a bondslave and an overcomer.

Name ____

Address ____

City, State ______________________________ Zip __________

Home phone (   ) ______________ Business phone (   ) __________

Occupation _______________________________________

COMMITMENT TO BE A BONDSLAVE AND AN OVERCOMER TO THE GLORY OF GOD THE FATHER, AND HIS SON, JESUS CHRIST

TO THE GOD OF ETERNITY,

I am voluntarily becoming a bondslave of Yours. I have no property nor possessions of my own. I have no time nor rights of my own. I am willing to permanently be Your slave.

I am willing to put on Your armor and to fight against Your enemies. I am willing to do absolutely anything You tell me to do, even if it goes against my knowledge of what is good. I am willing to die for You. Nothing is more important than doing Your will–not my family, my (former) possessions, my job, nor even my own life.

Through Your power I will be an overcomer, not to my glory, but only to Your glory and the glory of Your Son and my Savior, Jesus Christ.

I make this lifetime commitment, not because I have to, nor because of rewards. I make it because of my love for You, because I desire to please You, and because I want to be as close to You as possible throughout eternity.

Signed ______________________________ Date ____________

Witness _____________________________ Date ____________

JOIN WITH US

If you would like to join with other committed bondslaves to keep in touch and to possibly help each other, send us a copy of this page. We feel that the Lord is raising up an army and we want to be part of His special troops. Perhaps this part of God's army will become known as "The Omega Force." At some point, we may have a conference just for bondslaves that will not be announced to anyone else.

We are going to need each other when persecution starts. Let's help one another to be good soldiers for Jesus Christ.

To: James McKeever, P.O. Box 1788, Medford, Oregon 97501

☐ Yes, I would like to keep in touch with others who have also made a commitment to be a bondslave and an overcomer.

Name ____

Address ____

City, State _______________________________ Zip ____________

Home phone ( ) ______________ Business phone ( ) __________

Occupation ____

TO THE AUTHOR

Some of the materials available from Dr. James McKeever are shown in summary on the reverse side. Please indicate your area of interest, remove this page and mail it to Omega Publications.

Dr. McKeever would appreciate hearing any personal thoughts from you. If you wish to comment, write your remarks below on this reply form.

Comments:

ORDER FORM

Omega Publications
P.O. Box 4130
Medford, OR 97501

BC-201

$_____ Please send me _____ copies of your popular ***Victory Bible Reading Plan*** ($1) (also available in Spanish)

Please send me the following materials by Dr. McKeever:

(Prices subject to change without notice)

Qty		
____	$_____	***You Can Overcome*** ($6.95)
____	_____	***Become Like Jesus*** ($6.95)
____	_____	*The Rapture Book* ($6.95)
____	_____	*Financial Guidance* ($7.95)
____	_____	*Believe it or not . . . It's in the Bible* ($7.95)
____	_____	*The Future Revealed* ($6.95)
____	_____	*Revelation for Laymen* ($5.95)
____	_____	*Claim Your Birthright* ($7.95)
____	_____	*Supernatural Power* ($9.95)

Please send me Dr. McKeever's video tape:

____ _____ ***Judgment Upon America*** ($29)

☐ Send complete listing of video tapes available

Please send me the book by Stuart Gramenz:

____ _____ ***How to Heal the Sick*** ($7.95)

TOTAL AMOUNT ENCLOSED $________

Please send me more information about:

☐ Dr. McKeever speaking at our church or conference

☐ Cassette tapes

Send the materials I have indicated to:

Name______________________________

Address______________________________

City, State____________________ Zip________